Money Adviser 2001

10 Steps to Increase Your Wealth

Andrew Feinberg
and the Editors of MONEY

MONEY BOOKS

Time Inc. Home Entertainment
1271 Avenue of the Americas / New York, NY 10020

MONEY MAGAZINE

MANAGING EDITOR Robert Safian **EXECUTIVE EDITOR** Eric Gelman, Denise B. Martin **ASSISTANT MANAGING EDITORS** Glenn Coleman, Alan Mirabella, Sheryl Hilliard Tucker **EDITORS-AT-LARGE** Jean Sherman Chatzky, Michael Sivy **SENIOR EDITORS** Marion Asnes, Jim Frederick, Jon Gertner, William Green, Scott Medintz, Ellen Stark, Teresa Tritch, Walter Updegrave **SENIOR WRITER/COLUMNIST** Jason Zweig **ASSOCIATE EDITORS** Kathatine B. Drake, Michael J. Powe **SENIOR WRITERS** Peter Carbonara, Jerry Edgerton, Amy Feldman, Pablo Galarza, John Helyar, Amy Dockser Marcus, Pat Regnier, Penelope Wang, Suzanne Woolley **STAFF WRITERS** Jon Birger, Joan Caplin, Brian L. Clark, Lisa Cullen, David Futrelle, Leslie Haggin Geary, Lisa Gibbs, Laura Lallos, Jeanne Lee, Nick Pachetti **WRITER-REPORTERS** Alec Appelbaum, Adrienne Carter, Jeff Nash, Ilana Polyak **CONTRIBUTING WRITERS** Paul Lukas, Bethany McLean, Joseph Nocera, Andrew Serwer, Rob Walker **ART DIRECTOR** Syndi C. Becker **DEPUTY ART DIRECTORS** David E. McKenna, MaryAnn Salvato **ASSOCIATE ART DIRECTORS** Marci Papineau, Michael Scowden **DESIGNERS** Semi Kang, **INFORMATION GRAPHICS DESIGNER** Myra Klockenbrink **TECHNICAL PROJECTS COORDINATOR** Tommy McCall **PICTURE EDITOR** Jane Clark **DEPUTY PICTURE EDITOR** Cathy Mather **FEATURES PICTURE EDITOR** Betsy Keating **ASSISTANT PICTURE EDITORS** Melanie Skrzek, Shawn Vale **SENIOR STAFF REPORTERS** Judy Feldman, Roberta Kirwan **STAFF** Andrea Bennett, Erica Garcia, Grace Jidoun, Patrice D. Johnson, Katherine Zamira Josephs, Daphne D. Mosher (mail), Natasha Rafi, Stephanie D. Smith **GROUP EDITORIAL PRODUCTION MANAGER** Allegra-Jo Lagani **COPY CHIEF** Patricia A. Feimster **OPERATIONS CHIEF** Lionel P. Vargas **STAFF** Sally Boggan, Martha E. Bula Torres, John D'Antonio, Judith Ferbel, Emily Harrow, Carol Robinson, Eve Sennett, Libby Stephens **PUBLIC RELATIONS DIRECTOR** Patrick Taylor **PUBLIC RELATIONS MANAGER** Robyn Kenyon **COORDINATOR FOR PERSONAL-FINANCE GROUP** Jamie Ringel **ASSISTANT TO THE MANAGING EDITOR** Lysa Price **ADMINISTRATIVE COORDINATOR, DESIGN** Llubia Reyes **STAFF** Merrily Brooks, Maitreyah Friedman, Amy Wilson **CORRESPONDENTS** Linda Berlin, Barbara Hordern, Ann S. Knol, Stephen Marsh, Melanie J. Mavrides, Laura Mecoy, Marcia R. Pledger, Elizabeth S. Roberts, Carol F. Shepley, Nancy Stesin, Jeff Wuorio **DIRECTOR OF IMAGING** Richard J. Sheridan **IMAGING STAFF** Janet Miller (manager), Michael D. Brennan, Edward G. Carnesi, Jeffrey Chan, Janet Gonzalez, Marco Lau, Angel A. Mass, Kent Michaud, Stanley E. Moyse, Claudio M. Muller, Paul Tupay **DIRECTOR OF TECHNOLOGY** John J. Ruglio **TECHNOLOGY STAFF** Al Criscuolo, Arthur Wilson (technology managers), John Deer, Ken Klokel, Michael Sheehan, Marvin Tate **EXECUTIVE PRODUCER, MONEY WEBSITE** Craig Matters **VICE PRESIDENT, INTERACTIVE DEVELOPMENT** Mark Gilliland **DESIGN DIRECTOR** Caldwell Toll **TECHNOLOGY DIRECTOR** Mark Thomas **SENIOR EDITORS** Alexander Haris, Anthony Mitchell, Susan Price, Peter Valdes-DaPena **SENIOR PRODUCER** Waits May **SENIOR WRITER** Borzou Daragahi **PROGRAMMERS** Steve Leung, Kim Tan, German Todorov, Tim Ungs, Georgi Vladimirov **PROJECT MANAGER** Ainsley Fuhr **PRODUCTION ASSISTANT** Savy Mangru **ADMINISTRATIVE ASSISTANT** Patricia Egbert

TIME INC. HOME ENTERTAINMENT

PRESIDENT Rob Gursha **EXECUTIVE DIRECTOR, BRANDED BUSINESSES** David Arfine **EXECUTIVE DIRECTOR, MARKETING SERVICES** Carol Pittard **DIRECTOR, RETAIL & SPECIAL SALES** Tom Mifsud **ASSOCIATE DIRECTOR** Kenneth Maehlum **PRODUCT MANAGER** Niki Viswanathan **ASSOCIATE PRODUCT MANAGER** Sara Stumpf **ASSISTANT PRODUCT MANAGER** Michelle Kuhr **EDITORIAL OPERATIONS DIRECTOR** John Calvano **ASSISTANT EDITORIAL OPERATIONS DIRECTOR** Emily Rabin **BOOK PRODUCTION MANAGER** Jessica McGrath **ASSISTANT BOOK PRODUCTION MANAGER** Suzanne DeBenedetto **FULFILLMENT MANAGER** Richard Perez **ASSISTANT FULFILLMENT MANAGER** Tara Schimmimg **EXECUTIVE ASSISTANT** Mary Jane Rigoroso

MONEY BOOK SERIES

DESIGNER Laura Ierardi, LCI Design

ISBN: 1-929049-21-8
ISSN: 1522-7618

We welcome your comments and suggestions about MONEY Books. Please write to us at:

MONEY Books
Attention: Book Editors
PO Box 11016
Des Moines, IA 50336-1016

If you would like to order any of our hardcover Collector's Edition books, please call us at 1-800-327-6388
(Monday through Friday, 7:00 a.m.–8:00 p.m. or Saturday, 7:00 a.m.–6:00 p.m. Central Time).
Please visit our website at www.TimeBookstore.com

Contents

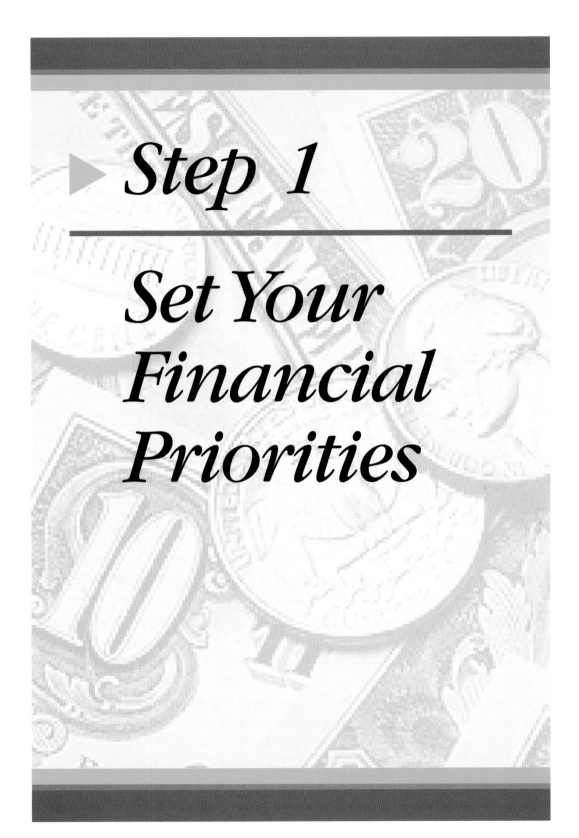

▶ Step 1

Set Your Financial Priorities

*T*hese days, when most people think about the accumulation of wealth, they think primarily about investing. Given the eye-popping returns of the stock market since 1982, how could it be otherwise? Except for a few imperfect years here or there—1984, 1987, 1990, 1994 and, egad, 2000—the upward march has been virtually relentless. And, indeed, in *Money Adviser 2001: 10 Steps to Increase Your Wealth*, we discuss detailed investment moves designed to fatten your portfolio this year, and for many years to come.

However, the editors of MONEY believe that doing well as an investor is only one aspect of wealth creation. Developing strategies for handling *every* aspect of your finances is critical if you want to achieve your financial goals. That explains why we've devoted so much of this book to presenting other strategies for accumulating riches, saving money and preserving the wealth you've worked so hard to acquire.

But the fact is, most of us have never spent much time thinking in a systematic way about which financial objectives matter most. Instead, we muddle through our financial lives, occasionally setting aside money for important long-term needs—like saving for retirement or protecting our assets with insurance—but more often just spending to meet the day-to-day expenses that always clamor for attention. There's nothing terribly wrong with that approach—except that it risks leaving the most important objectives unfulfilled.

So what are MONEY's 10 steps to wealth?

1. Set your financial priorities.
2. Hone your investment strategies.
3. Create a great retirement plan.
4. Protect what you have.

5. Preserve family wealth.
6. Get paid what you're really worth.
7. Raise money-savvy kids—and slash tuition costs.
8. Become a smart online consumer.
9. Make great real estate moves.
10. Save when you buy a car.

These steps, you might have noticed, are also the titles of the 10 chapters in the book. By using the techniques discussed in each chapter, you'll have a much better chance of realizing your financial goals. But first, you have to know what those goals are.

What are your financial objectives? Most people, when asked that question, fall back on platitudes—things like achieving financial security, sending children to college or securing a comfortable retirement. Or, they voice fantasies that probably can't be achieved at all—like doubling their income overnight, retiring at 40 or winning at Powerball.

But setting reasonable financial goals will greatly increase your chances of getting where you want to go. To set achievable goals, follow the steps outlined below.

▶ **Narrow your objectives.**
You may not be able to achieve every financial goal you've ever dreamed of, but you can realize the most important ones if you identify them clearly in your own mind and decide which are most important.

▶ **Focus first on the goals that matter.**
To accomplish primary goals, you will often need to put equally desirable but less important ones on a back burner.

▶ **Be prepared for conflicts.**
Even worthy goals often conflict with one another. When faced with a conflict between goals of equal importance, you can sometimes choose by applying criteria like: Will anyone's health be affected by my choice? Will one of the conflicting goals benefit more people than the other? Which goal will cause the greater harm if it is deferred?

▶ **Put time on your side.**
The most important ally you have in meeting long-term goals,

like preparing for retirement, is time. The reason, of course, is that money stashed in a savings account or invested in stocks, bonds or mutual funds usually grows over time—sometimes substantially—to help meet your needs.

▶ Include family members.

If you have a spouse or significant other, make sure he or she is part of the goal-setting process or you will probably regret it later. Children, too, should have some say in goals that affect them.

▶ Start early.

The longer you wait to identify and begin working toward your goals, the more difficulty you'll have reaching them. (That's why this is the first exercise in the book!)

▶ Sweat the big stuff.

Once you have prioritized your list of goals, keep your spending on course. Whenever you make a large payment for anything ask yourself: "Is this taking me nearer to my primary goals—or leading me farther away from them?" If a big expense doesn't get you closer to your goals, try to defer or reduce it.

▶ Don't sweat the small stuff.

Although this lesson encourages you to focus on big-ticket, long-range plans, most of life is lived in the here-and-now and most of what you spend will continue to be for daily expenses—including many that are simply for fun. That's okay—so long as your long-range needs are also provided for.

▶ Be prepared for change.

Your needs and desires invariably change as you age, so you should probably reexamine your priorities at least every five years.

▶ *How Are You Doing?*

This book was written to help you achieve your financial goals. We encourage you to read every chapter, although we know not all of them will apply to your needs at this moment. So focus on what matters most to you first, then take a look at all the other

► *Calculate Your Net Worth*

Pull out your financial statements to fill in the current market value of your assets and the amount of your liabilities in the spaces provided. Complete this exercise at least once a year to track how much your wealth is growing.

	AMOUNT
ASSETS	
Cash and Savings (savings accounts, money-market funds, Treasury bills)	1.
Taxable investments (excluding retirement accounts)	
Stocks and stock mutual funds	
Bonds and bond mutual funds	
Stock options (if exercised today)	
Value of privately owned business	
Investment real estate	
Cash value of life insurance policies	
Other investments	
Total taxable investments	2.
Retirement Accounts	
IRAs	
Employer savings plans, 401(k), 403(b)	
Self-employed plans, Keogh, for example	
Annuities	
Estimated value of company pension	
Total retirement accounts	3.
Home and Personal Property	
Home	
Vacation home	
Cars, recreational vehicles	
Art, collectibles, jewelry and furnishings	
Other personal assets	
Total home and personal property	4.
TOTAL ASSETS (Add lines 1, 2, 3 and 4.)	5.
LIABILITIES	
Mortgage debt (balance of mortgages and home-equity borrowings)	
Car loans/lease	
Student loans	
Credit-card balances	
Other loans (401(k), installment, personal lines of credit and the like)	
Other debt	
TOTAL LIABILITIES	6.
NET WORTH (Subtract line 6 from line 5.)	7.

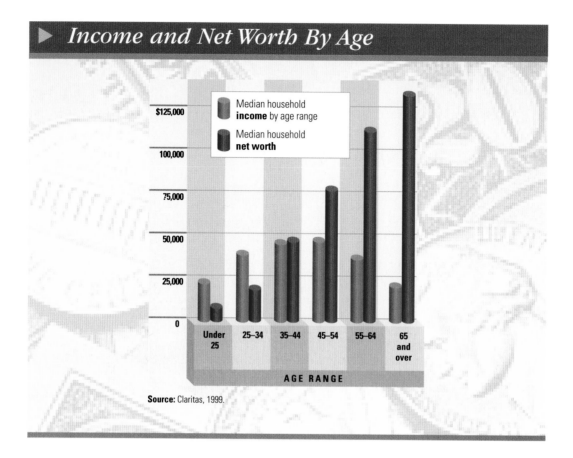

Median household **income** by age range

Median household **net worth**

$125,000

100,000

75,000

50,000

25,000

0

Under 25 | 25–34 | 35–44 | 45–54 | 55–64 | 65 and over

AGE RANGE

Source: Claritas, 1999.

wealth-building strategies we offer. But no matter how you proceed, we strongly encourage you to begin by calculating your net worth (your assets minus your liabilities) to see how you stand right now. (See worksheet on page 5.)

Ten years of surging stock prices and a robust economy have left quite a few Americans with growing incomes and an impressive nest egg. But now that the market has cooled off, many investors sense that the music might stop—and no one wants to be left without a chair. Assessing your net worth provides you with a snapshot of how you're doing at a particular moment— and often the news is better than you think. Ideally, you should calculate your net worth once a year to see how your money is growing and to get a sense if you are on track to meet your goals.

We believe that the strategies in this book will make that exercise a much more pleasant one for decades to come.

Step 2

Hone Your Investment Strategies

*T*o achieve or maintain wealth, you need to create a diversified investment portfolio designed to meet your specific goals. The purpose of this chapter is to give you ideas for maximizing the returns in every segment of your portfolio—from high-octane technology stocks to growth funds to good old dependable (well, sometimes) bonds. We even offer ideas for boosting your returns on cash (which many investors wish they had more of in 2000). We save the discussion of asset allocation for Chapter 3, but feel free to skip ahead to the diversification strategies outlined in the box on page 81.

The tools described below will help you assemble the core elements of a solid portfolio—stocks, mutual funds, bonds and cash. Much has changed in the investment world of late and this chapter focuses on profiting from those changes. Worried about another tech meltdown? We show you smart ways to play the sector. Fed up with high mutual fund fees? We give you savvy alternatives. Unsure how to play bonds? We cut through the confusion.

We believe that the strategies covered in this chapter will help you create a truly smart portfolio, one that will serve you well year in and year out. And we'll begin by focusing on what we think is in store for the markets in 2001.

▶ *What's Ahead for 2001*

A year ago the U.S. economy was rocketing along; today, many experts fear it is limping into a recession. Are we entering a pause that refreshes or might we suffer the ravages of a hard landing that will throw millions of people out of work?

We actually believe that the current environment is more benign than it might initially seem (especially to technology investors). The transition from rapid growth to much slower growth is often painful, at least for a while. But if the economy continues to grow and inflation remains subdued—as we expect—2001 could be a fine year for stock and bond investors.

The really shocking development of the past year isn't the contested election—it's the mangled market. As the economy slowed and companies started announcing profit shortfalls, stocks swooned. After five years of cranking out annual gains ranging from 20% to 86%, the Nasdaq index dropped more than 35% through early December and 50% from its 52-week peak. And the less racy Dow Jones industrials, coming off a five-year run of gains averaging more than 24% annually, dropped more than 11% from the all-time high reached in January 2000. All in all, a pretty bleak picture.

Or is it? For all the political uncertainty and talk show blather, Congress will continue to function. It may even operate more smoothly than usual, since small bands of moderates will hold the balance of power in both houses. Most important, Alan Greenspan will still be chairman of the Federal Reserve.

Uncertainty over the election chopped $1.5 trillion off the value of stocks by early December. And the markets could well be volatile for a few months more. But the fundamental forces powering the bull market—low inflation, steady profit growth and rising productivity—remain intact. So the market's long-term prospects look excellent. Meanwhile, as traders zig and zag, serious investors will be able to pick up topnotch stocks for far less than they're really worth. Concerns that profit growth will flag have been causing selective sell-offs in various stock groups (see the charts on page 10), so that at least a few top stocks are bound to be cheap at any particular time.

Greenspan is more important than ever. The current Fed chairman, of course, has long been considered the man with the most influence on the markets. The prospect of a deeply divided government only increases his importance. So what's his next move likely to be?

Since 1994, Greenspan has kept interest rates unusually high by historical standards as part of a campaign to grind down inflation to almost nothing (see the charts on page 11). He stepped up that campaign in late 1998, hiking short-term rates nearly two percentage points by early 2000, because of his concerns that inflation pressures were building. In particular, he

The crosscurrents that buffered the market in 2000 caused enormous divergences from one sector to another. Consumer stocks hit bottom in the spring, when investors began to worry that an economic slowdown could crimp earnings. Tech stocks,

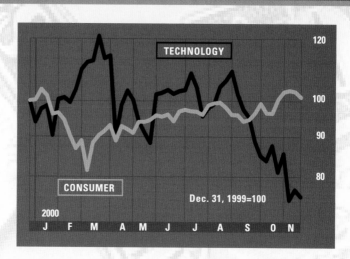

which had greater momentum, broke down later in the year, sending investors scrambling for safe havens and pushing consumer stocks back up. Other defensive groups, such as energy, also rallied, helped by soaring oil prices. By contrast, telecom firms were badly hurt in the second half as overcapacity led to rampant price-cutting that sapped profits.

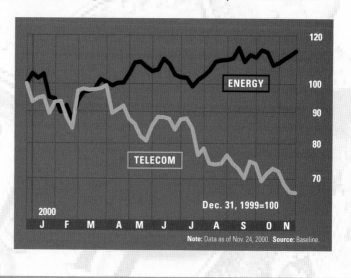

Note: Data as of Nov. 24, 2000. Source: Baseline.

thought that the steady reduction in unemployment to less than 4% signaled potential labor shortages that might drive up wages and trigger a new price spiral.

Now it looks as though high rates might cool down the economy too much. Over the past couple of quarters, growth in the gross domestic product has dropped from 5.6% to 2.4%, and it's projected to run about 3% in 2001. That's been enough of a

Money has been tight since Federal Reserve chairman Alan Greenspan began raising interest rates in 1994. The charts show how yields on Treasury bills and bonds compare with expected yields based on past inflation trends. Short-term rates are still very high relative to inflation, and bond yields are somewhat elevated as well. Since inflation remains moderate, interest rates have room to fall across the board. And if the economy continues to slow, Greenspan may cut rates much more than anyone expects.

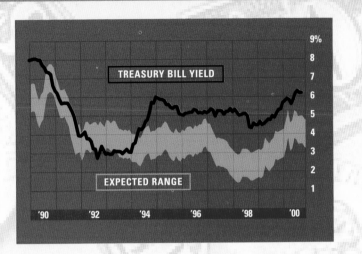

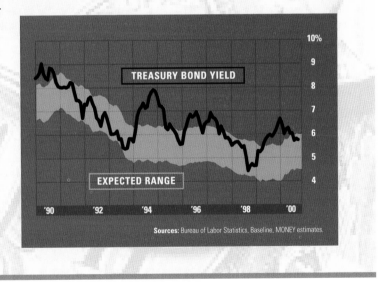

Sources: Bureau of Labor Statistics, Baseline, MONEY estimates.

slowdown to cause earnings shortfalls and price declines for many stocks. Share prices should rebound if GDP growth stabilizes as expected.

Recently, however, investors have begun to worry that the economy could slip from a slowdown into a recession. Consumer debt is at a 20-year high, and consumer confidence has fallen to its lowest level in more than a year.

Apparently, the Fed recognizes the danger that interest rates have been kept too high for too long. In December, Greenspan indicated that he clearly understood the risks of a slowing economy, and hinted that the Fed would act to deter a potential recession.

Greenspan will probably postpone any major policy shifts until early this year. But there's good news hidden in this scenario. When Greenspan gets to the point that he feels comfortable taking his foot off the brakes, he may actually be disposed to reduce interest rates more than anyone expects. From the Fed's viewpoint, the most important fact about a weak and divided Administration is that it is likely to use most of the surplus to reduce the national debt. And that's likely to do two things: act as a brake on the economy and bring down interest rates.

Gridlock is good for bonds. It's a reality of politics that no politician is content to leave money lying around. Liberals usually find some worthy reason to expand social programs, while conservatives typically bulk up the military or return money to the voters through tax cuts (and those refunds are mostly spent by consumers). But gridlock means that neither side will likely be able to pass an ambitious plan for what to do with the surplus, which could total more than $500 billion over the next two years. Any surplus that isn't spent or used for tax cuts automatically reduces the outstanding national debt. The net result could be a 10% to 15% reduction in the dollar value of Treasury bonds outstanding to less than $3 trillion.

According to basic economics, that will have two important consequences. First, bond buyers will be competing for a smaller pool of Treasury issues. That will bid up prices and reduce yields, which would create an extremely favorable market for the highest-quality government, corporate and municipal issues. In fact, the process has already begun—long-term Treasury bonds returned more than 12% in the first 11 months of 2000. Second, the application of the surplus to debt reduction (rather than spending) would slow the economy more than most investors expect and could easily lead to smaller gains in corporate profits (see the chart on opposite page).

A slowdown helps cool inflation pressure. Inflation currently remains remarkably mild despite $36-a-barrel oil—only a buck below its high—and unemployment of less than 4%. In fact, core inflation at the wholesale level, excluding volatile food and

Profit Slowdown

Corporate profits soared through much of the 1990s, except for a brief dip in 1998. But 2001 earnings are likely to be subpar before recovering in 2002. That could easily mean earnings disappointments and temporary sell-offs for top blue chips.

Fortunately, profit growth over the next five years should be strong because of technology and the likelihood that inflation will remain tame. So you should be able to do some great bargain hunting over the next six months.

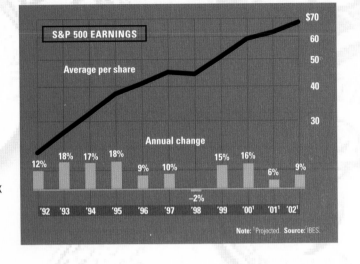

S&P 500 EARNINGS

Average per share

Annual change

12% 18% 17% 18% 9% 10% -2% 15% 16% 6% 9%

'92 '93 '94 '95 '96 '97 '98 '99 '00¹ '01¹ '02¹

$70 60 50 40 30

Note: ¹Projected. Source: IBES.

energy prices, actually declined slightly in October. Part of what's holding down inflation is the boom in computer technology, which continues to make businesses more efficient. That produces major gains in productivity, which will help to stem inflation over the next four years. In fact, while productivity increased an average of 1.5% annually from 1974 to 1995, the rate of gain rose to 2.5% in the late 1990s and is currently running around 3%.

The market fragmented as it fell. When economic trends are continuing in a well-established direction, most stock groups are priced fairly and move more or less together. But at turning points such as the one we're in now, different stock groups suffer at different times and bounce back with varying delays. When the market is deteriorating, it doesn't rot from the head like a fish, it wilts from the outside in, like a lettuce leaf that starts turning brown around the edges.

Rising interest rates started the market's rot, which began among stock sectors that are usually viewed as defensive. Consumer stocks, energy and health care all hit bottom between

Investing in companies that are growing faster than the market average is the simplest and safest way to reach your financial goals. These 100 big, financially solid stocks, selected by MONEY's stock guru Michael Sivy, all offer double-digit annual returns, based on projected earnings growth and dividends. Even without P/E increases, these stocks should match or outpace the S&P 500, which has returned an average of about 12% annually over the past 75 years. You increase your odds of beating the market if you can pick up these stocks when they're unusually cheap. Stocks with a PEG ratio (price/earnings ratio divided by expected earnings growth rate) of 1.5 or less are often the best buys, while those with PEG ratios of two or more may be overpriced. Of course, it's also important to see where a stock has traded over the past year and to compare its P/E with its multiples in the past. For more updated statistics on the Sivy 100, including yearly trading ranges, go to www.money.com/sivy.

STOCK	PRICE	P/E RATIO	GROWTH RATE	PEG RATIO
Abbott Laboratories (ABT)	$52.88	26.1	12%	2.2
Aetna (AET)	67.31	14.8	12	1.2
AFLAC (AFL)	69.75	25.1	15	1.7
Air Products & Chemicals (APD)	35.19	13.0	12	1.1
Albertson's (ABS)	24.69	9.8	12	0.8
Alcoa (AA)	29.00	11.8	12	1.0
American Express (AXP)	54.25	23.0	14	1.6
American Home Products (AHP)	58.88	26.9	14	1.9
American Intl. Group (AIG)	97.44	34.7	14	2.5
Anheuser-Busch (BUD)	47.13	24.8	10	2.5
Applied Materials (AMAT)	38.56	12.6	25	0.5
AT&T (T)	19.56	22.0	11	2.0
Automatic Data Processing (ADP)	64.94	43.2	15	2.9
Bank of America (BAC)	39.75	7.3	11	0.7
Baxter International (BAX)	85.31	24.8	13	1.9
Bellsouth (BLS)	40.56	17.0	12	1.4
Best Buy (BBY)	27.50	14.9	25	0.6
Boeing (BA)	65.81	17.9	15	1.2
Bristol-Myers Squibb (BMY)	67.38	26.0	12	2.2
Burlington Northern S.F. (BNI)	25.25	9.0	9	1.0
Chase Manhattan (CMB)	37.31	9.2	12	0.8
Cisco Systems (CSCO)	48.50	61.5	32	1.9
Citigroup (C)	48.94	15.9	14	1.1
Coca-Cola (KO)	62.19	35.9	14	2.6
Colgate-Palmolive (CL)	59.69	31.4	13	2.4
Comcast A (CMCSK)	$38.06	N.M.	16%	N.M.

STOCK	PRICE	P/E RATIO	GROWTH RATE	PEG RATIO
Compaq Computer (CPQ)	22.80	15.4	20	0.8
Conagra Foods (CAG)	25.38	13.6	10	1.4
Corning (GLW)	60.94	42.8	27	1.6
Costco Wholesale (COST)	32.63	21.9	15	1.5
Deere & Co. (DE)	41.94	15.8	10	1.6
Dell Computer (DELL)	18.44	16.6	25	0.7
Delta Air Lines (DAL)	48.25	6.1	12	0.5
Disney (DIS)	30.00	29.7	15	2.0
Dow Chemical (DOW)	32.69	13.8	8	1.7
Duke Energy (DUK)	87.25	19.3	9	2.1
Electronic Data Systems (EDS)	55.38	20.9	15	1.4
Emerson Electric (EMR)	74.44	20.2	12	1.7
Enron (ENE)	65.50	39.4	16	2.5
ExxonMobil (XOM)	88.81	20.7	10	2.1
Federated Dept. Stores (FD)	31.19	7.6	13	0.6
FedEx (FDX)	47.48	17.8	13	1.4
Gannett (GCI)	54.25	14.0	12	1.2
Gap (GPS)	24.75	18.1	20	0.9
Gateway (GTW)	19.12	10.2	22	0.5
General Electric (GE)	51.00	34.3	15	2.3
Gillette (G)	33.69	25.0	13	1.9
Halliburton (HAL)	33.88	24.4	15	1.6
Heinz (HNZ)	45.31	16.2	10	1.6
Hershey Foods (HSY)	63.00	23.6	10	2.4
Hewlett-Packard (HWP)	32.19	16.3	15	1.1
Home Depot (HD)	38.94	27.8	23	1.2
Illinois Tool Works (ITW)	56.06	15.0	13	1.2
Intel (INTC)	34.13	19.5	20	1.0
Intl. Business Machines (IBM)	95.63	19.0	13	1.5
Johnson & Johnson (JNJ)	97.75	25.6	13	2.0
Kimberly-Clark (KMB)	70.81	19.1	11	1.7
Eli Lilly (LLY)	90.06	31.6	15	2.1
Limited (LTD)	18.88	13.9	17	0.8
Lowe's Cos. (LOW)	38.88	14.6	22	0.7
Lucent Technologies (LU)	15.69	41.5	18	2.3
MBNA (KRB)	35.88	19.4	20	1.0
McDonald's (MCD)	30.94	18.6	12	1.6
Merck & Co. (MRK)	90.63	28.4	12	2.4

(continued)

STOCK	PRICE	P/E RATIO	GROWTH RATE	PEG RATIO
Merrill Lynch (MER)	$58.44	14.2	14%	1.0
Microsoft (MSFT)	56.63	29.6	20	1.5
Minnesota Mining & Mfg. (MMM)	99.63	18.9	11	1.7
Motorola (MOT)	18.56	15.7	20	0.8
Newell Rubbermaid (NWL)	19.50	10.7	15	0.7
Nike B (NKE)	43.69	18.6	15	1.2
Nortel Networks (NT)	37.75	38.3	26	1.5
Oracle (ORCL)	26.44	53.7	25	2.1
Pfizer (PFE)	43.50	33.7	21	1.6
Philip Morris (MO)	37.63	9.2	12	0.8
Procter & Gamble (PG)	73.94	23.3	11	2.1
Raytheon B (RTNB)	29.81	17.4	11	1.6
Safeway (SWY)	58.56	22.4	16	1.4
Sara Lee (SLE)	24.19	17.2	10	1.7
SBC Communications (SBC)	52.19	20.2	14	1.4
Schering-Plough (SGP)	53.63	28.2	15	1.9
Schlumberger (SLB)	66.75	34.1	20	1.7
Schwab (SCH)	27.31	36.1	20	1.8
Southern Co. (SO)	31.00	14.5	6	2.4
Sprint (FON)	22.94	13.8	11	1.3
Staples (SPLS)	12.31	15.2	25	0.6
Sun Microsystems (SUNW)	76.94	54.6	22	2.5
Sysco (SYY)	54.00	33.1	14	2.4
Target (TGT)	31.44	19.6	15	1.3
Texaco (TX)	59.31	14.3	8	1.8
Textron (TXT)	49.00	9.4	14	0.7
Tyco International (TYC)	54.31	19.8	20	1.0
UnitedHealth Group (UNH)	116.00	23.8	16	1.5
United Technologies (UTX)	70.50	17.3	15	1.2
Verizon Communications (VZ)	56.06	17.8	12	1.5
Viacom B (VIAB)	52.88	N.M.	28	N.M.
Walgreen (WAG)	43.25	50.1	17	2.9
Wal-Mart Stores (WMT)	51.19	31.0	15	2.1
Washington Mutual (WM)	45.44	11.1	13	0.9
Wells Fargo (WFC)	47.38	16.3	13	1.3
WorldCom (WCOM)	16.00	13.7	24	0.6

Notes: Data as of Dec 1, 2000. P/E ratios are based on estimated fiscal year 2001 earnings. Growth is the projected annual rate for the next five years. N.M.: Not meaningful. **Source**: Baseline.

February and April. Disappointments in first-quarter earnings triggered brutal drops in some top-quality shares. Procter & Gamble, for example, plunged by a third to less than $60 a share in March after warning that first-quarter results would come in below expectations.

At the same time that consumer stocks were troughing, tech stocks were peaking. The enormous earnings momentum that tech stocks had built up masked bad economic news—at least for a while. Consumer stocks, by contrast, quickly showed damage from the first hints of an economic slowdown. They also suffered from declines in the value of the euro that eroded profits earned overseas.

As evidence of an economic slowdown accumulated, technology companies also began warning that their earnings might fall short of initial projections. Stocks with particular profit problems were cut down like weeds. Dell Computer and Gateway, for example, fell more than 50% from September to December because of disappointing trends in sales of personal computers. But stocks throughout the sector were hurt as money managers and individual investors who were overloaded in tech began lightening up and shifting their money to more defensive groups. By Thanksgiving, even darlings like Cisco and Oracle were down a third or more from their highs earlier in the year. And there may be more of the same ahead. While some tech stocks are depressed, many others still trade at price/earnings ratios (P/Es) of 50 or more. Those that are down to bargain levels could fall further as growth in demand for their products continues to slow.

Consumer stocks, by contrast, benefited from investors' flight to safety. Procter & Gamble, for instance, gained 35% from its March 2000 low to $74 a share. And Anheuser-Busch has rallied more than 70% over the same period to $47. Those stocks now trade at more than 20 times next year's earnings, so they're no longer cheap. But such defensive issues may still be worth buying to balance a portfolio that has been overloaded in tech. And they'd be compelling if they pulled back to P/Es in the teens.

Energy stocks have also benefited immensely as a defensive sector, but they were helped even more by this year's sharp run-up in the price of oil. ExxonMobil has gained 20% since March to $89 a share. We doubt, however, that oil can remain above $30 a barrel for more than a year or two, simply because today's high prices will inevitably bring more supply onstream. In addition, an economic slowdown in the U.S. or abroad could reduce demand. So while the big oil stocks may certainly move higher in 2001, we think they are no longer screaming buys.

While constrained supply has pushed up prices in the oil business, oversupply has done the opposite in telecommunications. Fiercely competing phone companies have overbuilt their networks so much that they have been undercutting one another on pricing and cutting back on further equipment purchases. The result is that stocks throughout the sector—from AT&T and WorldCom to Lucent—have lost more than half their value since the spring. Statistically, we think stocks in the group are undervalued by a third, but because of turmoil in the industry, they may represent dead money for the next six months.

Bargain hunters should think small. The divergence among industry sectors is the most visible symptom of the roiling market, but there are others—for example, the fact that big stocks have fared so much better than small ones. As a result, stock market giants, despite their declines, generally remain overvalued, while mid-size and small stocks are priced quite reasonably. Of the 3,000 largest U.S. companies, those with a market capitalization (share price times number of shares outstanding) of less than $3.5 billion have average P/Es of below 18. The 600 stocks with much larger market caps have average P/Es in the mid-20s.

There are striking differences even within the big-cap group. The highest-priced blue chips, such as Cisco, at 62 times 2001 projected earnings, and Walgreen, at a 50 P/E, are trading at premiums far above long-term averages. By contrast, stocks with below-average P/Es, such as McDonald's at 19 and Du Pont at 16, have already gone through a partial bear market and are now only moderately overvalued by historical standards. The best bargains of all are mid-size and small-company shares.

Build a stash for bargain hunting. The most important fact for anyone managing a portfolio right now is that major sectors of the market are somewhere in the middle of a decline. We don't know how steep the drop will be, how much of it still lies ahead or which stock groups will be affected most. But unlike market dips over the past decade, this decline may inflict serious losses without an immediate rebound. Moreover, the risks are greatest for stocks with P/Es above 20. They're always riskier, of course, but since cheaper stocks have generally come back into line with historical norms, the disparities are greater than usual. That leads to these strategies.

▶ **Hang on to cash.** Don't be in a rush to put your money to work. The opportunities you spot won't disappear overnight. In this environment, you can afford to be very selective. The list of 100 stocks on pages 14 to 16 will help you identify such promising buys by comparing a company's projected earnings growth with the stock's P/E ratio. The online version of this table at www.money.com/sivy provides additional data.

▶ **Reduce your reliance on tech.** If you've been consciously diversifying over the past year, you probably are fairly well balanced for this market. If you're overweighted in tech stocks, you shouldn't rush to dump anything, but you should be trying to lower your portfolio's risk profile. You can do that by making sure that you have money in defensive sectors, particularly consumer products and energy.

▶ **Look at alternatives.** You should also consider fixed-income choices, including electric utilities, preferred stock and various bonds. There's also a case for putting 10% to 15% of your money in funds that focus on foreign stocks, especially European blue chips and companies in emerging markets.

Well-balanced portfolios ride out bad patches in the market without irreparable damage. So what's most important is being positioned to take advantage of any sell-offs to build the portfolio that will carry you safely to your financial goals.

▶ *A Case for Midcap Stocks*

Although big-cap stocks—particularly tech stocks—grabbed much of the attention in 2000, it was actually midcap stocks that provided investors with better performance (a gain of 12.93% for the S&P MidCap 400 Index through December 18, 2000, compared with a -9.97% return for the more famous S&P 500). We weren't looking to argue that this trend would continue when our staff began this process, but after all of our number crunching and guru interviewing and CEO vetting, we ended up with eight highly promising stocks—and all of them have market caps below $25 billion. Which makes sense, considering today's markets. Mid caps, as

▶ Our Best Investments

These stocks and funds can help you thrive in today's tougher market. Track our picks into the coming year (and take a look at how last year's choices fared) with our continually updated charts at www.money.com/bestpicks.

INVESTMENT OPTIONS	PRICE[1]	2001 P/E	EARNINGS GROWTH[2]	COMMENTS
Lehman Bros. (LEH)	$51.13	8	12%	A cheap financial stock with a big upside if the markets rebound
Lincoln National (LNC)	46.69	12	12	Not only an insurance takeover play but a turnaround story
CVS (CVS)	55.38	26	17	The No. 2 drugstore chain is fattening its profit margins.
Sanmina (SANM)	81.13	30	30	It makes complex parts for telecom and computer-hardware products.
Quest Diagnostics (DGX)	114.81	39	30	Gene-based tests mean big profit potential for clinical lab chain.
Alza (AZA)	41.31	42	20	Its new attention-deficit/hyperactivity drug is a blockbuster.
eBay (EBAY)	34.75	93	50	P/E is justified by big earnings growth and weak competition
Redback Networks (RBAK)	74.50	147	50	A leading vendor of high-speed Internet-access equipment

STOCKS

	PHONE (800)	EXPENSE RATIO	THREE-YEAR RETURN[3]	COMMENTS
Artisan International	344-1770	1.27%	27.5%	Nearly 60% of its $4.6 billion in assets are in undervalued Europe.
Excelsior Energy	446-1012	0.97	10.5	Extra-low expenses give this diversified fund's returns extra juice.

FUNDS

Notes: [1]Prices as of Dec. 1. [2]Three- to five-year estimate. [3]Annualized as of Dec. 1. **Sources:** Baseline, Morningstar.

indicated earlier, have lower P/Es than large caps, which would be fine if large-caps have superior earnings growth, but in fact the opposite is true: The S&P 400 boosted earnings 25% this past year vs. 17% for the 500. This is an important group for you to know.

Mid-size companies, of course, grow earnings from smaller bases than their large peers do, which makes it easier to post year-over-year increases. They're also more likely to be acquired—rewarding investors with huge gains—and they often don't have much exposure to international markets. "That's important when you consider how many big companies were adversely affected by the decline of the euro," notes Standard & Poor's senior investment strategist, Sam Stovall.

Our midcap stock picks hail from some of 2001's most promising sectors. Health care will remain hot, we feel, simply because the over-50 population will increase 30% over the next 15 years. Demographics also shaped our selection of financial services stocks—all those aging baby boomers bode well for sellers of insurance and investments. Wisely managed retailers should keep posting earnings gains in 2001. And ever-rising demand for oil, gas and electricity should continue fueling the energy boom. We're also believers in technology, despite the sector's hammering in 2000. Just as investors became overly enamored with tech stocks on the way up, they've become unduly pessimistic on the way down. Technology continues to be the growth engine of the U.S. economy, and opportunities abound—if you know where to look for them. We do. So on to our stocks, which are organized by price/earnings ratio, from lowest to highest, followed by our funds.

▶ **Lehman Bros.** Once known strictly for trading bonds, Lehman is now an important player in such ultralucrative businesses as underwriting stocks and advising on mergers. The biggest transformation has been on the bottom line. Corporate earnings have grown at a 36% annual clip since 1995—a rate double that of Merrill Lynch and only one percentage point behind the industry's growth leader, Charles Schwab.

Established stocks with this kind of track record almost always boast above-market price-to-earnings ratios, but as a midsize company in a volatile industry, Lehman has never gotten the respect from investors that it deserves.

In fact, at about $51 a share, Lehman is among the financial sector's most inexpensive stocks, with a P/E of just 8 vs. 14 for Merrill and 36 for Schwab.

If Lehman were to be sold, it probably could command a 50% premium over today's stock price. But even 50% might be selling Lehman short. If the markets rebound in 2001, Lehman could easily see its earnings rise 20% and its P/E return to its five-year average of 11. That would translate into a share price of $82.50, says Jeff Morris, portfolio manager of Invesco Financial Services: "Lehman Bros. could climb 60% or 70% without much trouble."

▶ **Lincoln National.** Not so long ago, it would've been preposterous to include a life insurance company in a list of top stocks. Aging baby boomers should have meant booms for life insurers, but over the past five years the industry's earnings have grown a mere 3% a year—vs. 8% for the S&P 500—while the average life insurance stock has had annual returns of only 9%.

Lincoln National used to be one of the worst offenders. Some say the company was grossly undermanaged. But new CEO Jon Boscia seems serious about cutting costs and boosting earnings.

Boscia has dumped health and property insurance units, focusing instead on higher-end life insurance and variable annuities. The shift paid off: Lincoln's return on equity is now 15% (up from 11%), and its earnings have grown 24% in the past 12 months. Throw in a 2.6% dividend yield and a 12 P/E, and the stock, recently at $46.69, looks like a classic value play.

Lincoln's low P/E and improving fundamentals make it an excellent buy-out candidate. If that happens, shareholders could reap gains of up to 75%.

▶ **CVS.** The prospect of a slower-growing economy in 2001 has some investors fearing a chill in consumer spending. But drugstores can be a good bet on retail while minimizing recession risks. Prescription-drug sales don't really rise or fall with the economy. Better yet, today's drugstores generate 60% of their revenues from consumer staples and other nondrug products that sell in good times and bad. That's why we like CVS, the nation's No. 2 chain, with 4,100 stores and $20 billion in sales. Earnings at CVS are growing a healthy 17% annually (slightly less than industry leader Walgreen's rate), yet the stock's 2001 P/E is 26 (compared with 50 for Walgreen). The lower valuation is one reason Bill Freiss, manager of Thornburg Value, calls CVS, recently trading at about $55, "a compelling buy."

Another reason is the company's push to build more of its stores outside malls. These stores tend to be more profitable locations than traditional sites in shopping centers.

▶ **Sanmina.** While Wall Street dumps on once-shining communications-hardware stocks like Cisco Systems and Nortel Networks, the building of the Internet's infrastructure continues. For a safer, more diversified way to play, drill down a layer to the suppliers. Fast-growing contract manufacturers like Sanmina specialize in assembling the complex hardware goodies (like printed circuit boards and backplanes) to help the Ciscos of the world cut costs. Demand is high—77% of hardware makers will increase outsourcing of this type of precise, complex manufacturing over the next two years, according to Merrill Lynch.

Sanmina has a customer list that's a who's who of tech hardware: Cisco, Lucent, Motorola, Nokia, Nortel, Siemens. Sanmina's revenues are buffered by being spread widely among them. Won't an expected slowdown in tech spending hurt Sanmina's margins? And if these companies can't maintain their projected growth rates, as some analysts fear, won't that hurt Sanmina's bottom line? No and no, insists CEO Jure Sola. The telecom industry currently outsources a mere 20% of production, he notes, adding, "If things slow down, they will outsource more to further cut costs."

Revenues and earnings are expected to increase 50% in 2001, yet the stock is down about 25% in the past month, recently fetching around $81. At that price, it's trading at 30 times projected 2001 earnings—on estimated long-term earnings growth of 30%. That's a P/E-to-growth, or PEG, ratio of 1, or less than half the current average for the S&P 500.

▶ **Quest Diagnostics.** When your doctor sends you to the local lab for blood work, chances are it's Quest Diagnostics, the largest chain of clinical laboratories, that's behind the needle.

Quest's core business—tests for cholesterol and the like—looks more promising than it has in years. After HMO price cuts in the mid-1990s squashed profits, Quest has spent the past few years renegotiating contracts for higher payment rates. In addition, insurers are approving more diagnostic testing to help catch illnesses before they become serious.

But the big reason we like Quest is that advances in genomics are expected to soon generate new and highly profitable tests that use genes to predict and diagnose disease. Quest is working with biotech leader Genentech, for instance, to offer a test to identify breast cancer patients who can benefit from Genentech's therapies. In the not-so-distant future, predicts Quest CEO Ken Freeman, health-care providers will create a personalized medical profile based on an individual's genetic makeup. "These are true breakout opportunities for the company."

Quest's gene-related business, while only 10% of revenues, is growing 50% a year. Analysts like Merrill Lynch's Tom Gallucci expect Quest to boost earnings at least 30% annually for the next several years. At almost $115, or 39 times earnings, it's no bargain, but Gallucci believes the company's volumes are growing faster than Wall Street thinks.

▶ **Alza.** Any parent who's had to shovel medicine into a sick kid twice or thrice a day should have no trouble understanding why sales at boutique pharmaceutical company Alza are skyrocketing. Alza's drugs use technologies that reduce the number of daily doses by precisely controlling the release of medication into the body. Their latest offering: Concerta, a drug to help control attention-deficit hyperactivity disorder. Children need take it just once a day, compared with two or more times for the popular Ritalin. By November, after just two months on the market, Concerta already had captured 10% of new prescriptions for attention-deficit hyperactivity disorder, and analysts see sales of the drug ballooning to more than $100 million in 2001.

Linda Miller, co-manager of John Hancock Health Sciences, says those estimates are too timid. Alza has plenty of other pills popping. Sales of the incontinence medicine Ditropan, for example, more than doubled in 2000.

For now, Concerta and Ditropan sales should drive 24% earnings growth next year. Alza revenues already top $1 billion, making the company one of the leading mid-size pharmaceuticals. The stock already had tripled for the year as of early December, to about $41, and it's not cheap either, carrying a P/E of 42. But Alza's accelerating growth justifies that valuation. Says Miller: "Analysts are going to have to increase their estimates, and I don't think the market has reflected that yet."

▶ **eBay.** Everyone knows most dotcoms lost between 50% and 95% of their value in 2000. But before writing them all off, try to recall what made the Web such an appealing investment in the first place. The dream was that the Net's low fixed costs would transform media and retailing, allowing start-ups to compete with established giants. What boosters forgot to consider is how the Web's nonexistent barriers to entry would inflate marketing costs and eviscerate profit margins.

Now consider eBay. Auctions, like all markets, require liquidity to be effective. Sellers attract buyers, who attract more sellers. The more buyers and sellers a marketplace has, the more liquid that market is and the harder it is for a newcomer to break in. That's why eBay already controls 80% of online auctions and

Best Bond Buys

Seems the Fed no longer needs to squelch inflation by raising interest rates. There's even talk that it may cut rates in 2001 to stop a slower-growing economy from slipping into recession. That's good news for investment-grade bonds, where prices move in the opposite direction from interest rates.

We loved Vanguard Intermediate-Term Tax-Exempt last year—it's up nearly 7% since, placing it in the top 20% of similar funds—and we love it now. The 0.18% expense ratio is a good 0.8 percentage points lower than what similar funds charge. The average holding is rated AA, and many are insured against default. If interest rates do climb, this fund certainly takes a hit, but the intermediate time frame (its average bond is due in 10 to 15 years) won't expose its holdings to as much interest-rate risk as it would if it held longer-dated bonds.

For a taxable alternative, look no further than Bill Gross. Famous for his Pimco Total Return, he also manages two lower-cost alternatives, Fremont Bond and Harbor Bond, that are similarly run clones for other fund companies. No load. Low $2,000 minimums. And not a bad price. Each has a five-year return in the top 3% of taxable bond funds.

BOND FUNDS	PHONE (800)	EXPENSE RATIO	THREE-YEAR RETURN[3]	COMMENTS
Fremont Bond	**548-4539**	**0.60%**	**6.5%**	**This Bill Gross vehicle was up more than 10% for 2000.**
Harbor Bond	**422-1050**	**0.61**	**6.6**	**Another Gross fund that mirrors Pimco Total Return**
Vanguard Intermediate-Term Tax-Exempt	**662-7447**	**0.18**	**4.5**	**One of the best bets in tax-exempt investing**

Note: [1]Annualized as of Dec. 1, 2000. **Source:** Morningstar.

why its profit margins keep rising. It's also why eBay is the rare Internet company that's built to last.

Already profitable, eBay grew earnings an incredible 1,200% in the third quarter of 2000. For the year, profits were expected to rise 420%, and for the next five years, Wall Street predicts 50% annual earnings growth. Given eBay's fattening margins and its rapid expansion into new regions (such as Europe) and markets (used cars), this 50% projection seems reasonable.

If we're right about the growth rate, eBay is a good deal at a beaten-down $34.75 a share. The 93 P/E may look expensive, but it's a reasonable multiple for a company with triple-digit earnings growth and a well of potential advertising revenue that, to date, has gone untapped. In a weaker economic environment, eBay may thrive as shoppers flock to secondhand merchandise in an attempt to save money.

▶ **Redback Networks.** Caught in the telecom debacle, Redback Networks' shares plummeted from a springtime high of $198 to $74.50 in early December. "We're not concerned about a decline in service-provider spending," Redback CEO Vivek Ragavan insists. "In our space, they are spending more because our products lead to revenue generation."

Over the past 12 months, Redback's sales soared 340% to $190 million. By the end of 2001, that number should hit $650 million, with gross profit margins approaching 63%. Carriers are buying Redback because it helps them better manage the customers who use their high-speed Internet connections. What's really got savvy investors excited is Redback's SmartEdge machines, which take voice, video and data from the telco's central office, convert them into packets and route them along the telecom pipes that circle major cities.

Redback sells for about 147 times the 55¢ a share Wall Street calculates it'll earn in 2001. But fans of the company say that profit target is too conservative. "Redback's growth rate is higher than Wall Street estimates, so it looks expensive," says Rudy Torrijos, a tech portfolio manager for Neuberger Berman.

▶ **Artisan International Fund.** The typical international stock portfolio plunged 17.5% for the year through Dec. 1 vs. a 9.6% loss for the S&P 500. What went wrong? A double whammy: Nasdaq carnage spread overseas while the plunging euro dragged down fund returns when they were translated into U.S. dollars. Hardest hit: international growth funds, which had feasted most heavily on volatile tech stocks, with an average 21.2% loss.

But the slump offers an opportunity. In Europe, for instance, corporate profits are expected to jump more than 15% in 2001. "Continental Europe right now is particularly undervalued," says Leila Heckman, a managing director at Salomon Smith Barney.

One choice in this arena for 2001 is $4.6 billion Artisan International, a fund we recommended last year. Manager Mark Yockey seeks fast-growing companies but steers clear of high valuations. That strategy led him to trim his tech holdings earlier in 2000, a timely move that helped him sustain a relatively modest 13.6% loss for the year. Still, tech remains a solid 28% of his fund's assets, with stakes in Ericsson and Software AG. "The key is to own good companies that make something people will buy," explains Yockey. "Now's a great opportunity, because dozens of good names have been obliterated in the market downturn." Overall, nearly 60% of Artisan International's assets are in European stocks.

▶ **Excelsior Energy Fund.** If you've stared dumbfounded at your heating bill lately, you probably can guess how much energy stocks soared throughout 2000. And it looks as if shares of natural gas explorers and oil companies will keep climbing well into 2001. But energy, with its gambles and confusing science, can scorch stock pickers. Trust a fund that knows the terrain: Excelsior Energy, which offers strong performance and a very low price.

The $88 million fund realized a 27.2% return over the past 12 months by balancing workhorses like ExxonMobil with comers like Nabors Industries, which explores for and produces oil and natural gas. Portfolio manager Michael Hoover expects commodity prices to stabilize in the coming year yet still rest well above their 1999 trough. As investors grow accustomed to those prices, Hoover predicts higher P/Es for major oil companies. And he's even more bullish on natural gas, used to generate electricity. Hoover, who's run the fund since 1995, also expects a "second leg" of drilling to boost exploration and marketing companies.

Excelsior has an expense ratio of 0.97% vs. an average 1.77% for natural resources funds.

▶ *The Best Mutual Funds*

It's easy for mutual fund investors to become intoxicated by a fund's recent returns. Is there any fund investor who has never had the urge to buy what's hot and avoid what's lagging? That's a completely natural feeling—and a very dangerous one.

As an antidote to that approach, we recommend buying funds that have outperformed their peers over time, in both up and down markets. Our favorite list of such funds, we must confess, is the MONEY 100 (see pages 28 to 30), which contains many excellent vehicles that can meet your needs, regardless of your goals. For the most recent data and performance information on these funds, head to www.money.com/money100.

FUND NAME	STYLE[1]	% ANNUAL EXPENSES	MINIMUM INITIAL INVESTMENT	NET ASSETS (MILLIONS)	TELEPHONE (800)
LARGE-CAP					
Alleghany/Montag & Caldwell	Growth	1.1	$2,500	$1,654	992-8151
Clipper	Value	1.1	5,000	813	776-5033
Dodge & Cox Stock	Value	0.6	2,500	4,219	621-3979
Domini Social Equity	Blend	1.0	1,000	1,420	762-6814
Dreyfus Appreciation	Blend	0.9	2,500	4,163	373-9387
Excelsior Value & Restructuring	Value	0.8	500	1,205	446-1012
Fidelity	Blend	0.6	2,500	17,027	544-8888
Gabelli Westwood Equity	Value	1.5	1,000	177	422-3554
Harbor Capital Appreciation	Growth	0.7	2,000	9,722	422-1050
Janus	Growth	0.8	2,500	49,058	525-8983
Kemper-Dreman High Return	Value	1.2[4]	1,000	1,367	621-1048
Legg Mason Value	Value	1.7	1,000	13,332	577-8589
Marsico Focus	Growth	1.3	2,500	3,332	860-8686[8]
Masters' Select Equity	Blend	1.3	5,000	477	960-0188
MFS Capital Opportunities A	Blend	1.2[4]	1,000	2,483	637-2929
MFS Mass. Investors Trust A	Blend	0.9[4]	1,000	7,591	637-2929
Neuberger Berman Partners	Value	0.8	1,000	2,307	877-9700
Nicholas	Blend	0.7	500	4,900	227-5987
Oakmark	Value	1.2	1,000	2,215	625-6275
Oppenheimer Main St. G & I A	Blend	0.9[4]	1,000	8,912	525-7048
Rainier Core Equity	Blend	1.1	2,500[6]	1,009	248-6314
Safeco Equity	Value	0.7	1,000	1,907	624-5711
Schwab 1000	Blend	0.5	2,500	5,278	435-4000
Selected American Shares	Value	0.9	1,000	3,798	243-1575
SSgA Growth & Income	Blend	1.1	1,000	443	647-7327
Stein Roe Young Investor	Blend	1.2	2,500[7]	1,110	338-2550
TCW Galileo Select Equities N	Growth	1.4	2,000	47	386-3829
TIAA-CREF Growth Equity	Growth	0.5	250	842	223-1200
TIAA-CREF Social Choice Equity[2]	Blend	0.3	250	—	223-1200
Torray	Value	1.1	10,000	1,923	443-3036
T. Rowe Price Equity Income	Value	0.8	2,500	10,261	638-5660
Vanguard 500 Index	Blend	0.2	3,000	107,365	851-4999
Vanguard Total Stock Mkt. Index	Blend	0.2	3,000	19,720	851-4999
Vanguard U.S. Growth	Growth	0.4	3,000	20,061	851-4999
Vanguard Windsor II	Value	0.4	3,000	23,218	851-4999
Washington Mutual Investors	Value	0.6[4]	250	49,507	421-0180
White Oak Growth Stock	Growth	1.0	2,000	3,702	462-5386[8]

FUND NAME	STYLE[1]	% ANNUAL EXPENSES	MINIMUM INITIAL INVESTMENT	NET ASSETS (MILLIONS)	TELEPHONE (800)
MIDCAP					
Brandywine	Growth	1.1	$25,000	$6,597	656-3017
First Eagle Fund of America Y	Blend	1.4	1,000	457	451-3623
Franklin California Growth A	Growth	1.0[4]	1,000	2,209	342-5236
Gabelli Asset	Blend	1.4	1,000	2,014	422-3554
Homestead Value	Value	0.7	500	357	258-3030
Janus Special Situations	Growth	1.0	2,500	1,849	525-8983
Longleaf Partners	Value	0.9	10,000	3,172	445-9469
Mairs & Power Growth	Blend	0.8	2,500	485	304-7404
MAS Mid Cap Growth Inst.	Growth	0.6	2,500[6]	1,842	354-8185
Nicholas-Applegate Growth	Growth	1.5[5]	1,000	450	551-8643
Oakmark Select	Value	1.2	1,000	1,502	625-6275
Oak Value	Blend	1.1	2,500	309	622-2474
RS MidCap Opportunities	Growth	1.5	5,000	305	766-3863
Sound Shore	Value	1.0	10,000	1,500	551-1980
Strong Opportunity	Value	1.2	2,500	2,808	368-1030
Strong Schafer Value	Value	1.4	2,500	448	368-1030
T. Rowe Price Mid-Cap Growth	Growth	0.9	2,500	6,042	638-5660
T. Rowe Price Value	Value	0.9	2,500	804	638-5660
Tweedy Browne American Value	Value	1.4	2,500	905	432-4789
Weitz Value	Value	1.2	2,500[6]	2,472	232-4161
SMALL-CAP					
Acorn	Growth	0.9	$1,000	$4,021	922-6769
Artisan Small Cap Value	Value	1.4	1,000	177	344-1770
CGM Focus	Blend	1.2	2,500	56	345-4048
Clover Small Cap Value	Value	1.4	2,500	29	226-9558
Delafield	Value	1.2	5,000	70	221-3079
Eclipse Small Cap Value	Value	1.2	1,000	203	872-2710
Fasciano	Growth	1.2	1,000	300	848-6050
Fremont U.S. Small Cap	Growth	1.5	2,000	78	548-4539
MAS Small Cap Growth	Growth	1.2	2,500[6]	473	354-8185
Royce Premier	Value	1.2	2,000	565	221-4268
Third Avenue Value	Value	1.1	1,000	1,639	443-1021
T. Rowe Price Small Cap Stock	Blend	1.0	2,500	1,962	638-5660
Vanguard Small-Cap Index	Blend	0.3	3,000	4,104	851-4999
Wasatch Core Growth	Blend	1.4	2,000	189	551-1700
Westport Small Cap R	Blend	1.5	5,000	100	593-7878[8]

FUND NAME	STYLE[1]	% ANNUAL EXPENSES	MINIMUM INITIAL INVESTMENT	NET ASSETS (MILLIONS)	TELEPHONE (800)
INTERNATIONAL					
Acorn International	Foreign	1.1	$1,000	$3,405	922-6769
American Century Intl. Growth	Foreign	1.5	2,500	5,122	345-2021
Capital World Growth & Income	World	0.8[4]	250	11,511	421-0180
Deutsche International Equity[3]	Foreign	1.5	2,500	2,567	730-1313
EuroPacific Growth	Foreign	0.8[4]	250	22,100	421-0180
Fidelity Diversified International	Foreign	1.2	2,500	5,945	544-8888
Hotchkis & Wiley International	Foreign	1.0	10,000	1,364	236-4479
Janus Worldwide	World	0.9	2,500	44,476	525-8983
Japan	Foreign	1.3	2,500	979	535-2726
Loomis Sayles Intl. Equity Retail	Foreign	1.3	5,000	15	633-3330
New Perspective	World	0.8[4]	250	35,806	421-0180
Putnam International Growth A	Foreign	1.3[4]	500	6,612	225-1581
Scudder International	Foreign	1.2	2,500	5,276	225-2470
SSgA Emerging Markets	Foreign	1.3	1,000	396	647-7327
Templeton Dev. Markets A	Foreign	2.2[4]	1,000	2,605	342-5236
T. Rowe Price Emerg. Mkts Stock	Foreign	1.8	2,500	207	638-5660
T. Rowe Price Int'l Stock	Foreign	0.9	2,500	12,900	638-5660
Tweedy Browne Global Value	World	1.4	2,500	3,236	432-4789
Vanguard Global Asset Allocation	World	0.6	3,000	108	851-4999
Vanguard International Growth	Foreign	0.6	3,000	10,824	851-4999
SPECIALTY					
CGM Realty	Value	1.0	$2,500	$397	345-4048
Columbia Real Estate Equity	Value	1.0	1,000	291	547-1707
Dresdner RCM Global Tech. N	Growth	1.8	5,000	355	726-7240
Hancock Financial Industries A	Value	1.4[5]	1,000	574	225-5291
Invesco Health Sciences	Growth	1.2	1,000	1,615	525-8085
Longleaf Partners Realty	Value	1.2	10,000	578	445-9469
T. Rowe Price Science & Tech.	Growth	0.9	2,500	15,543	638-5660
Vanguard Health Care	Blend	0.4	10,000	11,810	851-4999

Notes: [1]Styles for stock funds: Blend—buys stocks that mix growth and value characteristics; growth—buys companies with accelerating earnings; value—buys stocks that are inexpensive relative to earnings or assets; foreign—invests at least 90% of assets abroad; world—invests more than 10% of assets in the U.S. and more than 40% abroad. [2]Fund opened April 3, 2000. [3]Previously named BT Investment International Equity. [4]Plus 5.75% maximum sales charge. [5]Plus 5% maximum sales charge. [6]If purchased through Schwab OneSource, 800-435-4000. [7]Plans for minors can have minimums as low as $100. [8]Area code 888.
Source: Morningstar, Chicago.

The Smart Way to Buy Tech

Despite the drubbing technology stocks have suffered in the past year, investors continue to have an amazing level of confidence in the sector. "The future is in technology," we've heard many people say. "It's always going to go back up."

It's easy to understand why investors are so sanguine. Technological innovation has been the driving force behind the current economic boom, and the stunning performance of well-known tech stocks has made investing in the sector seem easy. If, for example, you'd invested $10,000 in Oracle in 1995, your stake would have been worth $140,000 five years later. Invested in Sun Microsystems, the same amount would have grown to $320,000. With EMC, you would have had $400,000.

But don't let the gaudy numbers fool you. Tech is actually the toughest sector of the market to play. The stocks are volatile and the best businesses are richly valued. Plus, technology itself changes so fast that it's difficult for laymen to keep up. For most tech investors, disappointment is as likely as success: In the past five years, only a third of all tech stocks beat the S&P 500. So it's crucial to know what risks you're exposing yourself to.

Our goal here is to deconstruct some dangerous myths that have grown up around tech investing and provide a sensible framework for approaching the sector.

▶ **MYTH NO. 1: You need to load up on tech stocks or you'll be left behind.**
Reality: Why not buy more of the fastest-growing businesses around? But before you sign up for 100 shares of Oracle, check out what you own now—because you may already be loaded with tech. If you own an S&P 500 index fund, for instance, the percentage of your holdings in tech has jumped from 18% in 1999 to 28% today. Actively managed funds are also packed with tech: American Century Ultra's stake is 39%, and it's even higher for Vanguard US Growth (55%) and Janus Twenty (59%). The point is that if much of your money is currently in growth funds and tech-tinged stocks, adding more may leave you overexposed.

▶ **MYTH NO. 2: Tech is the easiest way to get rich.**
Reality: In the 1920s, many investors realized that the automobile would have a profound impact on the U.S. economy.

Dazzled by high-growth tech companies, investors drove stocks like these to quadruple-digit gains. But their valuations have become dangerously inflated. As of September 2000, Ariba wasn't making a dime in profits, yet it traded at 229 times sales vs. two times sales for the S&P 500.

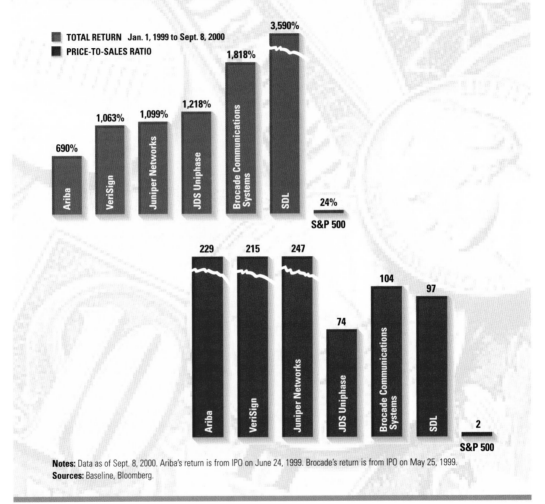

TOTAL RETURN Jan. 1, 1999 to Sept. 8, 2000
PRICE-TO-SALES RATIO

Total Return:
- Ariba: 690%
- VeriSign: 1,063%
- Juniper Networks: 1,099%
- JDS Uniphase: 1,218%
- Brocade Communications Systems: 1,818%
- SDL: 3,590%
- S&P 500: 24%

Price-to-Sales Ratio:
- Ariba: 229
- VeriSign: 215
- Juniper Networks: 247
- JDS Uniphase: 74
- Brocade Communications Systems: 104
- SDL: 97
- S&P 500: 2

Notes: Data as of Sept. 8, 2000. Ariba's return is from IPO on June 24, 1999. Brocade's return is from IPO on May 25, 1999.
Sources: Baseline, Bloomberg.

Yet parlaying that knowledge into winning stock picks was no easy task. As value investor David Dreman notes in his book *Contrarian Investment Strategies*, car makers like Dusenberg, Packard and Studebaker were all formidable competitors in their day, and it was hardly obvious that Ford, Chrysler and GM would be the ultimate victors.

Even for professional investors, the tech sector is something of a crapshoot. When Marty Whitman of Third Avenue Value saw how cheap the semiconductor equipment sector was in '98, he could have bet heavily on just one stock. Instead he bought a dozen. "It's just so hard to predict who's going to make it," he explains. "I expect to have a 30% strikeout rate."

Another thing to remember is that the tech market isn't a single entity. It stretches from chips to servers, telecom to dotcom. Within these subsectors, there are waves of boom and bust. For example, Internet content plays like iVillage and TheStreet.com once soared, only to lose more than 95% of their value later on. In 2000, the telecom sector, long beloved by Wall Street, crashed with a sickening thud.

Never lose sight of how quickly today's buzzword can become tomorrow's chopped liver. Procter & Gamble doesn't need to reinvent Tide every year to sell detergent, but Intel would wither away if it failed to upgrade its microprocessors. This constant threat of obsolescence makes tech a brutally tough business.

Meanwhile, other sectors can also give you great returns: For the first 11 months of 2000, financial services, health care and utilities rose significantly, while tech floundered.

▶ **MYTH NO. 3: Buy the market leaders; you can't pay too much.**

Reality: The stock market has come to be dominated by Goliaths like Cisco, Intel, Microsoft, Nortel, Oracle and Sun. These six companies have a combined market value of $1.8 trillion—three times the gross domestic product of Canada. So far, buying market leaders like these has worked—most of the time.

But not in 2000, when many of the largest, best-known tech stocks fell dramatically from their 52-week highs. Those taking a shellacking included Lucent (-74%), Nortel (-64%), Qualcomm (-63%), Dell (-61%), Intel (-51%), Microsoft (-47%), America Online (-47%) and even allegedly bulletproof Cisco (-45%).

The lesson is simple: Stocks with sky-high valuations are especially vulnerable because trigger-happy investors will bail out at the first sign of trouble. "The very visible names—the Ciscos, Suns, EMCs, Oracles [and] optical-networking names like JDS Uniphase—seem to me to be very, very expensive," warns Bill Miller of Legg Mason Value Trust. "Embedded in their prices are expectations that in the aggregate are unlikely to be met."

> **MYTH NO. 4: Don't worry about profits; if sales are soaring, you've got a winner.**

Reality: One peculiarity of today's market is that investors have fallen in love with profitless tech companies. Ariba and Commerce One, for example, have never made a dime. Yet, through September 2000, they had risen 690% and 528% respectively since going public in 1999.

In 1999's bizarro market, shares in unprofitable companies actually outperformed those of profitable ones by an average of 50 percentage points, according to Merrill Lynch. In 2000, that trend reversed. The lesson: Shares in money-losing companies can thrive for a while, but when assumptions shift—as they have for e-commerce stocks—the results can be devastating. Of the 148 tech companies whose stocks plunged 75% or more in 2000, 131 were not making any money.

> **MYTH NO. 5: If every analyst loves a stock, you're on solid ground.**

Reality: In the fall of 2000, Wall Street analysts were almost uniformly bullish about tech stocks. If you clicked on to **Yahoo**

Illustration by Ricardo Stampatori

Finance (www.yahoo.com), you would have seen that JDS Uniphase had garnered 30 "buy" recommendations from analysts, three "holds" and no "sells." One reason: Analysts are loath to alienate companies that could be a source of lucrative investment banking deals such as mergers. "Politically, you have to have a 'buy' rating," says Ken Pearlman, a former analyst who now manages money for Firsthand Funds. Nonetheless, many investors continue to regard analysts' glowing reports as signals to buy.

In 1999, analysts were especially hot on Citrix, which sells software that allows different operating systems to share data. Every one of these analysts failed to foresee that Citrix's earnings growth was slowing. Between March and August of 2000, the stock crashed 88%.

Investors looking for the real story on Citrix would have been better off scouring the insider-trading data on sites like **insidertrader.com**. There, they would have seen that Citrix's two top executives sold 230,000 shares in the two months prior to Citrix's decline. Now *that's* a sell recommendation.

▶ MYTH NO. 6: **Once a tech stock is out of favor, it's toast.**

Reality: Chip Morris, manager of T. Rowe Price Science & Technology, used to hunt for cheap tech stocks, but he recently abandoned that approach. "We're in a market that diverges to the extremes, so that doesn't play anymore," he explains.

In the short term, the rules of the game may have changed. But out-of-favor tech stocks have a lucrative history of bouncing back. Firms like IBM, Hewlett-Packard, Advanced Micro Devices and Apple all recovered sharply after being widely dismissed as dead in the water. Another benefit of buying what's unloved is that it often has less downside risk than voguish stocks that are priced for perfection.

Three paths to tech profits. If tech investing is so risky and complicated, should you just turn away? Hardly. Even in today's richly priced tech market, there are clearly areas of great opportunity. We've developed strategies that we believe are ideally suited to the current tech market. Our first strategy relies on sector funds run by a handful of the nation's savviest stock pickers; our second strategy focuses on overlooked or beaten-down companies with underappreciated businesses; and finally, we offer a strategy for investing in speculative stocks with the potential to be the next stock market stars.

1. **Hire a pro.**

Before you load up on individual tech stocks, ask yourself if you're really up to the task of analyzing these companies. (Care to define dense wavelength division multiplexing?) For many of us, it makes sense to hire a mutual fund manager who can spend all day analyzing companies and assessing their competition. They can also engage in the fast-paced trading that aggressive tech investing sometimes requires. Funds also often get access to racy IPOs that aren't available to individual investors.

The three funds we recommend below are all run by experienced managers with outstanding long-term records.

▶ **Dresdner RCM Global Technology** (www.drcmfunds.com; 800-726-7240) offers three approaches to tech within a single fund. Co-managers Huachen Chen and Walter Price own a core of market leaders like Sun. But they also have more aggressive plays like Ariba, which helped propel the fund to a 183% return in 1999. (For the first eleven months of 2000, the fund had a market-beating return of -5.9%.) Another portion of the fund is stashed in what Chen calls "real value plays." These currently include beaten-down Internet company eBay, which they expect to grow explosively, and Tyco, which sells everything from electronics to medical supplies and has a modest P/E of 21. While every tech fund is risky, this one is milder than most, thanks in part to this smattering of lower-priced stocks.

▶ **Firsthand Technology Value** (www.firsthandfunds.com; 888-884-2675) holds tech stocks for the long term—quite a rarity nowadays. The average tech fund has a turnover of 250%, meaning that it typically holds stocks for less than five months. By contrast, Firsthand has a remarkably low turnover of 40%. Manager Kevin Landis—a former Silicon Valley engineer—seeks out strong trends, then plays them by buying relatively cheap stocks that he views as undiscovered or unloved.

Landis' eye for value led him to snap up Applied Micro Circuits in 1997 and 1998 when it was hit by the Asian economic crisis. At its peak, the stock had risen 9,100% since he first bought it. Landis recently unloaded JDS Uniphase because it got too pricey, but even he has his share of stocks with sky-high P/Es. So far, he's played the tech boom as well as anybody: For the five years ended November 30, 2000, his fund has averaged 43.73% a year, beating all of its peers.

▶ **Turner Technology** (www.turner-invest.com; 800-224-6312) makes most other tech funds look tame. Lead manager Bob Turner makes masses of short-term trades to exploit the sector's volatility. Turner says his turnover could go as high as 1,000%. He typically owns only about 40 stocks, so the fund doesn't offer the comforts of broad diversification.

Turner's momentum-driven approach may sound scary, but it works—at least in a bull market. In the fund's first year (mid 1999 to mid-2000), it returned a phenomenal 224%. If the tech sector holds up, he stands a good chance of outperforming his peers. Just don't expect a relaxing ride.

2. Buy bargains.

One of the best ways to make money in tech is to buy stocks nobody else likes. Wireless stocks, for example, are being treated like toxic waste, but has much changed? Not really. Analysts estimate that 425 million mobile handsets were sold globally in 2000—not as spectacular as the 450 million that bulls had previously predicted, but still far better than the 270 million sold in 1999. All that's really different is that the herd has moved on to fresher pastures.

This exodus has created some compelling bargains, such as Motorola (MOT), where disappointing profits have sent the stock reeling 71% since March 2000. There are signs, though, that the company is on the mend. It's expected to boost handset margins in 2001, and its other businesses, such as set-top boxes for digital TV, are gaining ground too.

Another one-time wireless darling that was selling at an alluring discount in October 2000 is Sawtek (SAWS), which sells circuits that filter noise and unwanted radio frequencies in mobile handsets and wireless base stations. Sawtek's customers include Ericsson, Motorola, Nokia and Samsung. Their mobile phones typically contain $2 to $7 worth of Sawtek's filters.

It's a lucrative business. Sawtek earns more than 30¢ per dollar of sales and "throws off a ton of free cash flow," says Chris Bonavico of Transamerica Premier Aggressive Growth fund. In the past, the firm primarily made components for products that use Qualcomm's CDMA technology. But Sawtek is now branching out by selling components for products that use two other wireless technologies. That should help boost Sawtek's earnings growth rate to 47% annually for the next three years, says Chase H&Q's Ed Snyder. Yet the stock trades at only 26 times this fiscal year's expected earnings—strikingly cheap for an outfit that's growing this fast.

Lucent (LU) has plunged because management woefully underestimated demand for optical systems, sales of old-line products like traditional phone switches have sagged and the firm lowered its earnings targets. But Ned Brines, an analyst at Roger Engemann & Associates, points out that Lucent is still a "strong No. 2 in five important telecommunications businesses." These include booming areas like wireless and optical-communications systems. Right now, investors seem to be grossly undervaluing these businesses. Take Lucent's microelectronic unit, which sells optical components. In the past 12 months, it had sales of $4 billion and its earnings grew 38%. In 2001, Lucent plans to spin the unit off.

3. Roll the dice.

If you're an aggressive investor, it makes sense to bet a small portion of your portfolio on a couple of more speculative tech stocks. They may get creamed, but there's also a chance that you'll land a huge winner. The key is to identify companies with spectacular growth potential and jump in before they hit everyone else's radar screens.

One fledgling company that showed tremendous promise at the end of 2000 is Boston-based SpeechWorks International (SPWX), which went public in August 2000. It's still small, with a market value of $1.9 billion, and it's not making any money yet.

Illustration by Ricardo Stampatori

SpeechWorks is at the forefront, though, of a major emerging trend. Its speech-recognition software allows customers to obtain automated services from corporations by speaking in a natural voice over the phone. Companies that adopt speech-activated technology are able to cut costs because they don't have to hire as many operators to field customer calls. The technology can be used for an array of everyday tasks, from ordering clothes to checking flight schedules to trading stocks. "This is a huge growth area," says Joe McNay, chairman of Essex Investment Management, and SpeechWorks is a "true leader of the business."

One caveat: This stock is crazily volatile. After going public at $20, it zoomed to $108.50 within three days, then plunged to $45. It has since rebounded to $67—about 38% off its peak.

Another hot prospect at the end of 2000 was International Rectifier (IRF), a little-known outfit with a $2.2 billion market cap. By the end of 2000, this 53-year-old firm emerged as the premier maker of power chips. These devices take the alternating current flowing from your electrical socket and convert it into direct current so it can be used by a microprocessor or smart chip. It doesn't sound sexy, but it's a huge growth business, since popular gadgets like handheld computers, mobile phones and digital cameras all need power chips. Power chips are also used in generators and microturbines, which provide ultrareliable sources of power.

The company is growing at a dazzling pace. In its latest fiscal year, revenues soared 38% to $753 million. Wall Street estimates that it will earn $2.84 per share in the fiscal year ending in June 2001. The firm has no debt and $800 million in cash. Yet the stock has a modest P/E of 13—proof that you can find great tech stocks at affordable prices even in today's overheated market.

▶ Competition for Mutual Funds

The folks who run mutual funds have always been good at cooking up clever ways to gouge you on fees, confuse you about performance, make you pay unnecessary taxes and goad you into buying funds you don't need. Creating genuinely better ways to invest has ranked on many fund executives' to-do lists somewhere behind "schedule proctological exam."

Suddenly, however, true innovation has arrived in the fund business—mostly from the outside—and mutual funds are no longer the only game in town for long-term investors. Three intriguing new rivals offer exciting options for some investors with specific needs.

The ABCs of ETFs. ETFs (exchange-traded funds) are highly complex and can be fully explained only with gibberish like "creation units" and "redemptions in kind." Luckily, that complexity is irrelevant to you as an investor. You don't need to know exactly how a computer works to be able to send e-mail, and you don't need to master all the intricacies of ETFs in order to invest in them.

ETFs, which date back to 1993, are similar to regular index funds, but they trade on the American Stock Exchange just like stocks. Instead of buying directly from (or selling directly back to) a fund company, you buy or sell ETFs through a broker. The best-known ETFs are SPDRs (based on Standard & Poor's 500-stock index), Diamonds (based on the Dow Jones industrial average), QQQs (or "Qubes," based on the Nasdaq 100 index) and iShares from Barclays Global Investors, which track dozens of different stock indexes.

ETFs have some big pluses. First, they're cheap. Once you pay the broker's commission, an ETF may cost as little as 0.1% a year to own; a traditional fund can easily cost 15 times as much. Second, unlike many traditional mutual funds, ETFs won't whack you with capital-gains tax bills. If you're a buy-and-hold investor, you could keep one of these babies for decades and never pay a dime in capital-gains tax. (That's not a guarantee, but it's pretty close.)

What are the minuses? First, not all ETFs are cheap. For instance, the iShares Dow Jones Healthcare Sector Index Fund charges 0.6% in annual fees—nearly twice the cost of a traditional fund like Vanguard Health Care. If you pay a $14.95 commission to invest $1,000 in an ETF through an online broker, you've forked over 1.5% of your money; at a no-load mutual fund, buying and selling cost nothing. And dollar-cost averaging—investing a fixed amount every month—makes no sense with an ETF, since you pay a commission on each purchase.

The bottom line is that ETFs are a good option if you're in a high tax bracket and you're making a one-time lump-sum investment of at least $3,000—the level at which most online brokerage commissions drop under 1%. But if you want to invest additional money on a regular basis, then ETFs are not for you; even the low commissions at an online broker will eat you alive.

Building a portfolio DRIP by DRIP. Next let's look at microinvesting websites, which allow you to toss tidbits of money into individual stocks. Among the best are **www.buyandhold.com** and **www.sharebuilder.com**. These are online centers for "DRIP investing"—the dividend-reinvestment plans and direct stock-purchase programs that many companies offer so retail investors can buy shares without a broker.

Sharebuilder.com has no minimum balance; buyandhold.com lets you open an account with just $20. Sharebuilder.com charges $2 for each regular periodic purchase of any of the more than 2,000 U.S. stocks it offers, $5 for a one-time-only purchase and $19.95 to sell; buyandhold.com charges $2.99 each time you buy or sell any of 1,700 U.S. stocks. Both services will systematically buy shares for you weekly or monthly, reinvest dividends at no charge and let you buy your favorite stocks through automatic withdrawals from your bank account. Sharebuilder.com even lets you invest with payroll deductions.

The obvious drawback is cost. While $2 or $2.99 is a tiny amount of money, it's a monstrous percentage of a $20 investment. In fact, if you invest $20 a week, buyandhold.com's fee comes to 14.95%—nearly twice the highest mutual fund sales commission allowed by law. That's not cheap, but if you insist on picking your own stocks and have only a small amount of money to work with each month—say, $100 or less—then these microinvesting websites are probably the best choice you're going to find.

Fill your basket. Finally comes the most novel competitor, an online service called **www.foliofn.com**. Folio, which launched in May 2000, has gotten lots of glowing press, partly because its founder, Steven Wallman, is a former big cheese at the U.S.

► **For ETFs:**
www.amex.com/indexshares/index_shares_over.stm
www.ishares.com
www.spdrindex.com

► **For DRIPS:**
www.buyandhold.com
www.sharebuilder.com
www.dripinvestor.com

► **For Foliofn:**
www.foliofn.com

Securities and Exchange Commission, where he was a fervent advocate for retail investors. When Wallman says, "We've combined the diversification benefits of mutual funds with the customized service of a brokerage to rethink how you invest," he's not kidding.

Here's how Folio works: For a $295 flat annual fee (or $29.95 a month), you can assemble up to three investment baskets or "folios," each containing as many as 50 stocks. You can choose the stocks yourself, or select from nearly 80 prefab folios—one holds the 30 stocks in the Dow, another is a basket of 19 companies that sponsor or benefit from NASCAR racing. You can trade as often or as seldom as you like at no extra cost. What's more, you can buy or sell the entire folio, or one or more stocks separately—giving you much greater control over your tax bill than a mutual fund can offer. You can invest automatically every month, and Folio offers an excellent tax-tracking tool, a crucial feature for anyone with a do-it-yourself stock portfolio.

There's one odd wrinkle: Under its all-inclusive fee, Folio executes trades only twice a day, at 10:15 a.m. and 2:45 p.m. In other words, the costs of trading are automatically included in your account fee—so long as you trade only when Folio wants you to. (Why? By concentrating all its customers' dealings into these "trading windows," Folio can seek to match the maximum number of buyers and sellers in-house, which keeps everyone's brokerage costs low.) If, however, you want to trade immediately at, say, 9:47 a.m., then Folio will charge $14.95 to fill your order.

For risk-tolerant long-term investors, this wrinkle shouldn't be a problem; but if you are a hair-trigger trader, Folio is not for you. Also, Folio is not economical for small accounts. Even if you invest $10,000, Folio's $295 annual fee will eat up nearly 3% of your money. For initial investments of $25,000 and up, however, Folio looks good—and above $165,000, Folio is even cheaper than a SPDR or a Vanguard index fund.

▶ Four Ways to Play Bonds

For most investors, bonds are the afterthought of asset allocation. That's because, according to standard portfolio management advice, the role of fixed-income securities is to smooth out the volatility of a stock-packed portfolio. But because we may be headed for a few lean years, bonds may grow beyond their risk-reducing duties for your portfolio. Now that economic growth has

Illustration by Ricardo Stampatori

slowed, and interest rates have steadied, this may be an excellent time to spice up your portfolio with bonds. Below are four smart strategies for capitalizing on today's opportunities.

▶ **Take advantage of short-term Treasury yields.** Normally, the longer the term of a bond, the higher the yield. But two-year Treasury notes now yield more than 10-year notes and almost as much as 30-year bonds (mainly because investors see slow economic growth ahead). In mid-November 2000, you could get a 5.89% yield on a two-year note and 5.78% on a 10-year. This is the equivalent of eating your cake and having it too: You get higher yields without having to tie up your money for a decade.

Treasuries are the safest and easiest way to lock in a steady payout. You can buy them straight from the government for only $1,000, with no fees or expenses (www.publicdebt.treas.gov; 800-943-6864).

▶ **Lock in high muni bond yields while you still can.** Tax-free municipal bonds are traditionally the province of the wealthy. But not today: Tax-free municipal bond yields are so high relative to Treasury yields that they make sense for anyone in the 28% federal tax bracket or above. As a result, savvy buyers have been grabbing munis.

For example, the average 10-year AAA insured bond yielded about 4.93% in mid-November 2000—equivalent to a taxable 6.85% for someone in the 28% bracket. If you've hit the 31% or 39.6% brackets, the equivalent yields are 7.14% and 8.16%, respectively. Buy a bond exempt from state taxes too for an even bigger yield boost. (Go to www.investinginbonds.com to calculate yields for your state and tax bracket.)

If you have less than $75,000 to invest in individual bonds, consider a low-cost intermediate-term bond fund such as Vanguard Intermediate-Term Tax-Exempt (www.vanguard.com; 800-851-4999), recently yielding 5.1%, or Scudder Medium-Term Tax-Free (www.scudder.com; 800-225-2470), paying 5.02%. Both emphasize high-quality bonds and avoid big bets on the direction of interest rates. USAA Tax-Exempt Intermediate-Term (www.usaa.com; 800-382-8722) ventures into lower-quality bonds but has compensated with a higher payout, lately 5.37%.

▶ **Shelter your long-term savings from inflation.** Two fairly new types of government securities do what no bond has done before: give guaranteed protection against inflation, which

Q. One of my mutual funds went down last year, but my statement claimed that I owed capital-gains tax. Why did I have to pay taxes on a money-losing mutual fund?

A. It may not seem fair, but even funds that have losing years can hit their shareholders with a tax bill. That's because the taxes are based on the stocks the fund sold at a profit during the year, not the overall performance of the portfolio. Federal law requires that the fund distribute substantially all of those gains (minus any losses from stock sales) to shareholders. Two ways to minimize this problem: Stay out of funds with a history of high tax bills, and don't invest in a fund late in the year, just before the distribution date.

Q. I like to invest in foreign companies. What's the difference between an American Depositary Receipt (ADR) and a New York Share?

A. Both allow U.S. citizens to buy, hold, sell, trade and receive dividends of foreign companies in U.S. dollars. But New York Shares are generally unique to companies in the Netherlands. Two good websites to check for more information on buying foreign stocks: J.P. Morgan's www.adr.com and Bank of New York's www.adrbny.com.

Q. I'm an investor in a company that's holding its next shareholders' meeting in Hawaii. I'd go in a minute if my travel expenses were tax deductible. Are they?

A. Possibly, but don't pack just yet. The Internal Revenue Service deals with situations like this on a case-by-case basis. If you have a function to fulfill at the meeting—you're presenting or opposing a resolution, for example—you're probably eligible for some kind of tax break. However, to deduct air fare, you'd have to fly in and stay just long enough to attend the meeting, then fly home.

If you extend your stay for a vacation, you'd be able to deduct, at best, only your hotel room for the night before the meeting plus any taxis to get back and forth. Attending the meeting simply as an onlooker gets you no deductions at all.

erodes the value of both principal and interest over time. Our favorite is the I-bond, an inflation-protected savings bond, yielding 6.49% in November 2000, including the inflation adjustment. Like regular savings bonds, I-bonds pay no interest until you redeem them (and you owe no taxes until then). But I-bonds have a kicker: The payout increases to keep pace with the cost of living. The next time you find yourself shopping online, surf over to www.savingsbonds.gov, and use your credit card to save instead.

Treasury inflation-protected securities (TIPS) offer a similar guarantee and potential for greater total returns. But the inflation adjustments are taxed each year, so consider TIPS only for an IRA or other tax-sheltered account. The easiest way to invest in TIPS is via a mutual fund, like the new Vanguard Inflation-Protected Securities.

▶ **Make a bet on rate decreases.** Some aggressive investors are already preparing for the rate declines that occur after an economic slowdown has taken hold. These hardy souls are playing bonds for capital gains. If you want to do the same, consider long-term Treasury funds such as Vanguard Long-Term U.S. Treasury, which are quite responsive to rates. For a more dramatic play, try American Century Target Maturities 2020 or 2025 (www.americancentury.com; 800-345-2021); these hold Treasury STRIPS, zero-coupon bonds that shoot up when rates fall (and tumble when they climb).

Robert Kessler, of asset management firm Kessler Cos., thinks that we are entering an economic period similar to that of 1989-93, when a 15-year STRIP returned 16.2% annually vs. 14.5% for the S&P 500. If he's wrong, and rates keep climbing? The price of STRIPS will plunge, but investors who hang on will continue to enjoy yields of almost 6%. (STRIPS don't pay interest until maturity, but you'll owe annual taxes on imputed income, so they're best for IRAs.)

Even if you're not inspired by one of these plays, bonds have a place as part of a diversified portfolio. If you haven't included them in yours, now is the time. If you don't want to think twice, stick with the Vanguard Total Bond Market Index fund.

▶ *How to Pick the Right Money Fund*

You may not put much thought into how you invest your cash. Let's face it, money-market funds all look the same, so why devote much time to picking one? Here's why. The Federal Reserve's rate hikes have driven money-fund yields to their highest point since 1991. The average in November 2000 was 6.08% vs. 4.5% a year ago. The yield at the top fund has jumped from

▶ Three Money Funds to Consider

You can check money.com for the top-yielding money market funds. But always consider these three funds, which consistently top the charts while charging very low expenses.

	% YIELD	MIN. INVESTMENT	TELEPHONE (800)
Strong Investors Money Fund	6.72	$1,000	368-1030
TIAA-CREF Money Market Fund	6.59	$250	223-1200
Vanguard Prime Money Market Fund	6.55	$3,000	662-7447

Source: MONEY, as of November, 2000.

5.25% to 6.76%. Yet not every investor is getting the full advantage of high rates. The spread between the highest- and lowest-yielding money funds stands at two percentage points; the difference between the highest-yielding fund and the average is three-quarters of a point.

That gap between average and best may seem paltry, but over time it adds up. Take $25,000 invested in the top-yielding Strong Investors Money Fund, which pays 6.72%, vs. the most widely held fund, the Smith Barney Cash Portfolio/Class A Fund, which yields 6.12%, or just above average. In 10 years, you'd earn nearly $3,000 more in the Strong fund.

Now that the Fed may be nearly done with rate hikes, money-market yields may be peaking for the short term, which means picking the best one is more important than ever. Here's what to look for.

Favor low expenses above all. With all money funds investing in the same pool of short-term government and corporate securities, low management fees are one of the few sure ways to stand out. Virtually every top-yielding fund has expenses well below the current 0.5% average or waives them. Three top-yielding funds with consistently low expenses are Strong Investors Money Fund, TIAA-CREF Money Market Fund and Vanguard Prime Money Market Fund, which charge 0.14%, 0.29% and 0.33%, respectively. (For yields, minimums and phone numbers for these top-yielding funds, see the box above.) Expenses are also the reason you'll likely earn average yields at best in your brokerage cash account. The expense ratio for the Smith Barney Cash Portfolio is 0.59%, for example; the Schwab Money Market Fund's is 0.75%.

Don't get blinded by tax perks. The difference between the yields on taxable money funds and tax-exempt ones is so wide today that most investors are better off accepting a tax bill. If you're in the 31% federal tax bracket, the taxable equivalent yield for the top tax-free fund, Strong Municipal Money Market, is 6.03%, well shy of the 6.76% top taxable yield. Only those in the 39.6% bracket (taxable income over $288,350 for both singles and marrieds filing jointly) earn more with a tax-free fund—a taxable equivalent yield of 6.89%. "I'm stunned by how many investors will leave their investments in a tax-free fund purely to spite Uncle Sam," says iMoneyNet analyst Peter Crane. "They're really missing out." Top earners in high-tax states like California or New York may come out ahead in a single-state tax-free money fund. To figure out the taxable equivalent yield using your state and federal tax brackets, go to www.Investinginbonds.com.

Put risk worries aside. Another mistake is to accept the lower yield of a Treasury-only fund—5.6% on average—solely out of safety fears. Although you can theoretically lose money in a money fund, no retail investor ever has. In those rare cases when bond defaults might have let the share price drop below $1—as was the case after the 1994 Orange County bankruptcy— fund families have kept savers whole.

Don't sacrifice the service you need. Most money funds deliver the same core services: unlimited check writing, telephone transfers into other funds and 24-hour customer service. But there are a few notable exceptions. The top-yielding Strong fund limits you to three checks for as long as you own the fund (but allows unlimited phone and Internet transfers). If you want to use your money fund as your bank account, you'll want one with a debit card.

Lock in a rate when you can. One of the great advantages of money funds is that you can withdraw money anytime, penalty-free. But many savers leave cash untouched for months, if not years. If that's the case, shift some into a certificate of deposit so that you can lock in today's 7%-plus yields.

▶ The Top Financial Websites

The Web is aptly named—it's so easy to get tangled up. And the Web moves fast, growing by nearly 2 million pages every day.

But, once again, MONEY's staff spent months clicking and comparing our way through nearly 1,500 sites (disqualifying those that charge a regular subscription fee) to find the most useful investing and money-management tools on the Web. We found some terrific sites—and eliminated hundreds that will waste your time.

▶ The Supersites

Everyone needs a page to call home. And MSN MoneyCentral, Quicken.com and Yahoo Finance remain the best places to make your default stop whenever you first hit the Web. These information supermarkets are more than just an investor's paradise of one-click access to quotes, news and data. They're also stocked with advice and resources on virtually every personal-finance topic there is, from mortgages and credit cards to insurance, taxes and home buying.

But no one site can be all things to all people. Each of these three portals sports a distinct personality, and each one's unique strengths may appeal to some users more than others.

▶ MSN MoneyCentral (www.moneycentral.com)

MoneyCentral is the single best all-around financial destination on the Net. Its step-by-step planning guides and high-powered portfolio tracking and screening tools continue to be the site's hallmarks, easily outpacing those of its nearest competitors. But MoneyCentral has unveiled a number of significant improvements, with an emphasis on personalization. At My MoneyCentral, you can now aggregate information from multiple credit-card, brokerage and bank accounts, allowing you to check all of your balances on one Web page. MoneyCentral will also e-mail you reminders about upcoming bills and create a customized clip file of news stories from sources like the *Wall Street Journal* and MSNBC. Both real-time and extended-hours quotes on U.S. stocks are available for free, as are full financial data on companies located in France, Germany, Japan and the U.K.

▶ A Site We Call Home

Conflict of interest be damned. We can't help mentioning just one more financial website. At the site that bears our name, you'll find some of your favorite writers from the pages of MONEY, educational resources for newcomers, financial planning aids and a guide to the best of the Net.

As a MONEY reader, you may already be familiar with our Web sibling, **money.com** (www.money.com). If not, here's what you'll find. Along with the stock and fund quotes, business news headlines (from CNNfn) and the portfolio tools you'd expect, the site offers a regular lineup of columnists drawn from the magazine's ranks who offer advice and insight on blue chip stocks, the businesses of the New Economy, daily financial news and wealth-building personal-finance strategies. You can sign up for free e-mail delivery of all these columns.

The Money 101 section teaches newcomers the basics of everything from finding a home to managing your debt. Our calculators can help you buy a car, home or insurance policy.

There is one dent in MoneyCentral's armor (although, admittedly, it affects only 4% of all computer users). Most of its interactive tools do not work on Macintoshes.

▶ Quicken.com (www.quicken.com)

Quicken.com excels at offering basic, solid information on a broad range of topics. It is also exceptionally user-friendly. QuickAnswers—flash overviews of popular subjects—are available on each topic to save you the hassle of digging through the layers of info.

Quicken's editorial content isn't your typical regurgitation of yesterday's news. The IdeaCenter in the Investing section, for example, digests and analyzes recent stock picks from journalists and professional money managers.

And while Quicken's gadgets may not pack the punch of MoneyCentral's, they're well worth a look. Many of the tools use real-life data. The College Planner, for instance, incorporates actual college tuition figures to create a savings guide based on hard numbers rather than estimates. Quicken has caught the personalization bug as well, and it's easy to create your own personal-finance center at MyFinances.

▶ **Yahoo Finance (finance.yahoo.com)**
Need information fast? Yahoo Finance is the best bet. It lacks the bells and whistles of both MoneyCentral and Quicken, but that's often a blessing for the self-directed surfer. Its clean, spare design is free of intrusive advertising, making it easy to navigate the 10 primary sections, which range from Today's Markets and Mutual Funds to Loans and Insurance.

For a global perspective, visit Yahoo's International Finance Center. At this new addition, you can get economic profiles, news and exchange rates for countries all around the world. The upgraded Tax Center has a complete library of links to federal and state tax forms. Yahoo is quickly establishing a notable presence in the banking world as well, leading the pack in online account-aggregation and bill-payment services.

▶ *Investing Sites*

Directories: If you're looking for a Web directory a tad more expansive than our list, head to **Superstar Investor** (www.superstarinvestor.com), an obsessively detailed guide to virtually every significant investing site on the Web. This formidable collection of over 20,000 well-organized links is enough to satisfy any investor's needs.

For a compendium that's simultaneously broader in the kinds of subjects it covers yet more selective in the number of sites it recommends, try **CEOExpress** (www.ceoexpress.com). This carefully screened list covers general business and news, in addition to a full range of investing topics.

Financial News: Many destinations offer a daily dose of market chatter and business stories, but none do so as expertly as **TheStreet.com** (www.thestreet.com) and **CNNfn** (www.cnnfn.com). TheStreet vaulted onto our list this year by dropping its monthly $9.95 charge, giving everyone an all-access pass to the output of its 24-hour, business-news-only newsroom. The more polished CNNfn (owned by MONEY's parent company, Time Warner) spices up the standard news fare with relevant audio and video clips.

Stock Quotes and Data: **Market Guide** (www.marketguide .com) is the best place to look up stock prices and other fundamental data. That shouldn't be surprising once you consider that Market Guide feeds financial data to more than 135 major websites, including Yahoo Finance and Charles Schwab. Search by ticker or company name for free real-time quotes or a handy Snapshot that includes tons of information, ranging from P/E ratios and revenue figures to insider sales and institutional ownership.

MSN MoneyCentral (www.moneycentral.com) is also a good data source, especially for beginners. Its Research Wizard explains the fundamentals of any stock you select so you can learn the language of Wall Street. For the more advanced investor, the site also alerts you to key events, including earnings announcements and analyst upgrades or downgrades, for companies you select.

Company Research: You can now do a complete background check on a company via the Web. Among the handful of websites specializing in retrieving quarterly and annual reports from the Securities and Exchange Commission's EDGAR database, **10K Wizard** (www.10kwizard.com) is the easiest to use, allowing you to search for documents by company name, ticker symbol or keyword. Register for free at the site, and it will send you an e-mail anytime one of the companies you specify files a report.

BestCalls.com (www.bestcalls.com) maintains a calendar of upcoming company conference calls, searchable by name or symbol. Investors can then sit in on the meetings via telephone or streaming audio links at the site. Recent calls are archived for up to 90 days.

You can investigate up to 10 companies at a time with **Company Sleuth** (www.company.sleuth.com), which snoops around the Web and e-mails you daily updates on recent press releases, patents, trademarks, federal litigation, domain name registrations and other juicy tidbits.

Stock Analysis: To get the full picture of a company, you'll also want to exploit third-party resources for a different take on the numbers and news. **Multex Investor** (www.multexinvestor .com) is the leading source for those much hyped buy-sell-hold stock reports put out by brokerage houses and research groups. Multex Investor warehouses over 300,000 reports from hundreds of firms, including blue-chip names like J.P. Morgan and Bear Stearns. The catch: Most files cost between $4 and $150 to download. Even so, the site is worth a look. Each week, Multex

Investor posts a handful of free reports and hosts Q&A sessions with prominent analysts.

For whisper numbers (not-so-secret earnings estimates that differ from analysts' published expectations), go to **EarningsWhispers.com** (www.earningswhispers.com). To arrive at their figures, the site's team of editors polls a variety of sources, including industry experts and the analysts themselves.

ClearStation (www.clearstation.com) teaches technical analysis, the practice of studying a stock's historical charts to try to predict its future price movement. You can also surf the site's boards if you want a forum to share your newfound knowledge.

If a stock has been profiled at **Stock Detective** (www .stockdetective.com), you'd probably do well to avoid it. That's because the site highlights the biggest scams and the most suspicious stocks. Another attraction: its index of penny-stock promoters.

Portfolio Tracking and Analysis: The most worthwhile portfolio trackers can follow a stable of stocks from the date and price at which they were purchased, adjust for splits and dividends and point out holes in your portfolio. The high-powered tracker at **MSN MoneyCentral** (www.moneycentral.com) fits that bill and then some. It automatically updates prices every five minutes, categorizes your stocks by six criteria, including risk and market capitalization, and provides advice on how to better diversify your holdings.

Quicken.com (www.quicken.com) also has an outstanding (and Mac-compatible) tracker that uses icons to note if one of your stocks made headlines, was upgraded by a Wall Street pro or hit a 52-week high or low.

Stock Screeners: With more than 100 criteria, ranging from the obvious (price) to the obscure (receivables turnover), **MSN MoneyCentral's Stock Finder** (www.moneycentral.com/investor) is tough to beat for serious stock screening. Mac users, try **Wall Street City's ProSearch** (www.wallstreetcity.com) for advanced screens. Wall Street City flaunts an impressive set of more than 70 variables. Or run one of the 39 preset screens, including one that hunts for undervalued growth stocks and another that tracks possible turnaround plays. **Quicken.com**'s Stock Screener (www.quicken.com/investments) uses only 33 criteria, making it a good choice for quick, simple searches.

Charts: Virtually any finance site can draw you a chart, but the best ones let you customize the graphic with technical indicators such as moving averages and trading volume, compare stocks with one another or with indexes, and manipulate a wide range of dates. **MSN MoneyCentral** (www.moneycentral.com/investor) trumps the field in this category too: It allows a seemingly infinite variety of customization options and provides intraday pricing and volume information with a simple point of your cursor. **BigCharts.com** (www.bigcharts.com) boasts a range of offerings that's almost as varied as MoneyCentral's—and plays nice with Macs. BigCharts lets you alter a graph's look with nine different designs, from mountain and bar charts to candlestick and logarithmic charts.

Bulletin Boards: **The Motley Fool** (www.fool.com) has cultivated a sophisticated group of followers, many of whom espouse a long-term buy-and-hold philosophy. Noise is kept to a minimum by a self-policing membership and vigilant employees who stroll the most active boards looking for yahoos. It's harder to dig through the trash at **Raging Bull** (www.ragingbull.com), but the sophisticated level of the discussion makes the effort worthwhile. "Membermarks," a Siskel and Ebert-style peer review, honors the most respected posters.

    Silicon Investor (www.siliconinvestor.com) has among the most highly trafficked tech boards, and for good reason—the site tends to foster relatively intellectual stock discussions. Though posting messages will cost you $60 for six months, reading is free.

Online Brokerages: **Fidelity** (www.fidelity.com), **Merrill Lynch Direct** (www.mldirect.com) and **Ameritrade** (www.ameritrade.com) walked away with the three top slots in our 2000 brokerage survey, thanks to their knowledgeable customer service reps, timely trade execution and a full range of products and tools. Recent moves have reaffirmed their positions.

    Fidelity now provides real-time quotes and executes trades via Sprint PCS and Verizon Web-enabled mobile phones. Online limit orders remain high at $30, but the rate drops to $19.95 once you've executed 11 trades in a year. ML Direct slashed its minimum opening balance from $20,000 to $2,000, meaning even beginners may want to give it a look. Its $29.95 trade tariff is pricey, but users get unlimited access to Merrill's vaunted proprietary research reports. In the past year, Ameritrade has overhauled its infrastructure and expanded its customer service force. Given that the firm has kept prices low—only $13 for a limit order—we think this first-rate brokerage is a bargain.

Want an even cheaper way to invest directly? **Netstock Direct** (www.netstockdirect.com) is the premier place to participate in company-sponsored dividend-reinvestment plans and direct investment programs. The site provides access to over 1,600 plans, which sometimes require no more than $25 to start. Transaction costs are generally lower than with a broker.

Mutual Funds: Fund coverage on the Web has exploded in the past year; there are now hundreds of sites covering the $5 trillion industry. But **Morningstar.com** (www.morningstar.com) is still the king. A quick search unearths a report on any of the 5,548 funds the site covers. Dig through the front-page clutter for fund manager chats, daily industry news and tools like Fund Selector and Instant X-Ray to help analyze your options.

Looking for the next hot fund? **Maxfunds.com** (www .maxfunds.com) may already know about it. The hip, retro-looking site tracks 300 or so funds too new or too small to register on the radar screens of more traditional tracking services. **FundAlarm** (www.fundalarm.com) posts an informative listing of funds that have underperformed their benchmarks over the past one, three and five years. But FundAlarm's biggest draw is founder Roy Weitz's quirky, charming monthly column, a gossipy, insightful look into mutual fund industry mayhem whose audience includes scores of fund company executives and insiders.

International: **Worldlyinvestor.com** (www.worldlyinvestor .com) is the international investor's forum. Daily columns and e-mail newsletters dissect trends in stocks, bonds and mutual funds around the globe. The ADR Screener filters foreign stocks traded on U.S. exchanges by sector, country or return. **FT MarketWatch** (www.ftmarketwatch.com) is the place for up-to-the-minute news on offshore companies and foreign markets. A joint venture of the Financial Times and MarketWatch.com, the site combines insightful in-house commentary with a roundup of world news.

IPOs: Investors need to be pickier about snapping up IPO shares these days, so it pays to do your homework. Start at **IPO Central** (www.ipocentral.com) for a basic education on IPOs. Then cruise its other sections for company profiles and the latest news and statistics on hot offerings, top underwriters and lagging performers. To help get a feel for which new issues may be long-term winners, check out **Quote.com** (www.quote.com). It ranks recent IPOs' chances for success based on a variety of factors such as first-day gain, market cap and insider trading. It's also crucial to know when insiders can first sell their shares, as that may signal a possible sell-off or indicate when additional shares might become available. **UnlockDates.com** (www.unlockdates.com) keeps a database of IPO lockup periods and will alert you when the date approaches for any stock you choose.

Technology Investing: **CNET Investor** (investor.cnet.com) is a must for tech hounds. The site stockpiles articles from a variety of sources, including Bloomberg, and also offers its own crack coverage. Using one of CNET's 18 proprietary indexes, you can monitor the performance of, say, the wireless industry. The editors at **Next Wave Stocks** (www.nextwavestocks.com) believe that some of the best opportunities in tech are at companies with less than $10 billion in market cap. The Next Wave 100, a listing based on that philosophy, identifies emerging small and midcap players. In addition to the usual news you'll find at any tech site, Next Wave posts original Q&As with gurus like Roger McNamee of Integral Capital Partners and Softbank Venture Capital director Bill Burnham.

Miscellaneous: Curious about what EDGAR stands for? Not quite sure how return on assets differs from return on equity? **InvestorWords** (www.investorwords.com) defines more than 5,000 financial terms.

Everyone knows macroeconomics ultimately affects the markets. Keep track of the latest global data with the **Dismal Scientist** (www.dismalscientist.com), which gathers such information release dates for Germany's GDP figures, U.S. energy reports and French employment data, to name a few examples.

Banking: Virtual banking is far from perfect; it can be difficult to open an account, deposit funds or get in touch with a service rep. Despite those shortcomings, e-banks do offer among the highest rates and lowest fees in the business. While we wouldn't recommend making one your primary bank, they can be a good place to stash some extra cash. With a $500 minimum initial deposit, no monthly fees or minimum-balance requirement, recent interest rates of 6.25% on its checking accounts and 6.70% on its six-month CDs, **VirtualBank** (www.virtualbank.com) is a tantalizing choice. Customers also get free bill paying, postage-paid envelopes for deposits and reimbursement for $6 worth of ATM surcharges a month. If you want to shell out even less cash upfront, try **First Internet Bank of Indiana** (www.firstib.com), which requires a minimum opening balance of only $100 and still pays a decent interest rate on checking accounts (4.89% recently). Plus, you'll get many of the same perks.

Looking for the best rates on checking or savings accounts, CDs or money-market accounts, credit cards or personal loans? **Bankrate.com** (www.bankrate.com) lists rates for more than 2,000 banks across the country.

Calculators: **FinanCenter.com**'s (www.financenter.com) specialty is crunching numbers. With more than 100 calculators on subjects ranging from mutual funds to mortgages, FinanCenter has the most complete collection we've seen, including one to calculate the cost of raising a child.

Retirement Planning: To bone up on the basics, head to **MSN MoneyCentral** (www.moneycentral.com). It will walk you through the process of setting up a retirement plan, including calculating your living expenses and determining your income requirements. Or take advantage of the redesigned retirement tools at **American Express** (finance.americanexpress.com). One, for example, estimates how much extra money you'll need to put away every month if you put off starting your savings plan for a few years. **Quicken 401k Advisor** (www.teamvest.com/quick) gives free, personalized, fund-specific recommendations based on your employer's plan—more than 1,100 companies' plans are preloaded.

Taxes: At the informative Gary Klott's **TaxPlanet.com** (www.taxplanet.com), Klott, a former tax columnist at the *New York Times*, packs his site with the most recent tables, forms and updates. His year-round tax guide is chock-full of tips, and the articles link directly to the referenced IRS publications. If you are looking for a guide that is specifically designed for investors, you can head to **Fairmark Press Tax Guide for Investors** (www.fairmark.com). Whether you're a buy-and-hold strategist or a day-trader, you will find useful advice for offsetting capital-gains taxes or for writing off your home computer.

Step 3

Create a Great Retirement Plan

*I*f you ask most investors what they're saving for, the first word they're likely to utter is "retirement." It is the American Dream to retire happily, without a financial care. Of course, today's 30-, 40-, 50- and 60-year-olds may not actually stop working when they reach retirement age, but they sure would like to have the option of saying goodbye to their jobs.

In this chapter, you'll find clear strategies that can help deliver the retirement of your dreams.

▶ *Are You Saving Enough for Retirement?*

This is the most often asked—and perhaps the most difficult to answer—of all retirement questions. Coming up with the answer requires you to make an enormous number of assumptions—how much you'll earn as time passes, what you'll be able to save, how your investments will grow, how you'll spend your retirement, what will happen to the economy. It's enough to make you crazy. Plus, deciding how much to save inevitably involves trade-offs. Should you mortgage the present for an uncertain future? Would you prefer to live modestly today—or tomorrow?

But rather than throwing up your hands, start by calculating how much you are saving now. One benchmark to consider is the national savings rate: a meager 2.4% of household income. A more aggressive benchmark is what the average MONEY subscriber socks away: an impressive 14.8%.

Select a savings target. The next step is to choose a savings target for the future. Recognize that saving isn't a straight line. There are times—when college bills come due or the house needs a boiler—that finding $50 a month may be impossible. Other times, you may get a windfall. Still, most people are better off with a plan.

Sam and Diann West, both 43, regularly use online calculators to fine-tune their savings goal. The Lenexa, Kans. couple knew early on that they'd like to travel in retirement. "We're also planning to make sizable contributions to our church," says Sam. "We want the flexibility of living, not just simply being alive." Having a target has already helped them save $1 million toward the $2.5 million they figure they'll need to retire.

To come up with your own "magic" number, try our worksheet on page 89. Then consult the online calculators at www.money.com or at one of the other sites recommended on page 82.

Finally, be vigilant about bottom-up planning to make the most of the resources you have. Maximize contributions to your tax-deferred plans. Keep spending in check. Coming up with a few more dollars a month can prove significant over time. Thanks to the power of compounding, investing another $50 a month in a tax-sheltered plan for 20 years will add nearly $30,000 to your stake, assuming an 8% average annual return.

Stay financially flexible. Free yourself from high-interest debt by paying off a credit-card balance before you save. That guarantees a double-digit payback—and leaves credit available for borrowing in case of an emergency.

Select the right investments for retirement. The bedrock of any retirement portfolio should be stocks or stock mutual funds. Not because stocks have soared over the past decade. And not because stocks drooped in 2000, creating a potential buying opportunity. But because of inflation: Historically, only stocks have provided enough long-term growth to keep you ahead of inflation. That's why, even once you've retired, stocks should be a significant part of your portfolio.

But should stocks be your entire portfolio? No. As we've seen with the recent 50% Nasdaq drop, stocks' volatility can be painful. Bonds deserve a place in your portfolio. Figuring out how much to allocate to stocks vs. bonds is a critical decision. Too aggressive and you run the risk of being decimated when stocks go down. Too conservative and you may not be able to fund the retirement lifestyle you want.

How do you know how much risk you can tolerate? "What you've done the last few months is a test," says Scott Lummer,

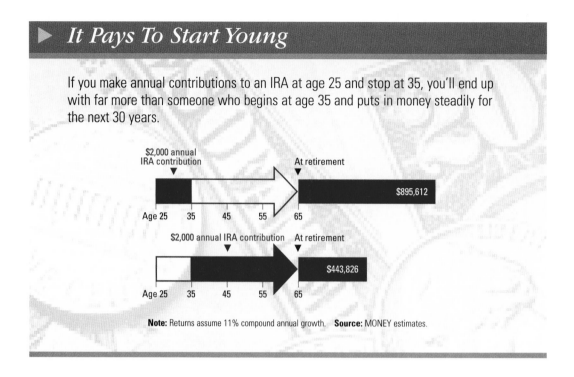

If you make annual contributions to an IRA at age 25 and stop at 35, you'll end up with far more than someone who begins at age 35 and puts in money steadily for the next 30 years.

$2,000 annual
IRA contribution ▼ At retirement ▼ $895,612

Age 25   35   45   55   65

$2,000 annual IRA contribution ▼   At retirement ▼ $443,826

Age 25   35   45   55   65

Note: Returns assume 11% compound annual growth.   **Source:** MONEY estimates.

chief investment officer of online advisory firm mPower. If the recent stock market pummeling kept you awake at night, you're probably too heavily invested in stocks.

▶ **You should recalculate your stock/bond mix at least once a year.** You may also want to check out a few online allocation calculators (see page 82) to see how your mix compares with the allocations suggested for your age and goals.

▶ **You should also calculate your exposure to specific industries periodically.** Lured by the promise of hot returns, many investors have too much of their money in high-priced tech stocks. We're not telling you to shun those high fliers, but recognize the risk you're taking. History has shown again and again that investors who disregard diversification get crushed.

If you decide you're overweighted in an industry or asset class, reshuffle within tax-deferred accounts so you don't take a hit from Uncle Sam. Or adjust your portfolio by putting any new money into underweighted areas.

Finally, one rule can be put bluntly: Don't trade more than is absolutely necessary. We understand the thrill of trading. But nearly every study of frequent trading has concluded that it's a loser's game. Transaction costs and taxes handicap your portfolio. Buy and hold may be a boring mantra, but it makes sound economic sense.

You don't have to beat the market to retire rich.

We'd all like to find the next great outperforming fund to power our retirement savings. But that's a game that's hard to win. Over the past 10 years, only one in four U.S. stock funds has beaten the S&P 500. And if you go out more than 10 years, the numbers drop further still. Indeed, of all the 847 U.S. stock funds that have been around for nine years, only one has out-earned the S&P in each of those years. That's why we'd make the foundation of any retirement portfolio a fund that virtually matches the market's return: an S&P 500 index fund, such as the Vanguard 500 Index (www.vanguard.com; 800-851-4999).

For a long-term investor, index funds have a built-in advantage: Their expenses are modest and their trading costs and taxable distributions are minimal. In addition, they are by definition broadly diversified.

You can even build an entire portfolio of index funds. If you already own an S&P 500 fund, you can capture the rest of the U.S. stock market with the Vanguard Extended Market Index. To home in on small stocks, add the Vanguard Small Cap Index. Or get the whole pie at once in the Vanguard Total Stock Market Index. For overseas exposure, try the Vanguard Total International Stock Index.

If the asceticism of index investing isn't appealing—or your company plan doesn't give you that option—examine the MONEY 100, our exclusive selection of low-cost, well-managed funds. This list, compiled and refined over three years, includes aggressive sector funds like T. Rowe Price Science & Technology (www.troweprice.com; 800-638-5660), value players like Clipper (www.clipperfund.com; 800-776-5033) and that one fund that has beaten the market in each of the past nine years, Legg Mason Value (www.leggmason.com; 800-577-8589). Updated data can be found at www.money.com/money100.

Consider annuities, but be very careful. Variable annu-

ities offer the same investing options as mutual funds, plus the tax deferral of IRAs and 401(k)s. So what's not to like? Onerous annual fees—2.1% on average—and surrender charges of 6% to 9%. Variables make sense only if you want a retirement income that you won't outlive. Through a process that goes by the ungodly name of annuitization, a 67-year-old man with $100,000 in a variable annuity could elect to receive payments for life that start at $621 a month. The amount will change over time, depending on the investment returns of the underlying funds. But the trend should be upward. For example, a steady 8% annual return after expenses would boost that initial $621 to $950 after 10 years and to $1,455 after 20 years. That would likely keep your buying power ahead of inflation.

When you should buy. If that prospect is appealing, the next question is when to buy a variable. If you're positive you'll opt for a lifetime income, you can buy one early on—in your forties or even earlier—and rack up tax-deferred gains until you annuitize. But if it turned out that you had to liquidate your

annuity within 15 years or so, the fees and the tax hit (as with other tax-deferred accounts, withdrawals are taxed at ordinary income rates, not the 20% capital-gains rate) would probably leave you with less money than if you had invested in a decent fund. A more prudent strategy: Wait until you're close to or in retirement to buy a variable—and then annuitize. If you do opt for a variable, go for one with low fees, such as those sold by eAnnuity (877-569-3789), T.D. Waterhouse (800-622-3699) and Vanguard (800-523-9954). (For more, see "One (Small) Cheer for Variable Annuities" at www.money.com/retirement.)

Illustration by Ricardo Stampatori

Should you be debt-free by retirement? It has a nice ring to it: debt-free. But whether you should be debt-free, in retirement or earlier, depends on the kind of debt. At one end of the spectrum is credit-card debt—typically high interest, with no tax perks. At the other is a low-rate, deductible mortgage.

If you're still saving for retirement, ask yourself whether you could earn more on the money than you're paying in interest. As Westerly, Rhode Island financial planner Malcolm A. Makin explains, "If I can borrow money at 6% and earn 8%, and I have plenty of cash flow to pay off that loan, I am golden."

High-interest debt doesn't pass that test—so get rid of it. The average standard credit card charges 17.4%, so a $5,000 balance would cost you more than $850 a year in interest.

With a mortgage, if you're far from retirement, the answer is equally clear. The cost of a 30-year fixed-rate mortgage is still a relatively low 7.67%, and the interest is tax deductible. Given that, there's little reason to prepay it.

Being retired may change your thinking. In retirement, however, you'll tend to think about these decisions differently. The reason: cash flow. Once you've stopped receiving a salary, you'll need to figure out where you're going to get money to pay the bills. Many retirees find enormous peace of mind in getting rid of their largest monthly expense. "You can make the numbers look however you want," notes Phoenix financial planner Stephen Barnes. "The bigger question is how comfortable do you feel carrying a mortgage?"

And repaying your mortgage opens up a potential source of cash: a reverse mortgage. With this loan, essentially a mirror image of a conventional home loan, the lender pays you. You must be 62 to qualify, and the older you are, the more you can borrow. The cash isn't taxed (it's considered loan proceeds) and the loan typically doesn't come due until you die, sell your home or stop living in it for 12 months. The drawbacks: high closing costs and the risk that you'll leave nothing for your heirs. For more, check out www.reverse.org.

▶ Saving for Retirement and College Tuition

Any parent who's snuck a look at the $23,000 average annual cost of a private college knows that saving for your kid's education can get in the way of retirement planning. When you can't find money for both, you may favor college savings. Don't do it. As David Rhine, director of family wealth planning at BDO Seidman in New York City, suggests, "Fill up your retirement bucket first." From loans to financial aid, there are plenty of ways to soften the cost of college. No one will award you a retirement scholarship. Even colleges recognize that retirement savings are sacrosanct; when determining aid eligibility, they don't expect you to tap your tax-sheltered retirement funds.

But don't neglect college planning altogether. While about 70% of students receive some sort of financial aid, according to the College Board, 60% of that assistance is in the form of loans, not grants. When you're scraping up money for college and retirement, you should stretch your dollars as much as possible by taking the following tax breaks.

▶ **Custodial accounts.** Once you set up what's commonly called an UGMA or UTMA in your child's name, you and your spouse can give up to $20,000 a year without triggering gift taxes. Until the child turns 14, the first $700 in income is tax-free; the next $700 is taxed at the child's rate; anything above that is taxed at your rate. Once the child is 14, all earnings are taxed at his or her rate (presumably lower than yours). The money can be used only for the child's direct benefit, however, and the child gets full control at age 18 or 21, depending on your state. Also, since it is in the child's name, it may reduce chances of getting financial aid.

▶ **State-sponsored savings plans.** The money you invest in these so-called 529 plans grows tax deferred until you withdraw it for college expenses, at which time it's taxed at the student's rate. While your state plan may offer additional benefits to residents, you don't need to invest locally; nearly half of the 41 state plans are open to out-of-state residents. For more, see page 157 or go to www.collegesavings.org.

▶ **Roth IRAs.** While we're not suggesting that you endanger your own retirement, don't forget that you can make penalty-free withdrawals from Roth IRAs for education expenses.

▶ *Will Social Security Be There for You?*

Some financial planners routinely advise savers to enter a goose egg on the Social Security line of a retirement worksheet. Assume no benefits, the argument goes, and save more on your own. Well, you needn't take such an alarmist approach. Rumors of the death of Social Security have been widely exaggerated. In fact, the system's trustees recently reported that the retirement fund has gained another three years of solvency; it won't come up short until 2037, at which time it'll be able to pay 72% of the promised benefits. That's a sizable gap, to be sure, but with 36 years for politicians to phase in corrective changes, it's one that can be bridged.

New rules take effect. Of course, future benefits may not be as generous as today's ($907 a month for a man, on average; $699 for a woman). Still, there's good reason to believe you'll collect something from Social Security—but perhaps not as soon as you'd expected. Under a 1983 law that took effect in 2000, the full retirement age (FRA) for Social Security is pushing past 65. If you turned 62 in 2000, for example, your FRA is 65 and two months. By 2005, the FRA rises to 66 for anyone born from 1943 through 1954. Thereafter, it goes up by two months a year until it hits 67 in 2022 for everyone born in 1960 or later.

The cost of retiring early. As the full retirement age goes up, the penalty for retiring early becomes steeper. You can still collect benefits as early as age 62, but they'll be permanently reduced based on when you start. When the FRA was 65, for example, the benefit at age 62 was 80% of what it would have been if you'd waited till 65. With an FRA of 66, it's 75% of the full benefit; and at an FRA of 67, it's 70%.

So does it pay to take Social Security early? The answer hinges largely on how long you live. If you carry the Methuselah gene, you'll get more money out of the system by waiting until your FRA to start collecting benefits. For example, if you have an FRA of 66 and take benefits at 62, you'd pull more out of the system until the age of 78. Then you'd begin to fall behind people your age who waited to collect the full benefit.

Also, if you live a long life, the benefit reduction that felt painless early on could pinch in old age, when your other assets may be dwindling. Moreover, for most retirees, Social Security is the only component of a retirement income that is automatically adjusted for inflation. Why reduce it?

Here's another reason to wait: If your benefit is larger than your spouse's and you die first, your spouse's benefit will be increased, but the size of the boost depends in part on when you claimed your benefit. Say you're on track for a full benefit of $1,100 a month at age 66, and your wife is on track for $700 a month. If you start collecting benefits at age 62, you'll receive $825 a month (plus inflation adjustments). When you die, your wife's benefit will bump to just $908 (plus the adjustments), rather than to the $1,100-plus level of your full benefit.

The earnings penalty. Finally, if you start your benefits early and keep working, the higher full retirement age means that you'll face an onerous earnings penalty—that is, you'll forfeit some or all of your benefits—for longer. In 2000, Congress repealed the earnings penalty for Social Security recipients who've reached their FRA—but not for younger people who are drawing benefits. Between the time you turn 62 and Jan. 1 of the calendar year of your FRA, you'll lose $1 in benefits for every $2 you earn above a certain annual limit. The limit, currently $10,080, is adjusted upward each year in line with the national average wage. In the months before your birthday in the year you reach your FRA, the penalty goes down: You'll lose $1 in benefits for every $3 you earn above an annual limit ($25,000 in 2001 and $30,000 in 2002, with yearly adjustments thereafter).

Estimating your Social Security benefit. We're glad we convinced you that there may actually be a benefit. To estimate the size of your future Social Security benefit, use the new retirement calculator at the **Social Security Administration**'s website (www.ssa.gov). You enter your past earnings, what you expect to earn between now and retirement, and your desired retirement age, and the calculator computes a future benefit. The site also provides information on other factors that can affect your benefit, such as military service and federal employment. (You can get an estimate in writing by calling 800-772-1213.) If you plan to work in retirement, check out the new calculator at www.money.com/retirement that analyzes the impact of income taxes and the earnings penalty on your benefit.

▶ Planning for Early Retirement

These days, more and more Americans seem to be looking forward to an early retirement. We know some people who have already tried to do it and failed. Why? Because they assumed that the stock market would continue to rise inexorably by at least 20% a year. When it didn't do that in 2000, they were forced to unretire.

So what can you do to achieve an early retirement that will not end at the first hint of a market decline? The short answer: do everything we've already recommended, but do it in overdrive. Retiring early is an aggressive act and requires aggressive preparation. So max out your tax-deferred accounts, load up on low-cost stock index funds, control your spending, avoid high-rate credit-card debt like the plague and don't even think about borrowing from any of your retirement accounts.

Then there are the special issues that early retirement presents. Here are three of the big ones—and strategies for addressing them.

▶ **Income.** The earlier you retire, the more important it is to put off tapping tax-deferred retirement principal. You want those funds to keep compounding as long as possible. Where will you get the money to pay the bills?

For Bruce Martin, 54, of Milwaukee, the extra income he needs for his semiretirement comes from real estate and stock investments. More than 20 years ago, he and his late wife Wanda took second jobs and saved $20,000, enough to buy a duplex they turned into a rental property. As their income and savings grew, they began planning to retire at 55. They calculated that they'd need $1 million. Martin now owns 37 buildings worth about $2 million; they generate enough income to pay for his living expenses and new investments.

▶ **Retiree benefits.** If you're set to receive a traditional pension, you probably know that your payouts are likely to be based on your three to five peak earning years. Ask your benefits department to compute how much you stand to lose by retiring early, and be sure you're comfortable with the numbers.

Withdrawals from 401(k)s and IRAs before age $59^1/2$ generally incur a 10% penalty as well as income taxes. If you're planning on, say, taking a lump-sum distribution from your 403(b) and investing the funds in an IRA, make sure you understand the withdrawal rules.

▶ **Health care.** When you walk away from commutes and long hours, you'll probably say good-bye to employer-sponsored health insurance. And even if you're allowed to participate in your former employer's plan, it will cost you. In 1999, 42% of eligible retirees paid the total tab for these premiums, up from 31% in 1997.

"I tell people, 'If you're going to retire early, budget for health insurance,'" says Dee Lee, a financial planner in Harvard, Mass. and co-author of *Let's Talk Money*. She generally advises clients to count on paying as much as $30,000 to $45,000 for medical coverage between ages 55 and 65.

Make sure you don't outlive your money. The first rule of making your money last is not to touch your retirement accounts until you have to—either to pay the bills or because the law requires you to do so. The reason? In a word: taxes. The longer you can continue to rack up tax-deferred returns, the better. An added bonus, especially if you're in a high tax bracket, is that sales from your taxable portfolio may count as long-term capital gains, at a 20% tax rate, while retirement plan withdrawals are taxed as regular income.

An even bigger issue than minimizing taxes is figuring out how much money you can withdraw from your portfolio each year without running out of cash. Once you decide how much you need to cover expenses—and to what extent a pension, Social Security or part-time work can fill the gap—you need to come up with a withdrawal strategy that doesn't deplete your account too quickly.

Don't be overly optimistic. T. Rowe Price retirement specialist Joseph Healy warns that many retirees are too optimistic when they think they can withdraw 8% or more from their portfolios each year. Part of the problem is inflation. The other, he believes, is basing plans on average returns and ignoring the sequence of annual returns. If a bear market occurs soon after you start taking withdrawals, you could run out of money much faster than you expected. According to T. Rowe Price calculations, a balanced portfolio of 60% stocks, 30% bonds and 10% cash earned an average annual return of 11.7% from 1969 to 1999. But an investor who began tapping a retirement account at a rate of 8.5% a year in 1969 would have been broke in less than 13 years because of the vicious bear market in 1973 and 1974. "You really luck out if you have a bull market in the early part of your retirement," Healy says. "But what do you do if you don't?"

The best policy is to keep withdrawals to between 3% and 5% during the first year, and then adjust for inflation. If a withdrawal rate of 5% sounds too low—on a $500,000 portfolio, it amounts to just $1,500 a month after taxes if you're in the 28% tax bracket—consider taking a part-time job after you've retired. Or postpone retirement and keep stashing money in your retirement accounts. Even a short delay can mean a substantial increase in your retirement savings. If you're making $90,000 and contributing 10% to your 401(k), with a 5% match and a 5% return, a $500,000 portfolio would be worth $580,734 in two more years. And that means your 5% withdrawal rate would give you an extra $242 a month after taxes.

▶ *Answering Your IRA Questions*

Individual retirement accounts (IRAs) are much more complex than they used to be. Recent years have seen the introduction of the Roth IRA, the Education IRA and the proliferation on non-deductible IRAs. The Roth, in particular, is a terrific savings tool, but the rules are complex. At MONEY, we get thousands of questions about different types of IRAs, and we thought it would be productive to answer some of these questions for you.

Q. I converted some of my traditional IRA to a Roth IRA, and then, just my luck, the market went down. Does it make sense to recharacterize my Roth back to a traditional IRA so I will not have to pay conversion taxes this year? That way I can consider reconverting the money to a Roth at another time. Are there any guidelines to follow for this?

A. Yes, you can recharacterize the Roth back to a traditional IRA and avoid the conversion taxes. However, before you do so, you must wait either 30 days or until the following calendar year, whichever period is longer.

But be warned: There are some risks to this plan if you definitely want that money in a Roth. First, if the market should soar again before you reconvert, you could end up paying more conversion taxes than you would have faced if you had left well enough alone. Another risk: A hike in your income could push you into a higher tax bracket, or even over the Roth IRA conversion-eligibility limit, which is set at $100,000 (adjusted gross income) a year.

Q. My annual income is around $155,000. If I fund my Roth IRA for the year 2001 now, and find out at the end of the year that my income is $170,000 (which is likely), can I withdraw this money without a penalty? Or should I wait until year's end to fund the Roth?

A. Wait. Assuming you are married, filing jointly, $155,000 puts you smack in the middle of the income phaseout range, so you can contribute only $1,000 to your Roth. (If your joint income is below $150,000, you can put in the full $2,000; above $160,000, you cannot contribute to a Roth at all for that year.)

If you fund the Roth now and your income goes above the limit, you have two options: 1) You can recharacterize the excess contributions (and interest) as a traditional IRA. If either you or your spouse has a retirement plan at work, you would have to make it a nondeductible IRA. 2) You can simply withdraw the excess contribution and related earnings. But you must pay income taxes on any earnings and, in most cases, a 10% penalty as well. That's why it's wiser and easier to wait.

Q. My Roth account consists of 120 shares of Microsoft purchased at $96 per share. Can I sell the stock now, claim a tax loss, then buy the stock back for my Roth account after the wash-sale period expires?

A. For investments held outside of an IRA, this could be a clever tax strategy. It will not work for you, though, since transactions within an IRA do not trigger a taxable event.

Q. My husband and I are getting divorced. What's the best tax strategy for dividing an IRA in his name? We are both retired. I'm 55, he is 65.

A. As the song goes, breaking up is hard to do, but even as tempers flare, staying focused on all things financial will keep Uncle Sam from benefiting from your misfortune. To avoid triggering unnecessary taxes, consider these two alternatives to splitting your nest egg: A direct transfer lets you simply move your share of the holdings from his IRA into an IRA account in your name. Or if your husband has more than one IRA, he can sign over one of his accounts to you. He must agree to give you 100% of what's in that account though. Whichever method you happen to choose, have the exact terms of distribution clearly outlined in your divorce or separation agreement.

Q. Can a revocable trust be the beneficiary for a Roth IRA, a traditional IRA and a 401(k)?

A. Yes. However, the trust document must accurately fulfill Internal Revenue Service qualifications and address tax-law provisions, such as minimum required distributions, explains C.P.A. Ed Slott, editor of *Ed Slott's IRA Advisor*. But most boilerplate and revocable trust "kits" do not fit the bill, which is why you should consult an attorney with expertise in IRA trusts. To start your search, contact the American College of Trust and Estate Counsel at 310-398-1888 or www.actec.org.

Q. Can I contribute to a Roth IRA if I'm not working?

A. That depends on how you define working. In order to contribute to a Roth, you need to earn at least the amount of your contribution in taxable compensation, which includes wages, tips, professional fees, bonuses, commissions and alimony. But dividends, interest and capital gains don't count, no matter how hard you worked on your investment choices.

Q. I must take money out of my IRA when I am $70^1/_2$. Can I roll over some of the minimum required distribution into a Roth?

A. No. Until age $70^1/_2$, you can convert a portion or all of your traditional IRA to a Roth (which, of course, means a tax bill on your gains). The year you turn $70^1/_2$, however, the rules change. Not only do you have to take withdrawals from your IRA, but you can't fund a Roth with your minimum required distributions. Only withdrawals exceeding the minimum are eligible for a Roth.

Illustration by Steven Biver

Q. My 19-year-old daughter converted a traditional IRA to a Roth and opened a second Roth. Can she commingle them? Can she make deposits into both?

A. You can combine the rollover and the new Roth into one account. But while one Roth means less paperwork, it could also mean headaches if you take any money out soon. New Roth contributions can be withdrawn anytime, with no penalty; rollover contributions, however, cannot be tapped penalty-free in the first five years unless you're over $59^1/_2$ or using the money for certain medical or college expenses or a first-time home purchase. (Earnings are subject to different rules.) So keep careful records.

And, yes, you can contribute to two Roths, as long as your total IRA contributions don't exceed the maximum ($2,000 if your adjusted gross income is $95,000 or less for singles, $150,000 or less for marrieds filing jointly; the maximum decreases at higher income levels).

Q. Can I use the entire amount (investment plus earnings) in a Roth for college expenses without paying taxes? Or just the initial investment?

A. You can withdraw after-tax contributions anytime without paying a penalty, and once your Roth has been open for five years, you can withdraw earnings penalty-free for college expenses as well. But you will owe taxes on the earnings unless you are over $59^{1}/_{2}$.

Q. I converted my traditional IRA to a Roth and I make annual contributions. One C.P.A. says that I must wait five years to take tax-free distributions. Another claims that a five-year clock starts ticking each time I make an annual contribution. Which C.P.A. should I fire?

A. Give the second one his walking papers. You must wait five years after your conversion to avoid taxes on withdrawals of earnings. You must also be $59^{1}/_{2}$ years old, or the distribution must be due to disability or death, or for a first-time home purchase. Subsequent annual contributions do not trigger additional five-year clocks.

Q. I would like to tap the money in a 403(b) retirement account I have with an ex-employer, but I'm not $59^{1}/_{2}$, so I'd be subject to taxes and a penalty. What if I roll over the money to a Roth IRA first, then withdraw the money? I'd owe taxes on the rollover, but there is never a penalty for withdrawing contributions to a Roth, right?

A. You cannot roll over a company plan to a Roth without first rolling it into a regular IRA. However, your scheme still wouldn't work. Your rollover money wouldn't be a Roth contribution. It would be considered a conversion.

▶ *The 60-Minute 401(k)*

Retirement planning options, we're happy to report, are getting better every day. Companies keep improving their 401(k) plans, offering dozens of new investment choices for their employees.

Some 401(k) plan literature details so many different investment possibilities that you may be reminded of the wine list at a four-star restaurant.

Unfortunately, such abundance can be intimidating and confusing. For too many people, a 401(k) plan seems less a benefit than a burden. And many of us, apparently, don't want to bear so much responsibility for our financial future. A recent survey for Mutual of Omaha shows that nearly half of 401(k) participants can't name a single investment option in their company plan, and 75% spend less than 10 hours a year evaluating and tracking their investments.

As it happens, though, that may be more than enough time to create a solid retirement strategy and pick the right funds from your employer's 401(k) plan—if you take the right approach. Don't believe us? Read on.

If you have just an hour or so, you can cut through the clutter and create a solid, sophisticated portfolio. Of course, the more time you put in, the more you'll get out of it; if you can, linger on those steps that will help you make the most of your employer's plan—whether a 401(k), 403(b) or 457—and check out our "Overtime" tips. But our 60-minute basics are the bedrock. (In fact, they provide important lessons for choosing investments outside a retirement plan as well.)

Perhaps you've already devised a strategy for your retirement plan. We'd encourage you to put in an extra 60 minutes now anyway. For one thing, the runaway tech-stock prices of the past few years may have tilted your balanced portfolio too far toward today's riskier names. For another, you may not be aware of the best investment options that your employer has added recently.

Let's consider a hypothetical 401(k) plan with 103—yes, 103—investment choices. The goal here is simple: to come up with a plan with a good chance of giving you the retirement you want. It's not a test to see if you can pick the five future top performers from a 401(k) lineup.

The process used to get from 103 funds to five is outlined below, in nine distinct steps. It's a program that anyone can follow.

▶ **STEP 1: Max out**
Take a few seconds to make sure you're contributing as much as your plan allows. Truth is, the amount you stash away now is far more important than your choice of large-cap stock funds.

▶ Tax-Deferred Plans

To get the most from your retirement savings, you should take full advantage of tax-deferred plans. But which ones? Here's an overview of the eight major plans. In all, your earnings grow tax deferred. With a Roth IRA, you also get tax-free withdrawals. But keep in mind that in exchange for the tax perks, you have to leave the money untouched until age $59\frac{1}{2}$ (with certain exceptions). Otherwise, you could owe a 10% early-withdrawal penalty, income taxes or both.

PLAN	WHO'S ELIGIBLE FOR FULL BENEFIT	MAXIMUM ANNUAL CONTRIBUTION	PRETAX CONTRIBUTION
401(K)	Employees of companies with plans, typically after one year of service	$10,500 or the plan limit[3]	Yes
403(B)	Employees of nonprofits	20% of gross income or $10,500[3]	Yes
KEOGH	Self-employed or small business employees	15% of net income or $30,000[3,4]	Yes
SEP-IRA	Self-employed or small business employees[1]	15% of net income or $25,500[3]	Yes
SIMPLE IRA	Self-employed or small business employees	$6,000 plus match of 3% of income	Yes
DEDUCTIBLE IRA	People not covered by pension or those who earn below certain income caps[2]	$2,000	Yes
ROTH IRA	Singles with adjusted gross income of $95,000 or less; couples with $150,000 or less	$2,000	No
NONDEDUCTIBLE IRA	Anyone with earned income	$2,000	No

Notes: [1]If compensation is $170,000 or less. [2]Eligible for full deduction if adjusted gross income (AGI) is less than $32,000 for singles, $52,000 for married couples filing jointly; if married and spouse is covered by an employer plan, you can take full deduction if total AGI is under $150,000. [3]Whichever is less. [4]25% if money-purchase plan.

"Savings have a huge impact," says Jason Scott of online 401(k) adviser Financial Engines. "Investors can make the biggest impact on their retirement portfolio by deciding to retire later and save longer, although that's not a palatable option for most people. But the next biggest thing they can do is to save more, sooner."

If you recently switched jobs and were automatically enrolled in your new plan—common practice these days—don't assume that you're contributing the maximum allowed; you likely were signed on for only 3% or so. Or maybe you felt you couldn't afford to save the maximum when you signed up several years ago; if you've gotten raises since then, raise your contribution rate too.

At the very least, invest enough to receive the full employer match. Saving less is like turning down free money.

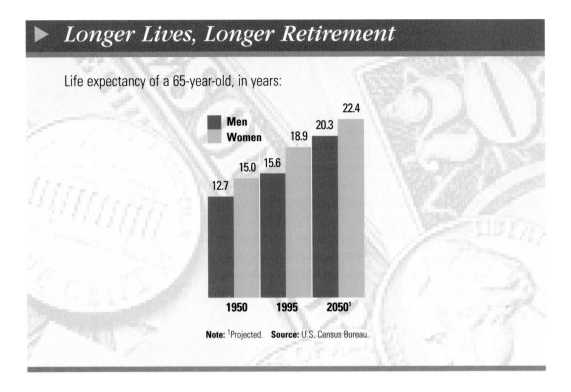

Longer Lives, Longer Retirement

Life expectancy of a 65-year-old, in years:

- Men
- Women

1950: Men 12.7, Women 15.0
1995: Men 15.6, Women 18.9
2050[1]: Men 20.3, Women 22.4

Note: [1]Projected. **Source:** U.S. Census Bureau.

▶ **STEP 2: Allocate those assets**

Go grocery shopping without a list, and you're liable to go home with two flavors of Godiva ice cream, a jar of raspberry mustard and no milk or cereal. So don't browse among all those fascinating funds without a clear idea of what you need. If you reach for the flashiest returns, you may end up with three tech-heavy funds and not a single sensibly diversified large-cap stock fund, a staple of a well-balanced portfolio.

Some plan packages have an easy-to-use asset-allocation worksheet in which you can enter such basic information as your desired retirement date, the size of your emergency fund for immediate needs until then and your ability to stomach losses. Fidelity's Web tools (available to all at www.401k.com) yield a detailed breakdown after a similar probe. For a young, aggressive investor who should have 85% of her money in stocks, the site suggests: 50% large-cap stocks, 20% midcap and small-cap, 15% international stocks, 10% investment-grade bonds and 5% high-yield bonds. There are other online tools, which provide similar results, at some of the sites listed in the resources box on page 82. Or consider one of Fidelity's sample allocations on page 81.

STEP 3: **Start cutting**

Now it's time to look over your specific investment options. First move: Toss aside the choices that don't match up with your asset allocation. You might throw out your plan's money-market and capital-preservation funds because you don't need cash dampening an aggressive portfolio. You might also reject the 14 hybrid offerings that combine stocks and bonds. If you stick to funds that own one or the other, that makes it easier to calibrate and control your overall asset allocation.

Finally, consider excluding your plan's bond funds—our hypothetical plan has 18 bond funds. That's because you can make the most of the 401(k) tax deferral by socking all your money into stock funds. After all, it's easy to shelter bond income from taxes in investments made outside a 401(k) by buying tax-exempt municipal bond funds. (For other strategies to boost your overall retirement savings, see "How to Compensate for a Crummy 401(k)" on page 78.)

We've now pared down the list from 103 choices to 69. Not bad for a few minutes' work. But there's still have slicing to do.

STEP 4: **Cut more**

Eliminate funds that might cloud the investment process. For example, there's no need to consider a convertible securities fund (which shares characteristics of both bonds and stocks) or a fund whose name is confusing, like Fidelity Export and Multinational. (Does it count toward international? In 60 minutes, we don't have time to find out.) You might also avoid funds that target specific foreign countries or regions. You can get diversified exposure in a one-stop international fund. We now have 60 choices left.

STEP 5: **Hunt for bargains**

You know the boilerplate: "Past performance does not guarantee future results." But there is a way to determine which funds are likeliest to outperform: Look at expense ratios. As Vanguard's Jack Bogle says, "I've never seen a case where the lowest-cost quartile of funds in a group did not outperform the highest-cost quartile in the long run." The argument is confirmed by the research of academics.

Your plan packet might not include expense ratios, but you can find them at fund websites or at Morningstar.com. Go through the list of funds and eliminate those with above-average annual expenses, using these benchmarks:

- Bond funds: 0.85%
- Domestic stock funds: 1.19%
- Small-cap stock funds: 1.37%
- International stock funds: 1.56%

If these expense figures are lower than other averages you may have seen, it's because they exclude the highest-cost types of shares (such as B and C classes). A good 401(k) plan these days is a Price Club of fund investing—your company buys in bulk and gets a discount. Since any decent 401(k) offers funds with cheaper shares, why pay expenses higher than these?

▶ **STEP 6: Find any index funds**
This is a corollary to the bargain-hunting rule above: Index funds tend to outperform actively managed funds in the long run, partly because their fees are almost always much lower. The other reason to favor index funds is that most of us, pros included, can't consistently pick winners. Some money managers make a convincing case that indexing isn't the best strategy in less efficient markets, such as small-cap or international stocks. But it's hard to argue against indexing the large-cap market in the long run.

Expenses will usually be lower for a "commingled pool" of big institutional money instead of an ordinary mutual fund serving individual investors (see "Everybody into the Pool" on page 80). Such an investment, with a large asset base and low marketing costs, may have an expense ratio as low as 0.1%.

By the way, if your plan doesn't have a large-cap index fund, make your displeasure known to the human resources department. An S&P 500 or Wilshire 5000 index should be standard 401(k) fare, and there's no reason not to have that option. Until you do, read on for tips on choosing actively managed names.

▶ **STEP 7: Check your master lists**
Compare your list of funds to those recommended by reliable sources, such as the MONEY 100 list of top mutual funds (see page 28 or go to www.money.com) or Morningstar.com.

▶ **STEP 8: Trust the old standbys**
What about small-cap funds? John Rekenthaler, Morningstar's director of research, notes that you're unlikely to go wrong with a fund from heavyweights like Fidelity, Vanguard and American.

The quality of 401(k) plans varies widely with the benevolence—or employee-retention savvy—of the companies involved. While the government sets a limit on annual contributions ($10,500 for 2001), your company plan doesn't have to let you save that much. Nor does your employer have to kick in matching contributions.

In addition, only about half of plans surveyed by the Profit Sharing/401(k) Council of America offered 10 or more investing options in 1999, though at least that's up from 16% in 1996.

If you aren't satisfied, march down to HR and cite those statistics. Meantime, make the best of what you've got.

► If you cannot save enough
If you can't contribute as high a percentage of your income as you'd like, decide to save more on your own while keeping taxes in mind. You can avoid taxes on investment earnings with a Roth IRA. We may soon see legislation upping the yearly $2,000 contribution limit to as much as $5,000 and raising the eligibility cutoff for joint filers from $160,000 to $220,000 in adjusted gross income.

If you want to save above and beyond the $2,000 limit, you could go with an annuity, though the higher fees might offset any tax advantages. You might consider instead a low-expense, low-turnover, tax-managed mutual fund. Vanguard is an obvious choice, and its tax-managed lineup includes large-cap, small-cap, international and balanced funds.

Then there are muni funds. Since municipal bond income is exempt from federal and sometimes state taxes, these investments belong in a taxable account. That frees up your Roth IRA shelter for a fast-trading stock fund or taxable bond fund.

► If you don't have good choices
Perhaps your plan is saddled with terrible investment options. You should still participate, at least up to your employer match: You can't beat that guaranteed return. Then look elsewhere.

Compare Your Plan

Percentage of 401(k) assets **in cheaper institutional** funds

1996 — 23%
2001[1] — 39%

Note: [1]Projection.
Source: Cerulli Associates.

12
The average number of **investment options**

40%

Percentage of plans that make employees **eligible within three months** of hire

The most common **employer match**?

50¢
on the dollar
up to 6% of pay

Source: ProfitSharing/401(k) Council.

You can make up for any deficiencies in your employer's plan by supplementing it with outside savings. Don't have a decent small-cap fund or even a single international option? Save extra in Vanguard Tax-Managed Small Cap, and pick your favorite actively managed foreign fund for a Roth IRA account.

But what if you can't save another penny beyond what you're putting into your 401(k)? Consider diverting some of the money earmarked for your 401(k) into a Roth IRA instead. That's right, it could actually make sense to invest with post-tax dollars in a Roth rather than pretax dollars in a 401(k).

Joel Dickson, a principal in Vanguard's Portfolio Review Group, says that's because your Roth earnings will be tax-free when you withdraw money in retirement, while all 401(k) withdrawals (even the capital gains) are taxed as income. This strategy is not for everyone. Dickson warns that if you're at the low end of the 28% tax bracket, you might not benefit. If there's a good chance you'll end up in the lower 15% bracket when you retire, it makes sense to postpone taxes via your 401(k). "But higher-income folks are quite susceptible to tax-rate changes," he says, "and they may want to lock in tax rates today."

Once you've contributed to your plan up to the employer match, you might then divert dollars to any fund you choose, sheltered in a Roth account (if you qualify). You get to pick better funds, and you may come out ahead after taxes as well. (The higher-income investors who'd benefit most from this arrangement may still have money to save after hitting the Roth ceiling, and they can then go back and use up the rest of their 401(k) allowance.)

Finally, hang in there. Your 401(k) plan is only going to get better, predicts industry expert Ted Benna (who'll answer your questions in his column at www.401kafe.com). "Participants have pushed for change," he says, "and employers are starting to give employees choice and control."

These families boast three times as many funds with above-average category ratings as below-average funds.

"They attract top-quality people and have below-average expenses, which leads to better funds overall," he explains. "Besides having a higher percentage of winners, they have almost no real dogs. When they have a problem fund, they can throw resources at it, as both Fidelity and Vanguard have done in recent years. They have a will to win and higher standards than most."

Some 401(k) plan choices aren't actually mutual funds—they are what are called "commingled pools" of money run strictly for retirement plans and not available to the general public.

Check for such options in your plan, particularly if you work for a larger company (they should be marked as commingled pools or separate accounts). Richard Malconian of Barclays Global Investors makes an enthusiastic case for these vehicles (which Barclays offers): "They give 401(k) participants the same advantages that big institutional investors enjoy," he says. Namely, bargain-basement costs and, often, effective and predictable index-based investing strategies.

Unfortunately, information on these pools can be hard to come by, especially when they are actively managed. Pools that track a specific index, therefore, may be your best bet.

► STEP 9: **Checks and balances**

Instead of considering only whether funds buy large-cap stocks or smaller names, it can also pay to offset aggressive, risky growth styles with more conservative value-priced plays. In the real world, this would mean choosing a fund like MAS Mid Cap Growth, a great aggressive play, and pairing it with another fund such as Fidelity Low-Priced Stock, which holds cheaper and smaller names.

You could make a guess on style by the fund names, but that method has a high margin of error. Any good mutual fund website, however, should categorize each fund in a helpful way. (Of course, a broad U.S. equity index fund would cover both growth and value.)

► STEP 10: **Overtime**

Even if you don't analyze portfolios for fun, a little extra time can have a big payoff. Consider these three moves:

1. Work as a team. The couple that plans together retires sooner—and better—together. If your spouse has a 45% stake in Cisco, you both should organize around it: With so much of the family's assets in one tech stock, you ought to think twice about that hot specialty communications fund your own plan just added. Or perhaps your partner's plan has a low-cost large-cap index option, but no small-cap funds. A tool such as

These allocations are derived from the Fidelity website (www.401k.com). Like many one-size-fits-all models, they're conservative. Consider holding cash in another account, for instance, to make better use of your plan's tax deferral. To help you make allocation choices, decide which profile most nearly matches your own.

▶ Aggressive growth

For daring investors with plenty of time—say, 15 years or more—and the nerve to ride out dramatic dips. You aren't counting on borrowing from your plan to purchase a home, and you've got a stash of cash in an emergency fund. Extra small-cap and international exposure adds a kicker. There's no cash inside the 401(k) to hold the portfolio back—or to cushion a fall.

▶ Growth

You still have a way to go until retirement, and you are willing to take some risk. However, you don't want to go all out. Perhaps you've got a couple of kids and some debt besides your mortgage, so you'll want a buffer here. The big, broadly diversified stock stake has good growth potential. The 25% bond stake lends significant stability, so you could forgo that 5% dash of cash.

▶ Balanced

Maybe you are near or in retirement but are still gunning for growth to the extent you can reasonably do so. Or perhaps you are only in your late thirties but can afford to play it safer because you expect real estate income to help support you in retirement. Only half of the portfolio is in stocks, but a bit of smaller-cap and foreign exposure add flair. The bonds and cash provide a sober contrast.

▶ Conservative

Either you're terrified of taking on much risk (and you can set aside enough so that you don't have to), or you have saved enough to live off of now. There's still room for growth here, with 20% in stocks, because you'll be living a long and happy retirement. But volatile small-cap or international names aren't part of the plan. And 30% in cash is thick padding against rocky markets.

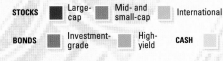

| STOCKS | ■ Large-cap | ■ Mid- and small-cap | International |
| BONDS | ■ Investment-grade | ■ High-yield | CASH |

Morningstar's ClearFuture or Financial Engines (see box on page 88 for more details) can help you map out your own 401(k) to complement your partner's picks.

2. Forecast your retirement prospects. Use online Monte Carlo simulation tools such as Financial Engines or Morningstar's ClearFuture. Or visit our own site, www.money.com, to use a version of the Financial Engines.

3. See how far your money will go. Think you're ready for the big day? T. Rowe Price's Retirement Income Manager can help you figure out how much you can safely withdraw from your plan each year. See the "Resources" box above for the website.

Now stop agonizing: If you've come this far, we bet that you're well on your way to the retirement you deserve.

▶ *Too Much Company Stock*

Your company's stock is probably accounting for a bigger and bigger chunk of the money in your 401(k) plan. That's swell if your company is, say, General Electric. But great growth can mean great risk, especially in a volatile market. There may be a smarter way to play your company stock.

Warren Glotzbach, a 49-year-old designer at Motorola, dreams of retiring in 10 years and building a second career as a rock-'n'-roll musician. To do that, the Delray Beach, Fla. dad needs at least $1 million in his 401(k). Key to his strategy: putting a sizable 25% of the money in his company's stock. It's a gamble that paid off last decade—Motorola shares soared 900% in the '90s—but in 2000 the stock fell 71% from its high as Wall Street pounded the company for earnings shortfalls. Glotzbach's 401(k) portfolio, which had surpassed $500,000, shrank as much as 30%. He remains undaunted. "It's like taking a roller-coaster ride in the front seat," he says of his Motorola megastake. "You hope you end up with a big smile on your face instead of flying off the tracks."

Glotzbach wants to diversify his 401(k) to reduce risk, but he also wants to snap up even more shares. "Motorola's trading at a bargain price right now," he notes. "This is a great company. It's had setbacks before, but it's always come back."

Call it the great retirement bet. Millions of people are wagering growing portions of their portfolios on the hope that a single stock—their company's—will rocket high enough to ensure a comfortable retirement. Risky? Obviously. Foolish? Not necessarily. While the traditional advice has been to invest no more than 10% of your total portfolio in company stock, the New Economy may demand new rules. In this environment, whether to invest in your company stock, and how much, depends on your particular situation. As Dee Lee, a planner in Harvard, Mass., says, "If I told Bill Gates that he shouldn't have 90% of his net worth in Microsoft, he would laugh in my face."

But what's right for Bill Gates probably won't work for you, so it's essential to understand your risks. Whatever the size of your company stake—10%, 20%, 30% or more—you need a portfolio strategy that will cushion your risk.

The company we keep. At larger 401(k) plans recently surveyed by benefits firm Hewitt Associates, 41% of total assets are invested in employer stock, up from 26% in 1995. At many big corporations, especially those that match contributions with company stock, the allocations can reach startling levels. At Anheuser-Busch, Abbott Labs and Procter & Gamble, for example, company stock accounts for 80% to 95% of total retirement plan assets.

The company-stock bet isn't limited to 401(k)s. As many as 10 million workers now receive stock options, up from just a million a decade ago. In addition, 8.5 million employees participate in ESOP and stock-bonus plans, and 15.7 million are in stock-purchase plans. Many folks take part in more than one of these programs, thereby compounding their exposure. Says San Francisco financial adviser Tim Kochis: "Many executives have the bulk of their net worth invested in their company."

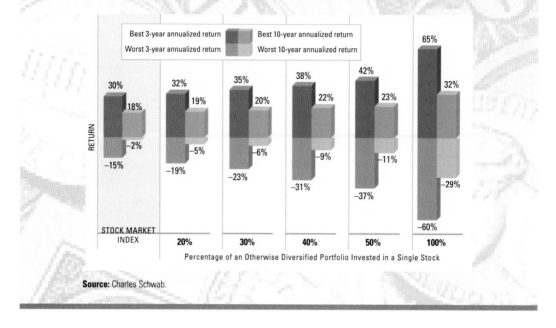

Powers of Concentration

Returns from rolling three- and 10-year periods from 1926 to 1998 demonstrate that the more a single stock dominates your portfolio, the greater the price swings—both up and down.

Best 3-year annualized return   Best 10-year annualized return
Worst 3-year annualized return   Worst 10-year annualized return

RETURN

STOCK MARKET INDEX

Percentage of an Otherwise Diversified Portfolio Invested in a Single Stock

Source: Charles Schwab.

Stashing more than 10% of your portfolio in any single stock is risky; if it's your employer's stock, your risk is intensified. You already have a huge stake in your company in the form of your human capital (the economic term for the value of the income you generate in your career). If your company does badly, you could suffer a double whammy, losing both your job and your nest egg. Remember when thousands of aging IBM workers were pushed into retirement in the early 1990s—just as the stock had fallen 60%?

It's also undeniable that company stock has been the engine driving much of our era's astounding wealth accumulation. Just look at the riches reaped by workers at GE (whose stock price has soared 859% over the past 10 years), Dell (28,843%) and Cisco (71,265%). All of which heightens what John Rekenthaler calls "risk of regret." Says Rekenthaler: "If GE employees had passed up the chance to own that stock for the past 10 or 20 years, they'd be kicking themselves right now."

Of course, that doesn't mean you should cavalierly plop 50% of your 401(k) into your company. Not every firm will be a Dell or Cisco—and even these winners saw their share prices falter in 2000. It's essential to understand what a big loss on your company stock would mean for your net worth and financial goals.

Risks vs. returns. Even a 30% weighting in a single stock can pump up a portfolio's volatility dramatically. Consider a study conducted by Schwab that examined the impact of a single large holding on a typical equity portfolio (see the chart on opposite page). Using randomly selected companies, Schwab researchers compared the range of returns with those of a market index over three- and 10-year periods from 1926 to 1998. An index portfolio, for example, gained as much as 30% over three-year periods and lost no more than 15%. By contrast, putting 30% of the portfolio in a single stock boosted the highest gain to 35% and intensified the worst loss to 23%. A 100% single-stock position generated a dizzying gain of 65% and a retirement-wrecking loss of 60%. "If a concentration in a single stock exceeds 30%, alarm bells should definitely be going off," says Mark Riepe, director of mutual fund research at Schwab. "Make sure you're really comfortable with the downside risk."

Unfortunately, most of us have the misguided notion that company stock is a relatively safe investment. A survey of 401(k) plan participants by UCLA accounting professor Shlomo Benartzi found that just 16% of respondents realize that employer stock is riskier than the overall market. "Because people think company stock is safe, they tend not to think of it as a 'stock,'" says Benartzi.

Employees also expect better performance from the stock than they get. An analysis of 154 401(k) plans with company stock from 1993 to 1997 found that participants typically earned only a market return on their shares while taking above-average risk. One reason: people tended to load up after a stock rose, and the subsequent returns tended to be far lower. Indeed, 63% of the companies in the study underperformed the S&P 500 over the four years; among those where employees held the highest allocations in company stock, 71% lagged.

What these studies show, most of all, is that the biggest problem with owning employer stock is not the stock, but the investors. There is a right way to handle a portfolio with company stock. Here's how.

▶ **Find out how much of your net worth is riding on your employer's stock performance.** Given the run-up in the market over the past few years, you may be surprised. If you have substantial stock options, the math is more complex; you may want to consult a financial adviser.

Then determine if you want to lighten up—and if your company plan will let you do so. There's no universal solution here. You must evaluate your financial goals, time horizon and taste for risk, as well as the fundamentals of your employer—a tech start-up will be riskier than a global pharmaceutical.

No matter how good you feel about your company, the key is to check your emotions. "You can't imagine how overconfident people can get," says Alan Benson Brown, a retirement planner in Hockessin, Del. "They think their company is the best in the world." The sudden fall of many high fliers in the past year should remind us that no company is bulletproof.

Of course, you may find you have no choice but to stick with your company shares. Stock options often take five years to vest, and 401(k) matches frequently can't be moved until you turn 50 or 55 or leave the company. Find out how soon you can sell your stock and shift money into less risky assets. Meanwhile, add as much as you can to your other savings, using the rest of your portfolio to produce the right mix.

▶ **Try to steer clear of funds that would tend to hold your company's stock.** For additional safety, avoid investments in your company's industry—chances are, when your employer hits a bump, so too will other businesses in its sector.

If you work for a large growth company like Intel and hold a lot of its stock, avoid large-cap growth funds and look to value funds that buy both large and small stocks, as well as those that invest overseas. Consider modest stakes in sector funds that focus on, say, health care or real estate, which historically have correlated poorly with technology—that is, they tend to go up when tech stocks fall and vice versa.

▶ **Develop a plan to to handle withdrawals.** When it comes time to retire, you have two choices: You can take your distribution in company stock or you can roll over your entire 401(k) into an IRA.

There's a tax break if you take your distribution in stock. You pay income tax only on the value of the shares when they went into your account, which may be far less than their current market value. When you sell, you pay only the long-term capital-gains rate, currently 20%, on the unrealized gain.

Tempting as that seems, it may not be the best move. In most cases, says adviser Bill Knox of Bugen Stuart Korn & Cordaro in Chatham, N.J., if you roll your stock over into an IRA and let your money grow tax deferred over the long term, you'll end up with a bigger nest egg. Plus, you'll have the opportunity to lower the portfolio's volatility. "People often get rich with concentrated portfolios," says Knox, "but they stay rich by diversifying them."

Still, if you need to draw money out of your 401(k) soon after you stop working, go ahead—take the company stock and enjoy the lower tax advantage.

▶ *Sites to Foretell Your Financial Future*

For the folks in your company's human-resources department, helping you with your 401(k) is simple. Perhaps a little too simple. They load you down with slick brochures about asset allocation, offer up a handful of funds and send you on your way. "You know how most people invest in their 401(k)?" asks Forrester Research analyst Jaime Punishill. "Their buddy tells them at the watercooler."

You can do better, and it doesn't have to cost a fortune. Two subscription-based websites, **ClearFuture** and **Financial Engines**, have taken a step beyond the usual free Web financial calculators. They provide sophisticated, individualized advice based on the choices in your company's retirement plan. Both have formidable pedigrees. ClearFuture belongs to mutual fund research firm Morningstar. Financial Engines was developed with William Sharpe, a Nobel prizewinning economist. (Full disclosure: Morningstar supplies MONEY with much of our mutual fund data, and Financial Engines has a partnership with our money.com website.)

The two sites work in roughly the same way. First, you enter information on your salary, goals and current investments. The sites then analyze the data to determine the likelihood that you'll meet your target. If you don't like the results, you can modify some criteria—pushing back your retirement age by a couple of years or increasing your 401(k) contribution—and see how such

Assembling a winning retirement plan can be a daunting task. But these two portfolio tools can set you on your way for a few minutes of your time and a few dollars a month.

NAME/ WEBSITE (WWW.)	QUARTERLY COST	MINUTES TO INPUT DATA	PROS	CONS
ClearFuture morningstar.com[1]	$7.95 for 401(k)	15	Setup is easy.	Offers only 401(k) analysis
Financial Engines financialengines.com	$14.95 for one retirement account; $39.95 for multiple accounts	25	Initial portfolio analysis is free.	More expensive

Note: [1]Click on "401(k) Advice." **Sources:** Morningstar, Financial Engines and MONEY estimates.

adjustments affect your chances. Finally, the services recommend a portfolio mix and specific funds in your plan.

To test these sites, we created a hypothetical investor. Bill is 45 years old, earns $70,000 a year and has $15,000 in a 401(k) to which he contributes 10% of his pay. His goal is to retire at 65 with an income of $65,000 a year.

ClearFuture, which charges $7.95 for three months of use, was the easier of the two sites to use. Setup took less than 15 minutes. Given Bill's ambitious plans, the initial 401(k) portfolios that ClearFuture returned couldn't help Bill reach his preferred retirement. Even the riskiest scenario, 100% in stocks, afforded Bill $38,000 a year at best. But by upping Bill's retirement age to 68, we found a portfolio with moderate risk that would likely meet his goal. Another couple of clicks, and we had a detailed portfolio of funds that Bill could buy.

Financial Engines is a bit more complex. Unlike ClearFuture, Financial Engines can analyze other retirement accounts like IRAs as well as 401(k)s. It can also use your current holdings as a starting point, whereas ClearFuture asks only for your current investment balance. Financial Engines takes a few more minutes to set up, but that's a natural consequence of entering a broader array of data.

Financial Engines' verdict for Bill was also pretty bleak. At first, the program gave poor Bill only a 5% chance of hitting his retirement target, even if he took on above-average risk.

When you consider what can change before you retire, estimating how much you'll need seems hopeless. Yet as a reality check, it's useful. This worksheet solves for two stakes. The first assumes you'll leave money behind; the second that you'll spend it all. Both assume 3% inflation, an 8% return and a life expectancy of 90. But beware: If a bear market hits early in retirement, these projections may prove too optimistic.

1. Enter your desired annual **retirement income**. (We recommend using 100% of pre-retirement income, less what you are saving.) $_____
2. Multiply line 1 by Factor A below, based on a target retirement age. This is the **income you'll want** in the first year of retirement. $_____
3. Subtract expected pension and Social Security income (available at www.ssa.gov). This is the **income your assets must generate.** . $_____
4. Multiply line 3 by Factor B, based on your age at retirement. The result is your **ideal retirement stake**, which should generate enough income without tapping your principal. $_____
5. Multiply line 3 by Factor C, based on your age at retirement. This is your **minimum retirement stake**, which should generate enough income only until age 90. $_____

YEARS UNTIL RETIREMENT	INFLATION FACTOR A	RETIREMENT AGE	FACTOR B	FACTOR C
0	1.00	50	24.2	20.7
1-5	1.09	55	21.8	18.6
6-10	1.27	60	19.9	16.2
11-15	1.47	62	19.0	15.5
16-20	1.70	65	18.1	14.1
21-25	1.97			

Source: Tarbox Equity Inc., Newport Beach, Calif.

Financial Engines did that much for free. Changing inputs such as retirement age and account contributions or getting fund recommendations costs $14.95 every three months. With a little tweaking, we found a scenario where Bill stood a 64% chance of retiring by age 70.

Both ClearFuture and Financial Engines base their forecasting and their fund picking on complex computations using historical data. So it's important to keep in mind that the impressively detailed predictions these sites spit out are ultimately just well-educated guesses. The sites' real service is that they force you to consider the hard questions about your retirement strategy, such as whether you're really saving enough and whether you can really handle the risk you are taking. If you still aren't sure about which funds you want to own, or how much of them, both sites do a fine job of presenting a realistic portfolio mix. Either one is a lot more thorough than that guy at the watercooler.

Step 4

Protect What You Have

We can't argue that insurance is fun; it isn't. Actually, it's a consumer's nightmare. It is costly, confusing and unrewarding—until you have to make a claim. And that's when you often find out whether you bought the right coverage from the right company.

Insurance won't make you wealthy, but it is an essential tool for preserving the wealth you have already accumulated. And if you can buy the same coverage you now have at a much better price, well, that *will* enhance your bottom line. Read on to find out how to cut your insurance bills while making sure that you're well covered for any eventuality.

▶ *Get the Life Insurance You Need*

If you want to disperse a crowd at a party, just bring up life insurance. It's that exciting.

Nonetheless, most people need some kind of life insurance, and the longer you wait to tailor your requirements to your budget, the more you will pay later—and the greater the risk of leaving your loved ones in financial danger.

Doing the numbers. If you do have people counting on you for your income—or, if you stay home caring for children, on your services—figure out how much money they would need to replace your contributions. To come up with a meaningful estimate, you'll have to think seriously about your lifestyle choices, goals and expectations. Will your spouse continue to work? How will the kids be cared for? Will the kids go to private colleges or public ones? At what age can they fend for themselves? After college? After graduate school?

How Much Insurance Do You Need?

The following simple worksheet, created with the assistance of the College for Financial Planning, assumes that once the children are independent, the surviving spouse will be self-supporting through retirement. Providing for the spouse would significantly increase the number of years used to calculate line 5. The worksheet doesn't take into account investment rate of return or inflation and may result in higher-than-realistic projections. But when it comes to life insurance, it makes sense to build in a little extra.

YOUR ESTIMATE

1. **Total assets that can easily be converted to cash**
   (investments, existing life insurance, equity in the family home only if survivors would want to move)   _____
2. **Survivors' future income**
   (until youngest child is independent, minus an emergency fund of three to six months' living expenses)   _____
3. **Expected liabilities**
   (outstanding debt, medical bills, funeral costs)   _____
4. **Net liquid assets**
   (add lines 1 and 2, then subtract line 3)   _____
5. **Survivors' living expenses**
   (75% to 85% of current expenses until youngest child is independent)   _____
6. **Higher education expenses**
   (until all children complete college and/or graduate school)   _____
7. **Projected expenses**
   (add lines 5 and 6)   _____
8. **Projected insurance needed**
   (subtract line 4 from line 7)   _____

To give you some guidance, we put together the worksheet above. You'll find other insurance calculators on the Net (see the box on page 95 for resources or go to www.money.com/life) and in personal-finance software packages. The results will vary—we found differences of several hundred thousand dollars when we tested four calculators—but all follow the same basic method: Total the assets and income that would be available for the years the family would need support after your death. (Our recommendation: Don't count the house if your family wouldn't want to move out after your death.)

Subtract the estimate of final expenses and the money the family would need for those years, probably 75% to 85% of current expenses. The shortfall between assets and expenses is the coverage you need—but be sure to calculate and update your coverage if necessary after major life changes, like a birth, divorce or remarriage.

Here are your choices for covering that shortfall.

▶ **Term insurance.** Most people are better off with the simplest—and cheapest—insurance product: term life, which provides a death benefit only during the period covered by the contract. If it's an annual renewable policy, you're generally guaranteed the right to renew, but your premium will go up. In a guaranteed level-term policy, the premium stays the same, but to renew at a favorable rate you usually have to take another health exam. (Note: some level-term policies don't guarantee the premium for the entire term, so check before you buy.) Premiums, expenses and commissions are lower for term than for whole life. No cash value builds up, but a convertible term contract allows you to convert to a cash-value policy later.

Term is unquestionably the best choice for most young families. But after age 50, premiums can run into thousands of dollars a year, even if you're in good health. By 60, premiums are often prohibitive. Even so, Glenn Daily, a fee-only insurance consultant, contends that convertible 10-, 15- or 20-year level-premium policies can meet most people's needs.

▶ **Permanent or cash-value insurance.** Consumer advocates are nearly unanimous in their criticism of cash-value insurance. So why mention it at all? Because it can make sense if you married or had kids late, have a much younger spouse, have maxed out on your tax-deferred savings, expect to incur federal estate taxes or are concerned about continuing a business.

Permanent policies provide a death benefit for as long as the premiums are paid, plus a savings or investment component that policyholders can borrow from or draw down as retirement income. Commissions and expenses slow the accumulation of cash value in the early years of the policy, so you should buy permanent life only if you'll keep the policy for at least 20 years.

▶ **Whole life.** Premiums are fixed, and in the early years are higher than the cost of providing the protection; in later years they're usually less. You have no say in how the insurer invests the funds; long-range returns are comparable to bond funds'. In participating policies, a share of surplus mortality charges is returned to the policyholder as dividends, which may be used to reduce the premiums. Nonparticipating policies have no dividends.

► **Universal life.** Universal life lets you adjust the death benefit and the amount and timing of premiums, so long as you keep enough cash value to cover administrative expenses and mortality charges. The part of the premium not going to the mortality charge is invested in a separate account of intermediate-term bonds.

Two caveats: Universal policies are very sensitive to interest rates. And cashing out, say, a whole life policy in order to buy a new universal (or variable) policy is not a good move. As Ronald Parry, a Covington, Ky., attorney who has represented policyholders in churning cases against insurers, warns, "The only reason to replace a policy is if the policyholder becomes convinced the company cannot pay the death benefit."

► **Variable and variable universal life.** All variable policies allow policyholders to invest their premiums in a stock portfolio.

The best deals at work are usually policies you couldn't buy as an individual, such as legal or dental insurance. Getting legal insurance may make sense if you expect to need basic legal advice soon, perhaps if you're buying a home or drafting a will.

When it comes to life and auto policies, your boss may or may not have the best deal, depending in part on how high a risk you are to insure. Since an employer's group life insurance rates are based on a large pool of workers, a young non-smoking employee might get a better deal as an individual, says Robert Sollmann, a senior vice president of Metropolitan Life Insurance. Similarly, a driver with a spotless record might do better on his own. To analyze any policy your employer offers, get independent quotes.

The value of the death benefit—and the cash build-up—fluctuates depending on the performance of investments you choose from a limited menu of stock and bond funds in a separate account. If you invest wisely and the market is up when you die, your beneficiaries may realize a windfall; if the market is down, they may wind up with a smaller death benefit than expected, though most policies do guarantee a minimum.

One hot commodity in today's life insurance market is variable universal. It combines the investing feature and the fluctuating cash value and death benefit of variable and the adjustable premiums of universal. (Variable life policies have a fixed premium.)

Both types of variable insurance carry mortality charges, expenses and commissions—often steep ones—that eat up returns. "So don't buy variable life to play the market," advises White Plains, N.Y. agent James Newhouse. "You buy life insurance to put the risk that you might die on the insurance company but [when you buy a variable product] you decide to take on the risk again."

Going shopping. Once you've determined how much and what kind of insurance you need, it's time to do some comparison shopping. For term insurance, 800 numbers and websites can provide dozens of quotes (see the box on the previous page). Group insurance offered by your employer is often a good buy, especially if you can take your policy with you if you change jobs. (See the box above for more advice about insurance offered at work.)

Life Insurance: Where Does the Money Go?

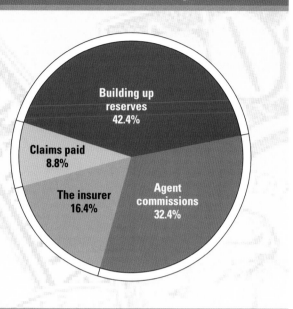

In the first three years of a typical universal life policy, barely half of your money is dedicated to policy-holder benefits. The rest is gobbled up by your agent or your insurer, which spends part of its share on marketing, administrative expenses and taxes, and retains the rest as earnings.

Building up reserves 42.4%

Claims paid 8.8%

The insurer 16.4%

Agent commissions 32.4%

Source: Brian Fechtel.

For permanent coverage, you'll probably need a broker. Contact the local chapter of the National Association of Life Underwriters or Society of Financial Service Professionals (888-243-2258; www.financialpro.org). Look for an agent with at least five years' experience and a C.L.U. or Ch.F.C. designation. If you're buying a variable policy, your agent must be registered to sell securities.

Be skeptical about policy illustrations when it comes to comparing costs of cash-value policies. Beware of "vanishing premium" pitches, which work like this: An agent tells you that your policy will "pay for itself" after, say, five years, because the illustration anticipates annual investment returns that are greater than the premiums. If those projections prove to have been overly optimistic, customers may find themselves on the hook for unexpected bills.

Call a low-cost, low-load provider like USAA Life Insurance (800-531-8000) or Ameritas Life Insurance (800-552-3553) for a benchmark quote. Most Americans who own permanent insurance could cut their premiums by about 40% and receive the same benefits.

When you have narrowed your choices to a few companies, check their ratings for financial stability. You'll find A.M. Best's Insurance Reports, Moody's, Standard & Poor's or Weiss Ratings at your local library. A.M. Best reports can be ordered over the Net (www.ambest.com). Choose only top-rated companies.

Tell the truth on your application. If you smoke, say so. If you die within the first two years of the policy and it's found that you lied on your application, the insurer can refuse to pay.

Finally, be sure you'll be able to keep paying the stiff premiums. It's usually a terrible deal to surrender a permanent life policy in the first few years, before you see the investment returns that come later. Yet some 25% of policyholders do just that, giving up or cashing out in the first three years. These buyers lose enormous amounts of money.

▶ The Ins and Outs of Auto Insurance

Some auto coverages are crucial and some are desirable, but others are unnecessary. Here are some strategies for prioritizing your auto insurance spending.

Cover your assets and your family first. Your most costly bills in an accident may very well come from the other people involved. That's why most states require *bodily injury liability* insurance to cover medical treatment, rehabilitation and funeral costs incurred by your own passengers, the other drivers and their passengers, and even injured pedestrians. This also covers lawyers' fees, and non-monetary losses related to pain and suffering. State minimum coverage limits are too low to protect the assets of most motorists. Unless your income and assets are minimal, buy at least $100,000 per person, $300,000 per accident.

Property-damage liability covers repair or replacement of other people's cars and property. State minimum limits average about $15,000. But with the cost of a new car averaging $22,000, buy at least $25,000 in coverage.

Uninsured-motorist and underinsured-motorist coverage pays for the medical, rehabilitation, funeral and pain-and-suffering costs of the victims in your car when it's struck by a hit-and-run driver or someone who's inadequately insured. This crucial coverage also insures your household members as pedestrians. Buy at the same limits as your bodily-injury liability.

Personal-injury protection (PIP), often known as "no-fault," covers medical, rehabilitation and funeral costs for household members, as well as some lost wages and in-home care. Unless your health and disability coverages are slight, buy the minimum required.

Consider these options—if your budget permits. *Collision* pays to repair or replace your car after an accident. If you have a new car with a loan, you'll be required to buy this coverage.

Comprehensive pays if your car or its contents are stolen, or your car is damaged by fire, water or other perils. Lenders will also require this.

For both coverages, you'll have to choose a deductible, and the higher the deductible you carry, the more you'll save. Try to carry a deductible of at least $500 on each coverage.

For cars worth less than about $3,000, comprehensive and collision probably aren't worthwhile. Over time, the premiums you'll fork over will probably exceed the payout, even if your car is totaled. And you can figure that in an accident that isn't your fault, the other driver's insurance will cover your car. For a quick estimate of your car's market value, consult the **Kelley Blue Book** (www.Kbb.com).

Coverages you can probably do without. *Medical-payments* pays the deductibles and co-payments not covered by your health insurer, or the insurer of any of your passengers. It also covers some funeral and rehabilitation costs. It's not useful unless you face very high health-insurance deductibles. In states where it's required, get the minimum.

Towing and labor only pays if you can't drive your car away from an accident. Members of auto clubs with such privileges don't need this coverage.

Rental insurance costs only a few dollars a year. But if you can depend on another car in a pinch, spare the expense.

Glass breakage coverage can add up to 20% to your comprehensive premium. When it's not built in to the premium, avoid it.

▶ *Protecting Your Home*

To preserve the wealth you've accumulated in real estate, you should insure your home for its replacement cost: that is, the cost to rebuild if it were totally destroyed. To do so, you must determine the average local building cost in your region and apply it to your home's size, style and quality of construction.

Sensible valuation tools. Your best resource in this task is—surprise—a builder. For a flat fee, you may be able to lure a local contractor to your home for an estimate. Try to find someone who builds custom homes that don't benefit from the economies of scale that tract homes offer. If you want the same antique moldings, stone fireplace and plaster-and-lathe walls as before, make sure the builder takes that into account. Otherwise, the estimate may reflect less costly modern materials.

If you can't get a builder, try these tactics.

▶ **Use a calculator.** A few websites will instantly calculate your cost to rebuild. You'll need to estimate the exterior square footage of your total living area, excluding basement. You'll also have to guess at the construction quality of your own home. One comprehensive site is the **Home Rebuilder Tool** (www .libertymutual.com).

▶ **Invite an agent to tea.** An agent who visits your home can eyeball the construction quality and enable you to point out special features. If you deal with a direct marketer with no local agents, you can better ensure proper coverage by accurately reporting your home's details—built-ins, antique wood and glasswork, upscale kitchen appliances and marble bath tile, for instance.

How much coverage do you need? For the majority of single-family homeowners, the most appropriate policy is the HO-3, sometimes called the special policy (in Texas, it's known as the HO-B). It insures against all major perils, except flood, earthquake, war and nuclear accident, making it very broad coverage.

You'll also need deep coverage, at limits at or near 100% of your home's replacement cost. By insuring at, say, 90%, you're making the reasonable bet that your home won't ever be a complete loss. Usually, the basement remains intact. Still, victims of the devastating Oakland Hills, Calif. fire in 1991 witnessed the destruction of even their basements. So if you want to play it safe, insure at 100%.

Insurers generally cover home contents at between 50% and 75% of the home's value. For a more exact estimate of your

How to Handle a Homeowner's Claim

The more information you can provide, the more likely you'll get your due. The insurer will send an adjuster to assess what was lost, stolen or damaged, and offer a settlement to replace or rebuild. Independently, you should get three estimates from local contractors whose reputations you've researched. But if you've faced a very big, traumatic loss and don't feel confident going it alone, consider hiring a public adjuster licensed by your state to walk you through the process.

Typically, they take between 5% and 15% of the settlement. Because the public adjuster works for you, he or she has no obligation to reduce costs for the insurer. Twelve states—Alabama, Alaska, Arkansas, Delaware, Idaho, Maine, Nebraska, New Mexico, North Carolina, South Carolina, Texas and Wyoming—don't have licensing laws that apply to public adjusters. But you can obtain the names of public adjusters in every state who have passed the voluntary certification process sponsored by the **National Association of Public Insurance Adjusters** (www.napia.com).

---

needs—and a written record that's useful when you file a claim—make a list of your home's contents. The industry-sponsored Insurance Information Institute (www.iii.org) provides a useful inventory.

As with auto insurance, it pays to pick a deductible of at least $500.

Buy the guarantees. Traditional guaranteed replacement cost coverage promises to pay whatever it takes to rebuild your home, even if it costs more than the original limits you purchased. That's key in the event labor and building costs balloon after a disaster. But in many states, large insurers now cap the guarantee at 120% to 125% of purchased limits.

Your safest bet is to seek a company with no cap. However, if you've properly valued your home's replacement cost, the caps shouldn't scare you. It's unlikely that building and labor costs will exceed 120% of your home's insured value.

If it's not built into your policy, ask for replacement cost coverage for your home's contents. Without it, you'll have to take the depreciated value of any object that's damaged or stolen.

You should also get a policy with *inflation guard*, an option that annually increases your premium at the rate of local building-cost inflation. *Ordinance-and-law coverage* is a rider that covers the costs of bringing your home into compliance with current building codes. It is a must if your home is more than a few years old.

Limit your liability. Your homeowner's policy protects against lawsuits for accidents that happen on your property. It also indemnifies you if your dog bites the neighbor. You should probably get more than the typical $100,000 limit.

In fact, if you have a higher net worth, buy umbrella liability coverage, which stretches both auto and homeowners liability limits above the underlying coverages.

▶ **Other options.** The homeowner's policy also provides for living expenses if you're displaced; replacement of structures such as garages and sheds; and limited medical coverage for someone injured on your property. Don't buy more than the minimum offered.

▶ **Floods and earthquakes.** Floods aren't covered by ordinary homeowner's insurance. Flood insurance is available through the **Federal Emergency Management Agency** (www.fema.gov). In California, you may need earthquake coverage; check www.insurance.ca.gov for a list of insurers who provide it.

▶ **Home business coverage.** Business property worth more than $2,500 isn't covered by a homeowner's policy, so buy a rider or separate policy to fill the gap. Business liability coverage must be purchased separately, too.

▶ **Riders for valuables.** A standard policy provides only minimal coverage for antiques, collectibles, furs, silver, jewelry, cameras, computers, musical instruments and firearms. The solution is to get a rider.

▶ *Picking an Insurer*

If you haven't shopped in three years for insurance, check what's out there. Get quotes from at least four carriers. First try a free database such as **InsWeb** (www.insweb.com), which offers quotes from up to eight insurers, or **Quicken InsureMarket** (www.insuremarket.com), which provides up to 16 quotes. The

Maximizing Your Savings

To save money on auto and homeowner's insurance, take the following steps:

▶ **Ask for discounts.** You can't change many of your risk factors—they're just who you are. But you can save money by taking advantage of discounts insurers offer for behavior that lowers your risk—from driving less than the average number of miles per year to quitting smoking. Certain types of people—senior citizens, for instance—also are eligible for price cuts. You'll also save by installing certain safety or protective equipment in your car and home. There's one catch: You have to ask. By one estimate, consumers lose some $300 million a year by not taking advantage of discounts.

▶ **Combine coverages.** Because it's cheaper to service two policies from the same customer, insurers often cut premiums by up to 15% if you link auto and homeowners policies.

▶ **Sweat the small stuff.** Frequent claims are red flags for insurers; some won't renew policyholders with more than two claims in three years. So try to carry more of the risk by covering claims under $1,000 yourself.

▶ **Raise your deductible.** The average driver files a collision claim once every three years, and a comprehensive claim once every 10 years. Increasing the collision deductible on your auto policy from $200 to $500 can save up to 30% annually, so given the likelihood of filing a claim, you might come out ahead with the higher deductible.

▶ **Pick your car carefully.** Car makes that cost a lot to repair or that are popular with thieves can cost more to insure. The *Consumer Insurance Guide* has a list of the most-stolen cars.

▶ **Park your teens in one car.** Name teenagers as the occasional drivers of your least-expensive car, and make sure they only drive that car.

▶ **Get your records straight.** Insurers have access to all sorts of personal information, including your motor vehicle record, credit record and your history of claims with other insurers. So it makes no sense to lie. But credit report mistakes need to be corrected because they may make you look like a worse risk than you are. If you haven't done so in a few years, consider obtaining reports from all three of the credit-reporting services, Equifax (www.equifax.com), Experian (www.experian.com), and TransUnion (www.transunion.com), since the reports can differ. Reports cost $8 apiece in most states. For a combined report, available online for $29.95, check out qspace.com.

larger the database, the better. If you're willing to pay for a more comprehensive database, look into **Consumer Reports Auto Insurance Price Service** (www.consumerinsure.org). The service's database compares up to 25 policies in 27 states. It costs $12 for the first vehicle, $8 for the second.

▶ **Use a "direct writer."** Companies like **State Farm** (www.statefarm.com) and **USAA** (www.usaa.com) that deal directly with consumers without using independent agents are called direct writers. In theory, they can pass on their savings by eliminating the middleman.

▶ **Read your junk mail.** Direct marketers like **Geico** (www.geico.com) and **Progressive Insurance Co.** (www.progressive.com) save on overhead—and pass on the savings—by marketing by phone, mail or the Internet.

▶ **Let your state be your guide.** Thirty-three state insurance departments and the District of Columbia offer shopping guides for auto insurance on the Web; 23 offer homeowner's guides. Your state's guide may identify little-known companies with competitive rates. **Insurance News Network** (www.insure.com) can link you to your state guide. (Illinois residents will have to go directly to the state website (www.state.il.us/ins).

▶ **Check affinity groups.** Your business association, club or employer may offer group auto insurance at a significant discount.

Assess an insurer's service and stability. No discount in the world will make up for a claim in purgatory or a botched car repair, so find out as much as you can about a company's service. *Consumer Reports* (www.consumerreports.org) periodically publishes service ratings for large insurers.

Ask the insurer for its financial ratings or check out one of the financial ratings services on the Web. An 'A' rating or higher from **Standard & Poor's** (www.standardandpoors.com) or an 'Aa' ranking or better from **Moody's Investor Service** (www.moodys.com) is a good indicator of strength. **Weiss Ratings** (www.weissratings.com), the most independent of the ratings services—and arguably the most stringent—posts a list of the current worst offenders.

Do You Need Long-Term Care Insurance?

The numbers sound scary—50% of Americans who reach the age of 85 eventually need long-term care to pay for an extended nursing home stay. And it is expensive: The average nursing home costs $50,000 a year. But that doesn't necessarily mean you should buy long-term-care insurance. If you have assets of less than $75,000 to $100,000, say health-care consultants, it's likely that you'll eventually qualify for Medicaid. And if you have more than about $600,000, you're better off investing the money until you need it. If you fall in the middle—and especially if longevity and chronic illness both run in your family—you should at least consider insurance.

And don't delay your decision too long: A policy that costs a 50-year-old $888 a year runs $1,850 for a 65-year-old and $5,880 for a 79-year-old. (This policy would take effect in 20 days and pay $100-a-day nursing-home or $50-a-day at-home benefits for four years, with payouts rising 5% annually.) Though rates can go up, you'll almost always come out ahead if you buy a policy when you're younger. Economics aside, you may not qualify for coverage when you're older.

One warning: Unless you're confident that you can afford the premiums for the long haul, don't sign on. You could waste thousands on a policy that lapses before you need it.

Focus on the essentials. Here's what to look for in a policy:

▶ **A financially strong insurer.** You want to buy from a firm that will be around if and when you need to collect benefits. Look for an "exceptional" Aaa or "excellent" Aa from Moody's (www.moodys.com), a superior A++ or A+ grade from A.M. Best (www.ambest.com) or between an A+ and B+ from Weiss Ratings (800-289-9222). For $49, Weiss sells customized reports for all long-term-care insurers in your area.

▶ **An inflation rider.** If you're under 70, you're probably not going to need the benefits for years, so you should buy a policy that keeps pace with inflation. But it will cost you approximately $500 to $1,000 more a year.

▶ **Ways to trim your premium.** The elimination period, which generally runs from zero to 180 days, is the time it takes for your benefits to kick in. The longer you can wait, the less expensive the policy. You can also save by limiting the length of coverage. Three to five years is usually adequate; the average nursing-home stay is $2^1/_2$ years, and 90% of patients stay less than four.

▶ **Cost and breadth of coverage.** Be sure to canvass nursing homes, assisted-living facilities and at-home nursing providers in your area to determine costs. Your state Office on Aging can help you track down estimates. Compare those numbers with the benefits of policies that you can afford. Be sure that home care and assisted living are covered as well as nursing-home fees.

▶ **Tax deductibility.** So-called *qualified policies* let you deduct part of your premium from your federal taxes if your medical costs exceed 7.5% of your adjusted gross income (AGI), but benefits are generally limited. Unless you're sure you'll meet the AGI limits and think you're likely to suffer from a protracted and debilitating illness, choose a nonqualified policy.

▶ Test Yourself

1. **Insurance policies cost pretty much the same and they are very much alike.**
   True
   False

2. **When shopping for life insurance, the best strategy is to:**
   A. Do what the agent tells you. After all, they are the experts and it is the agent's job to make sure you get the products that are right for you.
   B. Buy your coverage at work if possible.
   C. Figure out how much you need, then comparison shop using the Web and other resources.

3. **The purpose of life insurance is to:**
   A. Pay your funeral and final expenses
   B. Provide investment income and help fund retirement.
   C. Allow your dependents to maintain their lifestyle in the event of your demise

4. **The best time to get life insurance is when:**
   A. You are a baby
   B. You get out of college or start working
   C. You have dependents

5. **When shopping for life insurance on the Internet you should look for:**
   A. A low rate
   B. A company with a good rating
   C. A company with a low rate and a good rating
   D. A company that gives frequent flier miles with its policies

6. **How much bodily injury coverage you should buy?**
   A. $50,000 per person, $100,000 per accident
   B. Buy the state-required minimum
   C. None if you already have good medical and disability coverage
   D. $100,000 per person, $300,000 per accident

7. **A "direct writer" can save you money in theory because it:**
   A. Cuts out the independent agent's commission
   B. Generates annual dividends
   C. Has the best access to insurance databases
   D. Caters to affinity groups

8. **Which behavior is a red flag to an insurer?**
   A. Raising your deductible
   B. Shopping around
   C. Combining coverages
   D. Filing frequent claims

9. **For what value should you insure your home?**
   A. The mortgage amount
   B. The real-estate market value
   C. The value of its contents, plus 10 percent
   D. The cost to replace it

10. **"Guaranteed replacement cost" does what?**
    A. Ensures your totaled home is rebuilt, regardless of the cost
    B. It depends on the insurer's definition
    C. Rebuilds your home at 120 to 125 percent of the limits you purchased
    D. Rebuilds at 90 percent of your home's replacement cost

Answers

1. **False.** There's a huge difference in pricing and products when it comes to insurance.

2. **C.** The best approach is to do it yourself. Buy term and buy from a low-cost company that has a top rating.

3. **C.** The goal is to allow your dependents to maintain their lifestyle in the event of your demise. You want to have enough face value so that the proceeds of the policy could be conservatively invested to yield enough to cover the loss of your income.

4. **C.** The purpose of life insurance is to allow your dependents to maintain their lifestyle after your death.

5. **C.** This is the combination for a great deal on life insurance.

6. **D.** This is most appropriate for the typical consumer with assets to protect.

7. **A.** Direct writers don't use middlemen. That can mean the company passes on its savings to you in lower premiums.

8. **D.** Filing even small claims is a signal to an insurer that you're a poor risk.

9. **D.** One purpose of homeowner's insurance is to make you financially whole in the event of a disaster.

10. **B.** In spite of its name, guaranteed replacement cost isn't always guaranteed.

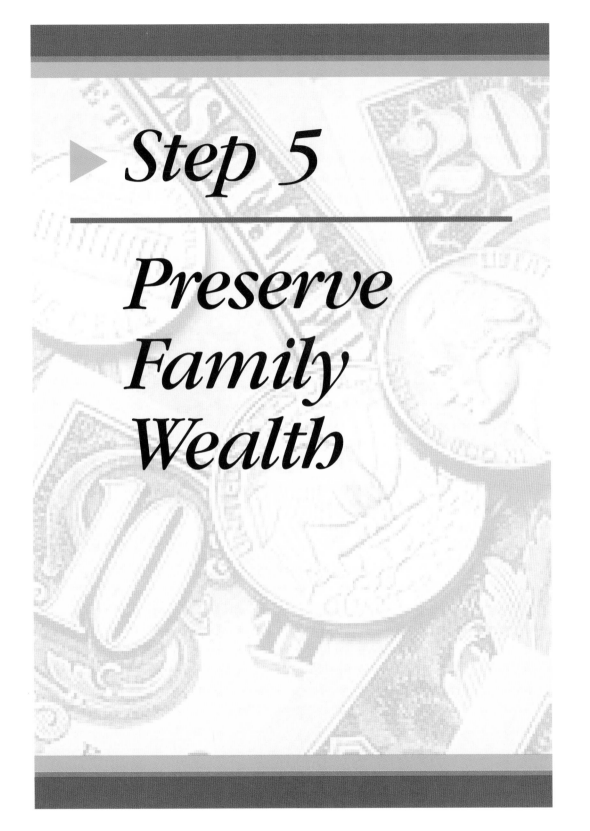

► *Step 5*

Preserve Family Wealth

*I*f you follow the advice in this book, you're likely to wind up with a sizable estate someday. Therefore, you need to know how to protect that money from the long arm of the government and how to pass it on to your heirs in the most effective way.

Of course, you, like tens of millions of other Americans, may face an entirely different set of estate planning issues as well because you will be on the receiving end of a bequest from a parent or another relative. This, too, may require more fore-thought than you might expect, and, as we shall see, may necessitate an awkward conversation with your parents. But such conversations are essential if you don't want Uncle Sam to get more than his fair share.

▶ *Realize Your Hopes and Dreams*

What are your hopes for the wealth you've amassed through a lifetime of hard work and smart investing? A financial safety net for your family? A college education for your grandchildren? Preserving a family business? Whatever your goal, you may not reach it if you don't take steps to protect what you own. You can't shield your estate from every threat, but you can keep it from getting mauled by federal estate taxes, which, at 37% to 55%, may be the biggest menace of all.

Know exactly what you have. The good news is that you can leave more than ever to your heirs tax-free: $675,000 this year, $700,000 in 2002 and $1 million from 2006 on. (As always, you can leave an unlimited amount to your spouse, as long as he or she is a citizen.) To determine whether your estate will outstrip the exemption, first tally up what you have now, including the value of your home, retirement funds, investments and life insurance death benefit. Of course, to get a snapshot of what will be left for your heirs, you'll have to estimate the future value of your assets—minus what you'll spend in retirement. Even if predicting your financial future seems as uncertain as reading tea leaves, the exercise is worthwhile. "Most people don't have a clue what they're worth, and they end up paying estate taxes because they didn't realize how much they have," warns New York City estate attorney Martin M. Shenkman.

Define your goals. Once you know whether your estate is likely to exceed the estate-tax exclusion, settle on your goals. If you want to make sure your kids can buy a home or put their children through school, consider making tax-free gifts now. By paring your estate, you may be able to reduce or eliminate estate taxes altogether. You can give an unlimited number of people up to $10,000 a year each without triggering federal gift tax; married couples can give up to $20,000 a year.

A trust may be just right for you. If you have substantial assets, the best way to preserve your hard-earned estate for your heirs is to establish a trust. Many people mistakenly think that trusts are only for "the rich." Not so. They are the right choice for millions of people who will face estate taxes, a number that has swelled because of the phenomenal rise in stock and home prices over the last two decades. Trusts are the most versatile tools in estate planning and they can help you do more than reduce estate taxes, including avoiding costly probate or controlling how your heirs spend inheritances. No matter what trust you choose, you'll need to work with a financial planner as well as an estate attorney. The one-time costs of drafting the trust documents range from $1,000 to $10,000, depending on the size and complexity of your estate. You may also have to pay ongoing maintenance fees.

Here are seven reasons you might want to set up a trust—and the vehicles that will best help you reach those goals.

1. Double what you and your spouse can leave tax-free. If your and your spouse's combined assets exceed the estate-tax exemption, there's a relatively simple way to double that tax break: Open *credit-shelter trusts*, also called *bypass trusts*, which

Everybody needs a *will*. Wills are especially important for people with young children, because they are the only legal way to transfer guardianship of minors, but it really doesn't matter how old you are or what you're worth. Your will is the device that lets you tell the world how and to whom you want to direct your assets. Die without one, and your property will be dispersed according to state laws—which typically split estates between surviving spouses and children, and not according to your wishes.

Is a will the way? But can a will accomplish everything you want it to? Until recently, a will was considered the cornerstone of any estate plan. For transferring sizable or complicated estates, however, estate-planning attorneys favor *living trusts*, which allow you to place your property that does not have a named beneficiary in the trust during your lifetime. You can change the trust terms at any time and serve as the trustee, so you don't give up control of the assets while you're alive. When you die, the trust assets are distributed to the beneficiaries you named, according to instructions you set forth in the trust document. Or you can instruct that the assets flow into a different type of trust, such as a *special-needs trust* for a disabled heir. Here's how wills and living trusts stack up in five key areas:

▶ **Probate.** Assets you transfer via a will must go through probate, the potentially costly and time-consuming court process of administering your will. Assets you transfer through a living trust avoid probate.

▶ **Privacy.** When a will is probated, its contents are made public. Since living trusts are not probated, there are no public records of the trust's terms.

▶ **Incapacity.** In a living trust, you can name a successor trustee to manage the trust assets if you become mentally or physically unable to do so. If you don't have a living trust, you will need to draw up a durable power of attorney to name someone to take charge of your assets if you become incapacitated.

▶ **Hassle.** With a will, you simply bequeath your separately owned assets that do not have a named beneficiary. In contrast, the property you want to put in a living trust must be retitled to the trust. Anything that is not so titled when you die will have to be probated.

▶ **Cost.** An attorney can draw up simple wills for a husband and wife starting at about $200. A living trust can run about $1,500. So weigh the benefits and costs before you decide what's best for you now. And remember, as your circumstances evolve, you should update your estate plan.

let a husband and wife claim one exclusion apiece. Credit-shelter trusts are "easy to set up and easy to manage," says Dee Lee, a financial planner in Harvard, Mass. "They're not so fancy or complicated that you can't live with them."

Here's how they work: You and your spouse must divide your assets. (It's possible, but more difficult, to fund credit-shelter trusts with jointly held property.) Then you each bequeath property worth up to the estate-tax exemption to a credit-shelter trust. If you die first, your spouse can tap the trust until his or her death, at which time the remaining assets go to your heirs tax-free. Plus, the surviving spouse can leave his or her own estate to the kids tax-free as long as its value doesn't exceed the exemption.

2. Support children from a first marriage. Tax avoidance isn't the only reason to set up a trust. For instance, what happens if your surviving spouse remarries and her new husband spends the money you hoped would go to your kids? A credit-shelter or bypass trust helps to safeguard your assets for your heirs. But remember, you can't put in more than the estate-tax exclusion. If you have remaining property, add a *qualified terminable interest property*, or QTIP, trust. "Usually bypass trusts and QTIPs go hand-in-glove," says New York City C.P.A. and attorney Stuart Kessler. "In most second marriages, I'd advise it."

Under QTIP rules, your spouse must receive income from the trust for life—and can tap the principal if you wish. Upon his or her death, the QTIP will pass to your heirs as part of your spouse's estate (so it may be taxable).

3. Shelter a life insurance policy. Your most valuable asset may be that rich life insurance policy you bought to protect your family. Well, you may have bought your loved ones a hefty estate-tax bill instead. Life insurance proceeds are taxable, even though many people think otherwise.

To make life insurance payouts estate-tax-free, move your policy into an *irrevocable life insurance trust*. The trade-off is that you must give up ownership of the policy, which means you can't borrow against it or change beneficiaries. Two more important caveats: You may owe gift taxes when you fund the trust and pay the premiums, depending on the policy's value and the number of beneficiaries. Second, if you die within three years of establishing the trust, the death benefit will be included in your estate.

4. Shelter a home or vacation dwelling. You can put the home in a *qualified personal residence trust* (QPRT), which allows you to give away your home, generally to your children, while you keep control of it for a period that you stipulate, typically five to 15 years. Because you manage your property through the trust for that time, the IRS assumes the value of the home to your children is only a small part of its fair market value. And that means it will gobble up a smaller part of your estate when you die, thus creating a tax break.

For example, say a 65-year-old man owns a house that is worth $500,000 today and will appreciate 4% a year over the next 10 years to a market value of $740,000. If he puts the house in a 10-year QPRT, the value that will count against his estate tax exemption will be just $190,765. (IRS tables are used to calculate this discount, so if you're interested in a QPRT, don't try this at home—see a planner.) One caveat: if you set up a QPRT and then die before the trust runs out, then your home will be included in your estate at its fair market value. (In the above example, if the man died after five years, when his house had increased to a value of $608,000, that full value would be counted against his estate-tax exemption.)

5. Provide for your grandchildren. If your children have already built up sizable assets, leaving them money may only shift estate taxes to the next generation. Fortunately, you have several ways to support your grandchildren, including direct gifts, custodial accounts and a *generation-skipping trust*, which will be part of your estate, not your children's, and therefore subject to estate taxes only once.

You can make a direct tax-free gift or fund a custodial account—best known by the acronyms *UGMA* and *UTMA*—if you don't want a young child to have the money right away. The child, however, does gain complete control of the money at age 18 or 21, depending on the state.

By contrast, if you set up a generation-skipping trust, you can control when a grandchild, or any other beneficiary at least two generations your junior, will receive the money and for what reasons. You can even let your kids collect income from the trust.

But tread lightly. If you put more than $1.03 million in the trust (or $2.06 million if you fund it jointly with your spouse), a 55% generation-skipping tax kicks in on top of the already hefty estate tax (unless the children's parents have died). This is designed to prevent very rich people from funneling all their money to their grandchildren.

6. Provide for children or grandchildren (with strings attached). The potential problem with traditional custodial accounts is that they let the child have full control of the stash at the age of majority, generally 18 or 21, regardless of whether he or she is mature enough to handle the money. However, if you establish a *minor's trust* to hold a child's assets, you can keep the money under wraps beyond the child's 18th or 21st birthday and influence how the money is ultimately used.

You could, for example, set up a college fund for a grandchild using a minor's trust. The trust documents could dictate that the funds must be used to pay for tuition, books, room, board and other living expenses while the child is attending a four-year college or university—and that the child receive, say, $10,000 upon graduation. Whatever is left in the trust might be distributed at age 30 or even 35. What if the child chooses not to go to college? Half the money might be distributed at age 30 and the rest at 35.

A caveat: While minor's trusts let you hold on to hefty sums for a long time, they're not entirely leakproof. In exchange for tax breaks on your trust contributions, you must generally give the beneficiaries limited access to the trust principal. Typically, the trustee would be required to notify the beneficiaries (through their parents) whenever subsequent contributions are made to the trust; they then have 45 days from the date of notification to withdraw an amount equal to the contribution. In practice, however, most beneficiaries never demand the money, so the brief window of opportunity to tap the trust is generally considered a risk worth taking to qualify for tax advantages.

7. Keep a family-owned business intact. Protecting a family firm from crippling taxes is tough for two reasons: The small business estate-tax exemption is only $1.3 million and, to qualify for the break, you must meet a slew of specific requirements. If you run your own business, a *family limited partnership* can help keep taxes from wiping out your legacy. With this complicated tool, you essentially transfer ownership of your business to a partnership that you control. Over time, you give family members limited interests. Because they don't control the business, their shares can be valued at less than fair market value—which can reduce your estate-tax liability. You may even avoid estate

If you have more money in your individual retirement account (IRA) than you'll ever need, you face a dilemma: Should you drain your Roth or traditional IRA, put it in a trust or leave it intact for your heirs? Here are the best ways to preserve the income tax benefits for your heirs.

The basics. Put off tapping an IRA as long as possible so that it can continue to grow tax-sheltered. If your spouse won't need the IRA, make your children the beneficiaries. Leave the account in your estate. Cashing in the IRA to put it in a trust will make the earnings taxable. If the IRA is sizable enough to trigger estate taxes, Ed Slott, a C.P.A. in Rockville Centre, N.Y. and editor of *Ed Slott's IRA Advisor*, suggests buying life insurance to cover the bill.

▶ **Roth IRA.** Bequeathing a Roth is relatively simple. You don't have to tap the account during your lifetime, so the entire IRA can flow to your beneficiary, who can choose to stretch the income-tax-free withdrawals over his or her lifetime.

▶ **Traditional IRA.** You must start tapping the IRA by April 1 of the year after you turn $70^1/_2$. To leave behind as much as possible, name a young beneficiary—your distributions can be based on your and your heir's joint life expectancy. (The IRS, however, considers a nonspouse beneficiary to be no more than a decade younger than you.) As for the distribution method, Lisa Osofsky, a partner at M.R. Weiser & Co. in New York City, suggests *term certain*, which results in a set number of payouts. That way your heirs won't have to cash out your IRA more quickly or even all at once when you die.

taxes if the discounted value of the shares is less than the estate-tax exemption.

Once again, family limited partnerships must be handled gingerly so that the potential tax savings don't vanish. The IRS stays alert for excessively discounted shares, so hire an expert to appraise the business and calculate the discounts.

▶ *Give Away Money While You're Alive*

Gift and estate taxes are basically the same assessment—your estate pays taxes after you die on gifts you made or stipulated while you were alive. You can give money away tax-free up to a

Okay, so you need to hire an accountant or financial planner to help you plan your estate and an attorney to draft a trust and will. But how do you know if the pros have the right expertise? Here are some rules to follow.

▶ What's the first thing to look for in a lawyer or planner?
Hire a pro who spends substantial time, roughly 40% to 60%, on estate-planning issues. You don't want a financial planner who devotes his practice to advising clients on investments or a lawyer who specializes in real estate.

▶ What about referrals?
Make sure other clients have financial profiles similar to yours. If you're worried about estate taxes, you don't want a lawyer or planner who works with smaller, nontaxable estates.

▶ Are special degrees and memberships important?
They're not necessarily so special. Membership in the American Bar Association's estate-planning arm or the National Association of Estate Planning Councils is a plus, but it doesn't mean much unless someone's actively involved to keep abreast of estate-tax issues. They should be participating in lectures or other activities that are challenging.

▶ Do I need to know about estate planning first?
Estate planning is not for do-it-yourselfers, but the more informed you are, the better you can interact with an expert. Educating yourself so you know the buzzwords will help you evaluate the estate-planning options that are available.

lifetime total of the estate tax exemption ($675,000 for 2001). Even after that point, however, gifting can cut your overall tax bill, because of the steep marginal rates of estate taxes. This is a complicated issue, so if you have a large estate and know whom you would like to designate as recipients of gifts while you're still alive, consult with your planner to see how much giving you should do.

You'll probably also want to make plans for your charitable donations that extend from today to beyond your death. Take heart, because when it comes to helping your favorite charities, these days anybody can be a Rockefeller. Gone is the era when you would have needed an eight-figure private foundation to consolidate your charitable donations into grants; several large financial services companies, including Fidelity (www.charitable gift.org) and Vanguard (www.vanguard.com), now provide convenient vehicles for giving. These *charitable gift funds* permit you to make a donation (minimum: $10,000 for Fidelity, $25,000 for Vanguard), grow your investment tax-free and then direct a contribution—in your name—to specific nonprofits whenever you like. Meanwhile, you can take an immediate tax deduction for your original donation.

Community foundations are also burgeoning. These are non-profit regional trusts run by private citizens that will welcome you for a donation of as little as $5,000 in cash, stock or property. Community foundations invest individual donations, pool the gains and allocate grants, usually to local nonprofits. In most cases, you can either suggest disbursements to specific organizations or ask a community foundation to put your contribution toward a cause you care about, then allow it to locate a worthy recipient.

Charitable gift funds and community foundations are encouraging families across America to get involved with philanthropy. They are easy to set up, don't cost much, offer control of your money and can be passed on to your heirs to continue the work you begin.

It's also possible to set up trusts in which a charity receives the income and your heirs get the principal after a specified period of time (a *charitable lead trust*), or in which a charity gets the principal after the income is paid out to your heirs (a *charitable remainder trust*). As always, the key is to establish your goals and then talk to your planner about how best to meet them.

▶ The Greatest Wealth Transfer

You may be in line to receive a portion of the largest transfer of wealth in human history. Research by John Havens and Paul Schervish, economists from Boston College, recently projected that wealth transfers by all Americans to all sources over the next 55 years will be at least $41 trillion.

The wealth that's changing hands is concentrated in a small number of portfolios. Of the amount to be received by baby boomers, one-third will go to the richest 1%. Another third will pass to the next wealthiest 10%, and the remaining third will be scattered among the bottom 90% of the boomer pyramid.

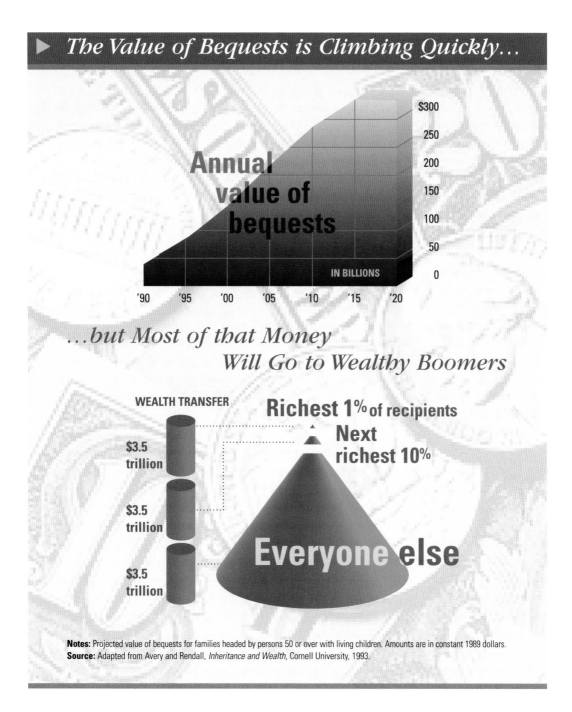

The Value of Bequests is Climbing Quickly...

Annual value of bequests

IN BILLIONS

$300
250
200
150
100
50
0

'90 '95 '00 '05 '10 '15 '20

...but Most of that Money Will Go to Wealthy Boomers

WEALTH TRANSFER

Richest 1% of recipients
Next richest 10%

$3.5 trillion

$3.5 trillion

$3.5 trillion

Everyone else

Notes: Projected value of bequests for families headed by persons 50 or over with living children. Amounts are in constant 1989 dollars.
Source: Adapted from Avery and Rendall, *Inheritance and Wealth*, Cornell University, 1993.

Whether you are a boomer or not, you can make sure a bequest makes a difference in your life by calibrating your expectations. Carefully managed, an inheritance can help you meet a specific financial goal or make meaningful—though probably not convulsive—changes to your lifestyle. Perhaps

Q. Can I leave my frequent-flier miles from the airlines and my credit-card reward programs to my heirs?

A. Frequent-flier miles are hot commodities, and ownership in cases of divorce or inheritance has been contested in court. A few airlines (including Delta, US Airways and TWA) let you transfer the miles but may require your heir to produce a death certificate and proof that he or she is indeed the beneficiary. Sadly, other companies (such as American Airlines, Qantas and American Express) stipulate that miles or points belong to the company and thus cannot be transferred, period. Although United Airlines agrees with this approach, the company will make individual exceptions—for a $75 fee!

To protect miles that you may want to pass on to an heir, establish joint accounts for frequent-flier or reward programs and name that beneficiary in your will. If there is no one that you fancy for the gift, suggests Randy Peterson of InsideFlyer.com, "consider leaving your miles to charity."

Q. Fulfilling my duties as the executor for my father's estate in Florida has cost me an entire month's income. Can I be paid for my work?

A. The typical fee ranges from 1.5% to 3% of the estate in probate, with independent consultants like yourself at the low end. Banks that provide fiduciary responsibilities, such as document and tax preparation, generally command the higher end of the fee spectrum. Remember: The executor fee is deducted from the taxable value of the estate.

you'll be able to afford a new car, take better vacations or start a business at home, but you almost certainly will not be able to replace your stream of income.

Of course, there is one catch to carefully managing your inheritance: You and your parents must be in accord about how and when they are going to divvy up all their property. And you can't be fainthearted about helping them get their estate in order. "If you thought talking to them about sex was tough," says financial planner Lee, "just wait until you try talking to them about estate planning."

Can we talk? Parents of any age can grow wary when children approach them about money. Nevertheless, the sooner you broach the topic of estate planning with your parents, and the more fully you explore it, the better. Once your parents are gone, you will have to do right by their wishes and take care of your family's needs. That's never an easy task; it may be nearly impossible without some instruction. In families with many siblings, or where there are divorces, remarriages and stepchildren, it's even more important to establish your parents' intentions.

So how do you ease into the most difficult discussion you may ever have? First, lead by example. Get your own estate in order, and it will be much easier to discuss planning without seeming as if your goal is getting your hands on your parents' money. You can talk to your parents about providing for the care of your spouse, setting up a living trust and seeking tax advantages as you work through these topics yourself. This shouldn't be any kind of ruse: If you are in your forties or fifties, you should be thinking about your own estate anyway.

Another way to prod Mom and Dad to do the right thing: Find their consigliere. Your parents may confide in someone about their financial affairs, even if they don't talk about money much with you. Let that person know you want to help with planning, and encourage him or her as well as your parents to widen the circle of their discussions to include everybody that will be affected by their estate.

If your parents are a bit bewildered by the task of assembling an estate plan, that's natural. To help them, try this tactic recommended by Norman Ross, vice president of Hirschfeld Stern Moyer & Ross, a New York City estate-planning firm: Suggest that they write down where they come from, where they have worked and what they have saved, and list their most significant purchases and investments. Encourage them to take stock of how they have come to accumulate their most important possessions. It's a simple way to connect the work they have done with the things in their lives that mean the most to them. That way, when they look at their inventory to divide up their estate, they will be working from a sense of pride in their accomplishments, not anxiety about death—and you may be fascinated by the details that emerge about their lives.

When your parents are ready for the nuts and bolts of estate planning, they'll need a good lawyer, someone who can create legal documents, offer advice when questions arise and help administer the disposition of their assets. It's also helpful to show them a clear reference guide. One excellent source is

Death and Taxes: The Complete Guide to Family Inheritance Planning by Randell Doane and Rebecca Doane. It's the kind of book that can lead to discussions that will help your family for generations.

▶ *Test Yourself*

1. **Which of the following is included in your taxable estate when you die?**
   A. Your home
   B. Assets in your IRA
   C. Proceeds from your life insurance policy
   D. All of the above

2. **Which estate planning technique effectively allows you and your spouse to double the amount of assets you can shield from estate taxes?**
   A. A credit-shelter trust
   B. An irrevocable life insurance trust
   C. A qualified terminable interest property (QTIP) trust
   D. A charitable remainder trust

3. **Ten years from now, how much of your property will be exempt from estate taxes?**
   A. 0
   B. $675,000
   C. $1,000,000
   D. It depends on your income tax bracket at the time of your death

4. **Why can you get a tax break with a qualified personal residence trust, or QPRT?**
   A. Because you are dedicating your home to a charitable cause
   B. Because the IRS acts as though the value of your home is just a fraction of its market value, since you give it away over time
   C. Because you agree to surrender control of your home over a 30-year period
   D. Because the value of your home ultimately benefits your grandchildren

5. **True or false: With a living trust, you escape estate taxes, but give up control of your assets while you are still alive.**

    True
    False

6. **Who needs a will?**

    A. Parents of minor children
    B. People with more than $650,000 in assets
    C. Retired persons
    D. All of the above

7. **If you give jointly with your spouse, what is the most you can leave to your grandchildren in a generation-skipping trust before triggering transfer taxes?**

    A. $675,000
    B. $1.03 million
    C. $2.06 million
    D. An unlimited amount

8. **If you have $800,000 in stocks and bonds, what amount can you leave to your spouse free of estate taxes?**

    A. 0
    B. $400,000
    C. $675,000
    D. $800,000

9. **If you want to direct assets to good causes after you die, which of the following organizations can grow your charitable dollars and pool them with money from other donors?**

    A. Irrevocable trusts
    B. Community foundations
    C. Qualified personal residence trusts
    D. "I love you" wills

Answers

1. **D.** Your taxable estate includes all of your assets when you die, including your home as well as your investments, retirement accounts and life insurance.
2. **A.** It is also known as a bypass trust.
3. **C.** The estate amount that is exempt from taxes will gradually rise from $650.000 today to $1 million by 2006.

4. **B.** People who use qualified personal residence trusts generally give their home to their children.
5. **False.** Living wills allow you to maintain control of your assets as long as you are alive, but not to hide them from taxes.
6. **D.** You need a will to direct the distribution of your assets when you die.
7. **C.** You are allowed to give up to $2.06 million jointly, or $1.03 million on your own, before steep generation-skipping taxes kick in.
8. **D.** You can leave an unlimited amount to your spouse tax-free when you die. This tactic, however, isn't a good estate planning tool, because it simply defers all of the tough decisions about your assets until the time of your spouse's death.
9. **B.** You can join one with a donation of as little as $5,000 in cash, stock or property.

Step 6

Get Paid What You're Really Worth

*Y*ou want more money. You don't want to bring your pets to work, and you don't need another week of vacation—you barely take all you're entitled to now. And let's face it: Flextime isn't going to help pay the tab for your kids' college education. Sound familiar? Well, if you want more than the skimpy 4.2% raises that corporate America is offering this year, start polishing up your negotiation skills. Although companies claim they're desperately trying to retain their best workers, hefty pay increases aren't on the agenda—unless you're talking high-tech careers.

"Global competition is forcing U.S. companies to keep fixed costs down," explains Steven Gross, a principal at the William M. Mercer human-resources consulting firm in Philadelphia. "Instead of bigger raises, employers are doling out bonuses and stock options to reward their high performers." In fact, Hewitt Associates (www.hewitt.com) found that in 1999, one-time bonuses rose almost four times as fast as salary increases.

If you're lucky enough to share the wealth of a prosperous company, incentive pay can drop a healthy piece of change into your pocket—and since options and bonuses are cheaper for the company than raises, they may be easier to get. That's because incentive or performance-based bonuses are often linked to such things as profits or productivity. Raises permanently affect the bottom line.

How do you angle for more pay at a time when most companies would rather pile on the non-financial perks, such as flextime or better food in the cafeteria? You ask for it. "People should navigate their careers as if they were running their own business, and that business is themselves," says Lewis Kravitz, an executive coach in Atlanta. "Your compensation should reflect your value to the company."

Almost a decade of corporate downsizing, salary freezes, cost cutting and Dilbert cartoons has convinced many of us that we're expendable and lucky to have a job—and maybe some of us are. But unemployment in late 2000 was at a 30-year low, and the tight labor market has left companies scrambling to find the brainpower and experience they need to thrive.

So, even if you're not a techno hotshot or the creative force behind your company's latest multimillion-dollar product, you're probably more valuable than you think. For instance, some recruiters say they are swamped with requests for middle managers who can lead project teams that cross functional lines.

Sure, there are timing issues, research requirements and a few negotiation tricks you should know before popping the money question, but you can do it. We'll show you how.

A little knowledge can be a lucrative thing.

Before you launch an intense lobbying effort to fatten your paycheck, build a rock-solid case for why you deserve a raise. And here's a hint: It's not because of the new house you just bought or the enormous tuition bills you face. Quite frankly, these are your problems, not your employer's.

"Your need is irrelevant to the company, even if your bosses like you," warns Robin L. Pinkley, who is a co-author of *Turning Lead to Gold: The Experts' Guide to Negotiating Salary and Compensation*. "To get more money, you must first determine what you're worth professionally—to your company and in the marketplace." In order to prepare for his own salary negotiation, Jim Cichanski, a vice president of human resources at a technology company in Atlanta, logged about 35 hours researching compensation packages for his peers in the same field.

Like Cichanski, start your investigation by priming your network of friends and business associates. "Within six degrees of separation, everybody knows somebody at a company similar to yours," says Eva Wisnik, a New York City career counselor. "Ask what their company would pay someone with your experience."

Professional associations can usually provide salary information that's broken down by years of experience, type of employer, geography and sometimes gender. (To learn how to best use salary websites for detailed compensation info, see "Use the Web to Get Paid More" on page 133.)

Headhunters are also good for up-to-the-minute salary intelligence. To get plugged in, introduce yourself to recruiters who

▶ *Rate Your Company's Benefits*

To assess how well the major features of your employer's benefits program rate against those of typical U.S. corporations, fill out the worksheet below by entering the correct number of points in the box next to each question and the total number of points in the last box in the right column. We developed the worksheet with the Vienna, Va. office of Milliman & Robertson, an actuarial and employee-benefits consulting firm.

HEALTH CARE

1. How much do you contribute each month for medical coverage?　　**POINTS**

SINGLE COVERAGE	FAMILY COVERAGE	POINTS
No medical	No medical	0
$41 or more	$151 or more	7
$21 to $40	$101 to $150	8
$11 to $20	$76 to $100	9
$1 to $10	$51 to $75	10
$0	$50 or less	11

2. How many medical plans can you choose from?

NUMBER OF PLANS	POINTS
None	0
One	1
Two	2
Three	3
Four or more	4

3. Does your company:

	POINTS	
STATEMENT	NO	YES
Offer a dental plan?	0	1
Pay for part of a dental plan?	0	1
Offer vision care?	0	1
Offer a flexible spending account?	0	1
Offer health care for retirees?	0	1
Pay for part of a retiree health plan?	0	1

DEFINED-CONTRIBUTION SAVINGS PLAN

4. How much does your company contribute to your employee savings plan—for example, a 401(k) or 403(b)—in both matching contributions and profit-sharing contributions if you make the maximum allowable contribution to the plan?

PERCENTAGE OF PAY	POINTS
No savings plan	0
Less than 3%	3
3% to 5%	7
6% to 8%	13
9% to 11%	18
12% to 13%	22
14% to 15%	25
16% or more	28

5. Can you change your investment election at any time?

ANSWER	POINTS
No	0
Yes	2

6. What percentage of final pay does your company's pension plan replace after 20 years of service?

PERCENTAGE OF PAY	POINTS
Company does not have a pension plan	0
Less than 10%	2
10% to 19%	10
20% to 29%	16
30% to 39%	23
40% to 49%	30
50% or more	33

7. Can you receive a lump-sum distribution from your pension plan?

ANSWER	POINTS
No	0
Yes	4

8. What level of employees is eligible for stock options?

ANSWER	POINTS
No stock options granted	0
Top managers only	1
Middle and top managers only	2
Professionals, top and middle managers	3
All levels of full-time staff	4

9. If you become disabled, how much is your long-term benefit?

ANSWER	POINTS
No coverage	0
49% of salary or less	1
50% to 59% of salary	2
60% of salary or more	3

10. Do you help pay for your long-term-disability benefit?

ANSWER	POINTS
Company does not offer plan	0
You contribute to cost of plan	2
Company pays full cost of plan	3

11. How much life insurance does your company provide?

ANSWER	POINTS
No coverage	0
Some coverage	1
Two times salary or more	2

Add up your points for questions 1 through 11 to calculate your total points.
Excellent Coverage: 70 points or more: Lucky you. Most of the ingredients of a great benefits package are there. **Typical Coverage: 40 points to 69 points:** Assess whether your package will provide enough retirement income **Minimal Coverage: 39 points or less:** Meet with your benefits administrator to make sure you understand your plan.

specialize in your field, suggests Laura Berman Fortgang, author of *Take Yourself to the Top: The Secrets of America's No. 1 Career Coach*. "Say you want a reality check," says Fortgang, "because in this market there's lots of room to move."

Finally, don't forget to take a look at other non-compensation financial benefits such as retirement and health plans to see how your company or potential employer stacks up. The worksheet on page 128 can help you make the assessment.

If you've got it, flaunt it. Once you have settled on how much you're worth on the street, document your contributions to the company. "Your track record is the best negotiating tool you've got," says Kravitz. "Past accomplishments are excellent indicators of future potential, but if you don't tell your manager what you've done, he's not going to look it up for you."

That's why Kravitz suggests that you keep a "Friday file." At the end of each week, jot down the progress and results of your most significant assignments. Provide details to demonstrate your value to the organization and to track how your job has evolved. (See "Five Traits Employers Pay More For" on the opposite page.)

Proving his ability to handle major projects helped Transamerica auditor Robert Schmollinger get more than the average 3% to 5% increase he heard the financial services company was offering. But it took some work. First the financial pro checked out several salary surveys to discover that he wasn't making the $58,000 a year that auditors with similar experience were earning. Then Schmollinger started flipping through his datebook to compile his most important assignments, which included serving on the team that implemented a new company-wide financial system.

Armed with an enviable portfolio of achievements and the salary research, Schmollinger presented his case after receiving a positive review from his boss. "Then I said right out that I wouldn't be satisfied with a standard 3% to 5% raise," he recalls.

"But I didn't volunteer a specific number. Instead, I asked that my compensation reflect my job performance." Impressed by his achievements and confidence, Schmollinger's supervisors took his request to the general auditor. Six weeks later, Schmollinger got a sweet 17.4% raise—far more than he expected.

If talking about yourself makes your stomach churn, follow the lead of Kirk Robey, a certified public accountant at EMO Computer Products in Naperville, Ill.: Hire a career coach to hone

Five Traits Employers Pay More For

Positioning yourself as a top performer is critical when you're asking for a raise. Although career strategists say that having a good attitude can go a long way when you begin negotiating for more money, these employees bring home the biggest rewards:

▶ Workers who produce impressive results but require very little maintenance.

▶ Individuals who take the initiative to learn more about their jobs.

▶ People who manage their boss as well as their subordinates.

▶ Pros who leverage their knowledge, not their years in the business.

▶ High achievers who develop brand-name appeal.

your presentation skills. "My coach encouraged me to emphasize projects that were extremely important to the company, such as improving banking relationships," Robey explains.

But remember, even a winning presentation can be defeated by poor timing. For instance, at companies where raises are tied to annual reviews, waiting for your performance review may not always be the best strategy. "To set yourself apart from the crowd, ask when you've finished a project and everyone's happy with your work," advises Robin Ryan, author of *24 Hours to Your Next Job, Raise or Promotion.*

Let your boss make the first offer. If the amount doesn't wow you, start lobbying. "Don't respond with a salary range, because you might wind up at the lowest end," advises Pinkley. "Instead, set a target and explain that your figure is negotiable. Then, position yourself as a top performer who deserves more than the average compensation."

Don't take "no" for an answer. No matter how deftly you ask for a raise, chances are your boss will try to stall you. But even canned responses—"That's the salary attached to this position" or "We don't pay Joe that much, and he's been here longer"—can provide a road map to a future raise.

First, clarify whether raises are based on seniority or merit. Unless yours is a union shop, performance is probably the real issue. In that case, suggests Cleveland executive recruiter Jeffrey

Christian, CEO of Christian & Timbers, figure out ways to increase your level of responsibility, broaden your skill set or take on higher-profile projects to better position yourself for a promotion that would include a raise.

If you really don't think your credentials are the problem, ask your boss what it will take to get a raise. Then set a later date to review the situation. He may come back with an offer of Fridays off or flextime in lieu of more pay. If you're unwilling to accept this, express your appreciation and suggest benefits that come from a budget other than payroll, such as membership in a health club or a car allowance.

The art of the counteroffer. Of course, nothing tells you more specifically what you're worth than another job offer. So if your research shows that you're significantly underpaid, start shopping around. But any career counselor will warn you that once you go that route, you must be prepared to leave. Counteroffers are flattering, but as David Yearwood, executive vice president and station manager for Fox 41 WDRB-TV in Louisville, explains, when they are introduced during salary negotiations, employers may view them as a threat to leave.

Keeping the discussion nonconfrontational worked out very well for public relations specialist Elhom Javadi. Six months after joining Aspect Development, a software company in Mountainview, Calif., Javadi received an even more attractive offer from Hewlett-Packard. H-P was ready to bump up her pay by $10,000, plus provide a slew of great benefits, such as on-site day care for her three-year-old son Leith.

"It was tough to ask for a raise so soon," Javadi says, so she supported her request by focusing on how well she was performing on her job. Three weeks later her company met Hewlett-Packard's offer. Between the salary increase and the $300,000 worth of stock options that Javadi already had from Aspect, she decided to stay.

Javadi credits her success to her straightforward, nonthreatening presentation of the attractive H-P offer. "Don't start rattling off all your issues," advises the savvy publicist. "When you're negotiating a raise, stick to finances." And most important, be sure that you want to stay at your current company. When you ask for a higher salary, you're offering total commitment to that job. If more money isn't worth the extra scrutiny, give yourself a break and move on.

▶ Use the Web to Get Paid More

Dozens of Internet sites, from online job-hunting bazaars such as **Monster.com** and **CareerMosaic.com** to niche sites like one devoted to engineering careers, **EETimes.com**, offer some salary information. But the best online sources are sites that focus exclusively on compensation for hundreds of professions, from senior accountants to warehouse managers.

These sites help you figure out what you're really worth on the open market—and they take much of the guesswork out of salary negotiations, whether you're dealing with your current boss or looking for a new job. "Having that knowledge means better bargaining, since the employee is no longer in the dark," says Bob Hughes, president of the salary site **CompGeo Online**.

We reviewed dozens of career sites, finally zeroing in on the nine specialized compensation sites that provide the most comprehensive salary and benefits data in an easy-to-navigate form. The sites we like best allow you to drill down into the numbers by specific job titles and by state, city, even zip code; most also give ranges for base pay and perks for a variety of titles on a career ladder, which can help you estimate future earnings potential. (For a ranking of the sites, see "Scorecard" on page 135.)

Get the lay of the land. The sheer volume of information on the Internet can be overwhelming, so it helps to understand how the compensation sites work and how they differ from one another before you begin clicking.

▶ **Free vs. pay sites.** Some salary sites charge users for compensation reports; others give away data for free and get revenue from advertising and fees from other sites. Plenty of the free information at sites like **Salary.com**, our No. 1 pick, is top-notch, especially for entry-level staff and middle managers. Executives, though, may find it worthwhile to shell out as much as $299 or even more at a site like CompGeo Online for the kind of sophisticated report that human-resources departments use to set pay scales.

▶ **Range of jobs.** Salary sites differ significantly in scope. The most useful ones generate reports for various ranks within each job category—from junior staffer to deputy manager to senior vice president—across a wide range of industries. Except for niche sites, those that cover a limited number of job titles usually lack detailed compensation information.

▶ **Search engines.** Better sites, such as **America's Career InfoNet**, give you more than one method to find the salary particulars you need. When you know what you're looking for, keyword search tools let you target relevant data quickly. If you're not certain which job title applies, pulldown menus of predefined job fields lead you to relevant facts.

▶ **Sources.** Salary sites obtain data from a variety of sources, including government labor statistics, company surveys and polls of professionals in the field. Although government stats tend not to be as current as company figures, they're usually more inclusive and far reaching.

The best sites let users know where their salary numbers come from—a valuable service that sheds light on how relevant and timely the information is. We preferred sites that rely on objective and extensive data from a variety of professional sources catering to specific industries to sites that rely on voluntary submissions for data, since this information may not be representative.

Bookmark our favorite salary sites.

▶ **Salary.com (www.salary.com).** Our No. 1 site offers the best of all worlds. With 1,100 job titles in its database, Salary.com is the powerhouse in the category, yet its streamlined design makes it a snap to use. Within two mouse clicks from the home page, the Salary Wizard search engine offers reports that include base pay and salary ranges for narrowly defined job titles in specific regions. Click again, and you get total compensation (including extras such as bonuses). Handy links let you see what you would make in various parts of the country or if you changed careers. Bottom line: This is the place to start your search.

▶ **America's Career Infonet (www.acinet.org).** Funded by the U.S. Department of Labor, the site covers more than 460 occupations, from oilfield roustabouts to motion-picture projectionists. If you're in an unusual industry or thinking about a

Scorecard: The Best Salary Sites

TOP FREE WEBSITES/ COMPANY OR AGENCY	EASE OF USE	NUMBER OF JOB TITLES	JOB DEFINITIONS/ EXPERIENCE	EARNINGS POTENTIAL[1]	REGIONAL BREAKDOWN	OVERALL RATING
www.salary.com Salary.com	●●●●●	●●●●● 1,100	●●●●●	●●●●●	Yes	●●●●●
www.acinet.org America's Career InfoNet	●●●●	●●●● 460+	●●●●●	●●●●●	Yes	●●●●◗
www.bls.gov/ocohome.htm U.S. Department of Labor Bureau of Labor Statistics	●●●●	●●● 254	●●●●●	●●●●	No	●●●●
www.erieri.com/doltrends Economic Research Institute	●●●●	●●●● 820	●●●●	●●	Yes	●●●◗
www.futurestep.com Korn/Ferry International	●●	●●● 308	●●●●●	●●●●●	Yes	●●●◗
www.jobstar.org JobStar California Job Search Guide	●●●	●●● 300+	●●●	●●●	For some jobs	●●●
www.wageweb.com[2] Human Resources Programs Development and Improvement	●●●●	●● 170	●●●	●●	No	●●◗
www.careerjournal.com Dow Jones & Co.	●●	●●●●● 2,000+	0	●●●	For some jobs	●●◗
PAY SITE **www.compgeo.net[3]** CompGeo Online Clayton Wallis Co.	●	●●●●● 1,000+	●●●●●	●●●●●	Yes	●●●●

Notes: [1]Provides salary data for several rungs on a career ladder. [2]Detailed reports available for annual membership fee: $169 (organizations), $219 (consultants). [3]This site only provides data for a fee ranging from $39 to $329, depending on the details you require. **Source:** MONEY research.

career switch, it's a great resource. Salary data is just three clicks off the home page. Type in a job title for a keyword search or select a predefined "job family" from the scroll-down menu one click from the home page. We like the links to other information, including skills needed for each job, job market outlook and job postings listed by state and profession.

▶ **U.S. Department of Labor (www.bls.gov/ocohome.htm).** This site is not perfect. We wish there were more charts to make the statistics easier to read. Limited salary reports cover just 254 jobs and offer only national median earnings. That said, the site's thorough job descriptions give rich detail about the nature of the jobs that are included and the education and skills needed for advancement, making it a good choice for entry-level and middle managers who are mapping out their next career moves.

▶ **Economic Research Institute (www.erieri.com/doltrends).** The site's search engine allows you to search by zip code or by state and city. Positions are listed alphabetically, not by industry, making it time consuming to obtain data for various jobs in a particular field. If you're willing to schlep through the entire alphabet, though, you'll find precise job titles that aren't often listed on other sites. For example, rather than a generalized listing for "doctors," we found reports for chiropractors, periodontists, pediatricians, dental ceramists (and their assistants) and on and on. Salary data are listed as averages, not as the more helpful ranges.

▶ **Futurestep (www.futurestep.com).** This is the site for ambitious mid- to senior-level corporate executives. Futurestep, which is a subsidiary of the executive search giant Korn/Ferry International, presents tailored earnings "profiles" for each user who registers at the site. Registration, which involves the types of work-style and personality tests administered by recruiters or career counselors, took us about an hour. Questions covered career and salary history, career objectives, personality traits and work priorities. Twenty-four hours later, you log back in to your secure account to retrieve a personal earnings estimate of what you're worth. You'll also get feedback, with a detailed analysis (you're "analytical," perhaps, or "collaborative") and a list of the careers for which you are best suited. We thought the report was trenchant and helpful for those who don't mind revealing information about themselves and being put in a database to be considered for openings being filled by Futurestep.

▶ **JobStar (www.jobstar.org).** This federally funded website is tailored to the California market, but its Salary Info link is a great tool no matter where you are. Placed on the home page, the link leads to roughly 300 industry-specific salary reports produced by professional organizations, publications or other niche websites. Think of the JobStar site as an online library to find professional groups nationwide, from geologists to graphic artists. But be warned: The quality of the reports varies greatly. Smart users will contact sources directly for more details.

▶ **Wageweb (www.wageweb.com).** If you're just looking for a quick hit of stats, Wageweb is very simple to use—but that's because there's so little free information there. The free reports for about 170 job titles are organized under eight broad categories (administrative, engineering, sales/marketing and so on) listed on the home page. For a $169 to $219 annual fee, members can obtain more detailed reports. However, since the data come from Wageweb subscribers and others, pay figures for any one job may come from fewer than 100 respondents.

▶ **CareerJournal (www.careerjournal.com).** If finding sophisticated career advice matters more than salary data, this site, run by Dow Jones & Co., publisher of the *Wall Street Journal*, is for you. The site's best features are articles that give incisive tips on, say, negotiating for a raise. Although there are some salary reports from reputable sources, such as the *Treasury Management Association Journal*, we found other data to be inconsistent and sometimes just plain useless. Many reports, for example, didn't break down salaries by region. In fact, the regional profiles link to general news articles about jobs in various areas, but not to specific compensation data.

▶ **CompGeo Online (www.compgeo.net).** This site is not free. Plus it's so ugly, it's tempting to log off immediately. (Was it the cluttered graphics or the prison-green, brown and purple color scheme that drove us to distraction?) Nevertheless, middle- to senior-level executives willing to ignore the poor design and spend some money can obtain extremely useful data.

The $39 reports don't offer much that can't be found on a free site. But when we spent $299 for a legal salaries report, we received a nearly 50-page trove of information that's normally used by human-resources departments and recruiters, with ranges of compensation for precisely defined jobs in various cities and towns nationwide. It also documented average pay increases and compared salaries by region and in public and private sectors.

You probably should download a sample to see what kind of information you'll receive for your money. That's because the explanation of what's contained in the reports at different price points can be quite confusing. This site gives you a chance to peek at the kind of information employers get all the time—but if slogging through mountains of detailed data gets you down, you may not appreciate the opportunity.

The sites may not offer absolutely everything you need, but they nonetheless provide excellent information for anyone who wants to increase his or her compensation.

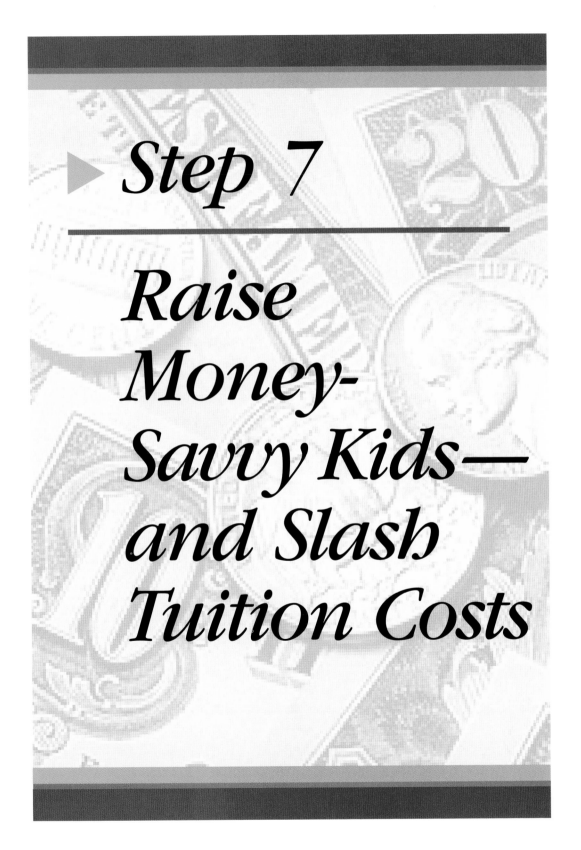

Step 7

Raise Money-Savvy Kids— and Slash Tuition Costs

*H*aving a child will provide you with extraordinary and innumerable riches—but it won't do wonders for your wealth. Frankly, we don't know many kids who have turned into profit centers.

But we do know some people who have handled the financial aspects of parenthood particularly well, and who have important lessons to impart. In this chapter, we will explore the best ways to teach children about money and the ideal approach to maximizing financial aid when it is time for your child to head off to college.

▶ *Lessons That Can Last a Lifetime*

Long before most children can add or subtract, they become aware of the concept of money. Any four-year-old knows where his parents get money—the ATM, of course. Understanding that parents must work for their money requires a more mature mind, and even then, the learning process has its wrinkles. For example, once he came to understand that his father worked for a living, a five-year-old asked, "How was work today?" "Fine," the father replied. The child then asked: "Did you get the money?"

Instant gratification aside, once they learn they can buy things they want with money—such as candy or toys—many children will begin hoarding every nickel they can get their hands on. How this urge is channeled can determine what kind of financial manager your child will be as an adult. It's important to work on your child's financial awareness early on, for once they're teenagers, they are less likely to heed your sage advice.

And besides, they're busy doing other things—like spending money.

The right way to make allowances. Perhaps the most important decision parents face regarding their children's attitudes toward money is how to handle allowances. The key to a successful allowance is structuring it correctly from the outset. Make it clear to your child what kinds of expenditures the money is for, and that they are expected to save some of it. Younger children—ages seven to 10—shouldn't be held accountable for items like school lunch money as part of their allowance, but it's not a bad idea for older kids, and has the added benefit of fewer payments changing hands.

Some experts think parents should not link allowance money to household chores. Children, they contend, should be expected to help out around the house and in the yard because they are members of the family, not because they are paid. Linking the allowance to household duties may sap this community spirit that you are trying to engender.

Yet with children over eight or nine years old, giving an allowance doesn't preclude paying them for specific chores, especially the occasional type that you might otherwise pay outsiders to perform, such as shoveling the sidewalk or washing the car. Why not keep the money in the family?

Some parents complain that giving their child an allowance will inevitably lead to demands for a raise or an advance. Jayne A. Pearl, author of *Kids and Money: Giving Them the Savvy to Succeed Financially*, would say these parents are missing the point. "Remember, an allowance is supposed to be a teaching tool," she says. "Negotiation skills are an important part of that, which they're going to need for dealing effectively with friends, teachers, and eventually, their boss."

So instead of grimacing when your child hits you up for a raise, decide when the time is right, and then engage them in fruitful negotiations. How long since the last raise? Will new expenditures be covered? What amount of the raise will be saved long-term for expenditures requiring your approval?

The most vexing decision on allowances is how much—a decision affected by personal values, family income and common sense. Don't let your child influence the amount by saying what their friends are getting: Any normal child will bring in high figures.

Many parents like to give their children the equivalent in today's dollars of the allowance they received at the same age. Assuming that these parents have more or less the same means as their parents did, this can be a comfortable solution.

The battle against instant gratification. If your child doesn't like to save, try the carrot—and then the stick. One way to encourage your child to develop sound money discipline is to make savings a condition of their allowance, so try to account for this when deciding on a weekly or monthly figure.

This, of course, means setting a budget—no easy task for people of any age. Kids' budgets will vary widely with needs and circumstances. The challenge is what to do when children run afoul of their own guidelines and end up dipping into savings illegitimately.

One answer is to require them save in a locked box so that each deposit is irretrievable. Yet, as this doesn't teach restraint and you won't always be around to oversee savings deposits, there are more instructive ways to make the point.

Illustration by Scott Menchin

Cultivate the saving instinct. Neale S. Godfrey, co-author of *Money Doesn't Grow on Trees: A Parent's Guide to Raising Financially Responsible Children* with Carolina Edwards, recommends what she calls the Bill-Paying Game, inspired by a scene in the film, *I Remember Mama.*

Count out a reasonable "salary" in play money, like that from a Monopoly game. Then, take some old bills and write the amount due on the back of the envelope of each. Show the child the entries in each for "date due," "minimum payment due" and "balance due," then let them decide how much to pay. If the allotted money is enough to pay the bills, everyone wins.

Use the leftover money to introduce the concept of savings. The younger your child, the more limited their concept of time. As a result, younger children aren't apt to realize the necessity of long-term savings. Indeed, for a six-year-old, long-term could mean spending the savings this weekend. Yet other children the same age tend to have an intuitive grasp of savings for savings' sake. Long before you give your child an allowance, their sav-

Every morning, the 26 kids in Jerri Cotter's second-grade class get down to business. The class veterinarian feeds the chinchilla. The paper pusher distributes worksheets. Every student in this bright classroom in West Middle Island School on New York's Long Island has a job.

For their efforts, the kids get paid 50¢ a week in plastic Cotter Cash, which they can bank or spend in the class store. Most choose the former, which allows them to earn interest at a very competitive 5% a month.

This economic microcosm sports penalties too. Forget your homework and you face a 10¢ fine. Lose your crayons and you have to buy new ones for $3. "It teaches children responsibility for their own behavior," says Cotter.

It also teaches them about money, which is not easy. Personal-finance courses are now offered to 60% of high school students, but only 21% have signed up. But nearly 30% of all high-school students have credit cards and, of those who do, more than a quarter carry debt from month to month. (Where did they learn this stuff?)

Cotter's daily program seems to be having much more impact than a simple lecture would. Why? Because there's a big difference between learning by listening and learning by doing. Her seven-year-olds understand interest not because someone told them what it is, but because they earn it. Fortunately, there's a lot about this program you can try at home.

▶ **A regular payday.** Allowances should come the same day every week to help kids budget.

▶ **A chance to earn more.** Consider paying a child for jobs that you'd otherwise hire an outsider to do.

▶ **Room to stumble.** Kids need to learn that money is finite. That's why, when they blow the budget—and they will—you need to be strong enough not to bail them out. Jerri Cotter's less frugal kids asked her to add credit cards and loans to the classroom. She said no.

---

ings sense will be clear from the way they deal with money from the tooth fairy or from Grandma's birthday cards.

If they've been receiving your sage financial teachings from an early age, older children shouldn't have trouble understanding the concepts of long-term and short-term saving. If not, illustrate the concepts using goals, as with a new video game a month from now versus a bicycle this summer, or college when they are 18. Remind of them of these goals to keep them from straying.

The more worthy and ambitious the long-term goal, the more you may want to consider matching grants to reward your child's savings discipline. These grants can be anywhere from 1.25-to-1 to 3- or 4-to-1, depending on the goal and your means. Matching grants are a great way to save for large items like computers, or even a first car.

Younger children understandably have trouble grasping off-site savings, so the best mechanism for them is often a piggy bank for coins and a wallet for bills. Count the money with them periodically, and tell them how close they've come to their goals. Above all, praise their progress.

Once children reach the age of nine or 10, they're more amenable to banks. Quantitatively adept children of this age can understand the concept of interest rates, especially when you demonstrate with coins to show how their money will grow.

Teach kids how to be good consumers. The best way to encourage sound spending habits is to exhibit them. When planning a trip to the grocery or discount store, get your children involved in making a judicious list and sticking to it. This will teach them to avoid the bane of all savers: impulse buying.

For big-ticket items like appliances, show them how to do the research: reading articles and reviews, phoning stores to see if your choices are in stock, negotiating with salesmen on price, going to several places to see what's available and compare values. Show them how to hunt for low prices on the Internet.

Don't forget the lessons that can be learned from tipping. Studies have shown that the quality of service received is not an important criterion for many tippers. Instead, people often tip to impress the waiter, or in accordance with their opinion of themselves. To ensure that your child tips for service, go over the good and bad points of your server with them, then arrive at an appropriate figure, for example, 20% for excellent service. Make sure they understand that, while the waiter relies on tips to make a living, poor service begets poor tips. This attitude toward value will carry over into purchases of consumer goods.

Giving a teenager the credit he may not deserve. The typical college freshman is burdened enough by scholarly responsibilities, homesickness and self-doubt. To keep your freshman of tomorrow from suffering the additional angst brought on by their first checking account, start them off soon-

▶ Plastic with Parental Guidance

Few parents relish lending their kid a credit card every time he or she wants to buy a new CD. But giving a teenager his or her own credit card on your account makes most parents just as uneasy. The VISA Buxx card (www.visabuxx.com) and American Express' Cobalt card (www.colbaltcard.com) are good solutions.

With these cards, parents transfer money into an online account, which kids 13 and older tap with a credit-card lookalike. Any store or website that accepts Visa or American Express will take the cards. (If there isn't enough money in the account to cover a purchase, the purchase will be declined. In this sense, the cards are essentially free, and flexible, secured cards.) You can track your kid's purchases with all the cards, but the Amex card has an added layer of protection; it cannot be used at pornography websites or those that sell liquor, guns or tobacco. The Amex credit card has no annual fee if you fund it via your checking account; annual fees for the Buxx cards range from zero to $24, depending on the issuing bank.

er—by their junior year in high school. Initially, keep it simple, avoiding frills and extras like overdraft protection; they need to experience the reality of bounced checks to understand their record-keeping responsibilities.

Many college freshmen today have credit cards, and if your kid is to be one of them, then this, too, has a learning curve that is best experienced under your tutelage. Before your kids acquire their first credit cards, they need a lesson in the evils of plastic. Tell them that this is where most individuals' finances go seriously awry, and illustrate your point with interest tables that show the damage that 18% annual interest, compounded over the years, can do to their savings potential. Also, tell them that credit is a privilege not a right, and that if they abuse it, they will lose their ability to get more.

After setting up rigid criteria for the use of a credit card, start them off with training wheels in the form of a secured card—in which the holder charges only up to a cash amount kept with the issuer. This way, they become accustomed to using the card judiciously without getting in hock. If their purchases are sound enough, then move on to an ordinary credit card, encouraging them to pay the balance each month to avoid interest charges.

When your kids go out to make purchases on this card, they may be tempted by same-as-cash purchase offers, in which buy-

Q. **I have been putting money away for our children's college tuition. The five kids are 7, 9, 10, 12 and 14, and the money is invested in various funds, in each of their names. One fund has done so well that that child's account far exceeds the others. Can I redistribute the money evenly?**

A. Nice idea, but since the funds are held in UGMA (Uniform Gifts to Minors Act) accounts, the money is no longer yours to redistribute. When you put money in a child's name using these types of accounts, the tax advantages are great, but—and here's the big hitch—that money is legally theirs when they reach 18 or 21 years of age (depending on the state).

To remedy the situation, you may want to put less money in the account in question going forward and a bit more money into the accounts of the other children.

Q. **I have a colleague who hires his children (ages 12 and 14) for routine household chores, pays them $2,000 a year and invests their income in Roth IRAs. Sounds like a great idea, but is it legit?**

A. Children can save money tax-deferred in a traditional IRA or a Roth at any age, as long as the income is for real work and the compensation is reasonable. So, for example, the Internal Revenue Service might disallow the Roth, making you subject to back taxes and penalties, if you paid a seven-year-old $60 an hour to clean her room—or do much of anything, for that matter. To be safe, keep careful records of the actual work and file an income tax return for your child, advises Karen Field, senior tax manager at KPMG—no matter how much they earn. Until age 19, work for the family is exempt from FICA taxes.

Q. **Can I use the entire amount (investment plus earnings) in a Roth to pay**

ers of items like appliances are allowed to borrow interest-free as long as they pay off the balance within a set period (usually six months). Financial planners like Eleanor Blayney of McLean, Va., advise against using same-as-cash. "It disassociates the cost from the benefit," she says.

Teaching your child how to invest. After teaching your children the hard lessons, show them the rewards of self control. Once your teenager gets a grip on credit, introduce them to the flip side—investing. After all, that's when they extend the credit and collect the interest. Since your teen may have too much

for my children's college expenses without paying taxes? Or can I just tap the initial investment?

A. You can withdraw after-tax contributions anytime without paying a penalty, and once your Roth has been open for five years, you can withdraw earnings penalty-free for college expenses as well. But you will owe taxes on the earnings unless you are over $59^1/_2$.

Q. Can an Education IRA be rolled into a Roth IRA, and if not, how long can the money stay in the account?

A. Absolutely not. An Education IRA is solely intended to save for college—not for retirement. Therefore, 30 days after the account holder's 30th birthday, the law requires a taxable distribution of any money left in the account. If the money isn't spent on qualified educational expenses within a year, the earnings on the account will also trigger a 10% penalty. But here's the good news: The account can be transferred to an eligible relative if he or she is under 30 years of age.

Q. I'm planning to give a graduation gift to a recent college grad who is in her early twenties. Can I set up a Roth IRA for her?

A. Great concept. Unfortunately, you cannot set up an IRA for anyone but yourself or your spouse. Instead, consider giving the grad money—up to $2,000 for each—and a strong nudge in the right direction to set up their own. But they must meet the Roth income requirements. If your grad qualifies, suggest that you make out the check to the fund company or brokerage of her choice, once she set up the account. You can also check your favorite fund to see if it offers gift certificates, which will encourage the recipient to set up an account.

money collecting no interest in checking and probably writes few checks, the best way to start is with a money-market account on which they can write checks.

From there, introduce them to simple, set-term investments like savings bonds and certificates of deposit. Though returns from these will be relatively small, they serve an important lesson and will build their confidence about investing.

Next, teach them about the stock market, but not as a prelude to picking stocks. Instead, advise them to get into some diversified mutual funds or an index fund. Some of the stock investing games available on the Internet are a fun and educational way to introduce a teenager to stocks. MONEY and *Fortune* magazines offer just such a game (www.stocktournament.money .com). There, anyone can sign up and run an investment portfolio—with simulated cash, of course.

Once you get your child to understand the ups and downs of the stock market, you've probably accomplished all that you can reasonably hope for, with one exception. Because your child may one day choose to buy individual stocks, you should briefly discuss the joys and the agonies that come with the territory. You might mention, for example, that a well-established company like Home Depot sold for just 38¢ per share in 1987 and now sells for about $45. On the other hand, many fledgling Internet companies that sold for more than $100 in March 2000 now fetch less than $10 a share. The message: Good investments prosper over time, while investments made on a wing and a prayer can cost you a fortune very quickly.

▶ *Getting the Most Out of Financial Aid*

You may be able to save a significant amount of money on your child's college education by understanding exactly how the financial aid game is played. The rules of the game have recently changed, and those who know the latest angles have a decided advantage.

Take charge of the process. When Miles Rodriguez entered his senior year of high school, he naturally turned to his school counselor for advice on college. He soon found out that he was on his own. "The counselor didn't even know who I was," says Miles, a former honors student at a magnet public school in Houston. When Miles applied for a prestigious Coca-Cola scholarship, he says that his counselor initially filed paperwork naming another student. And when he was sent a certificate for winning the first round in the selection process, the counselor didn't deliver it until he was well into the final round.

But Miles refused to let poor counseling keep him out of college. He talked another high school adviser into handling his recommendations. And his mother Renée helped him research possible colleges. His top choice: Rice University in Houston. He got in with a $12,000 renewable aid package and, despite the paperwork snafu, won a $1,000-per-year Coca-Cola scholarship, plus $7,000 in additional awards. "I never would have been able to do it if I had relied on the assigned counselor," Miles says. "We had to do most of the work ourselves."

Unfortunately, counseling experiences like Miles' are becoming more and more common. And what's at stake isn't just an acceptance letter to a top-choice school—it's whether or not you'll be able to afford to send your child to that top-choice school. In today's competitive financial aid process, you need a comprehensive plan that links the admissions process with your aid strategy. To get that, many families are now looking beyond overburdened high school counselors and hiring independent college advisers—or, like the Rodriguez family, taking charge of the process themselves. Which strategy is best for you? Before you decide, you'll need to consider the new landscape of financial aid. We'll help you understand when—and how—to look for extra help.

Have no illusions about the quality of guidance counseling. The much debated funding crisis in public education, which has led to overcrowded schools and poorly trained teachers, has had a less publicized but equally devastating impact on college counseling staffs. These days, topnotch college guidance is difficult, if not impossible, to find in many high schools. "There's a crisis in college counseling," declares Bill Fitzsimmons, director of admissions and financial aid at Harvard University. "The lack of access to information in many schools has made what is already an unlevel playing field even more unlevel."

A recent survey by the National Association for College Admission Counseling found that the average public school guidance counselor is straining under a caseload of 330 students, compared to just 161 in private schools. Worse, at many public schools, particularly in urban areas, caseloads can soar to between 1,000 and 2,000 students. Moreover, advisers have been saddled with administrative duties that leave little time for actual college guidance.

Meanwhile, the financial aid process has grown more complicated. Increasingly, aid is coming in the form of loans rather than grants or scholarships: In 1998, a full 58% of the average financial aid package consisted of loans, up from just 40% in 1980. What's more, the traditional division between need-based aid (based on your ability to pay) and merit aid (based on academic excellence) has collapsed, as colleges engage in a free-for-all for the best students. Clearly, private school students with expert college counselors have a big advantage.

An independent college counselor can help. It often makes sense to turn to an independent college counselor, usually a former admissions officer or high school adviser who now works as a consultant. Driven by a surging college-bound population, the ranks of these advisers are growing. All told, an estimated 1,000 college counselors, many of them part time, have set up shop around the country.

How can you tell if you should hire a personal college trainer to work with your child? Many public school advisers do a fine job with college planning and are respected by top colleges, so be sure to give your high school counselor a chance. A good public school adviser will start the college process during your child's junior year, offering advice and information on test preparation, college admissions and financial aid deadlines; a good counselor should also be willing to talk about the admissions records of previous graduates. If you don't see this kind of activity, or if your child's counselor is notably unhelpful or too busy for one-on-one college meetings, then it's time to consider striking out on your own.

First, bear in mind that hiring a professional is not the only option. If your child has special requirements—such as finding a school that allows her to major in music theater—you can narrow down the possibilities yourself by using the Internet. Nearly all colleges have their own websites, and detailed information on financial aid and scholarships is available on such sites as www.finaid.org, www.fastweb.com and www.collegeboard.org.

Of course, you may not have the time to spend researching colleges. Or maybe you just want the comfort of expert guidance when faced with the prospect of spending $100,000 or more on college. In either case, you may want to hire an independent adviser. Expect to pay a flat fee of $750 to $2,500, depending on where you live and the counselor's level of expertise; some will charge by the hour, typically $70 to $200.

The questions you need to ask about financial aid. Whether you hire a counselor or do the work yourself, you still need to understand the tricky financial aid application process. Don't rely solely on college marketing brochures or the advice of experts; check all information and requirements, such as deadlines

How to Choose a College Counselor

To pick the best adviser, start looking early, since most college counselors prefer to begin planning during your child's sophomore or junior year of high school. Here's a quick checklist of what to look for.

▶ **Credentials.** Anyone can hang out a shingle as an educational consultant, but, obviously, you want someone with years of experience. The Independent Educational Consultants Association (IECA) accepts only applicants who have worked for several years as school-based counselors or college admissions officers; members must also regularly tour colleges and meet with admissions officers. (To get a list of ICEA members in your area, call 800-808-4322.)

Keep in mind that advisers differ in background and training. Though most are knowledgeable on financial aid, some may also have expertise in assisting gifted students or those with learning disabilities. If you need specialized help, don't settle for a generalist.

▶ **References.** Any good counselor should be able to provide the names of several previous clients; be sure to call them to ask about their experiences. Also inquire about the prospective counselor's relationship with your school adviser. Remember that your school adviser will be the one sending out references and transcripts. A testy relationship could be a problem.

▶ **No guarantees.** No reputable independent counselor will promise admission to a specific college or a guarantee of scholarship money; if they do, walk away. Avoid any adviser who recommends a wholesale financial makeover to maximize your chances of financial aid. Pouring money into annuities or dumping your stock portfolio could improve your aid prospects, but you'll be no better off if your finances are tied into knots.

▶ **Clear costs.** All charges should be stated up front and in writing. Unless the help you need takes only two or three hours—say, you want to review five or six schools that are interested in recruiting your star soccer-player daughter—you're better off arranging a flat fee. A package deal may include guidance over several years, including regularly scheduled meetings and phone access. Some independent counselors may even help your son or daughter choose high school courses and summer work opportunities that can burnish a college application.

and required forms, with the college. To avoid some common pitfalls, here are six key questions to ask the financial aid officers:

▶ **Do you always meet full financial need?** Don't be surprised if the answer is no. Today only a few dozen well-

Illustration by Ed Milano

endowed colleges follow the traditional practice of providing enough financial aid to allow all students who are admitted to attend. So if a college claims that it meets full need, ask if that applies to everyone, including students admitted from the waiting list. Many top schools, including Brown, Carleton and Smith, follow a so-called needs-sensitive policy, notes Bruce Hammond, author of *Discounts and Deals at the Nation's 360 Best Colleges*. That means some 5% or so of those admitted—generally the less competitive students—are allowed in only if they can pay the full cost.

▶ **How are your financial aid packages structured?** Ask your prospective college how the amount of grant money, which does not have to be repaid, compares with loans or work/study jobs—obviously, the more grant money, the better. (Many schools employ so-called preferential packaging: The most desirable students get a bigger hunk of grant money and fewer loans or work/study requirements.) In addition, be sure to look past the first year's award. Even if the total aid package doesn't change after your son or daughter's freshman year, be aware that the loan portion will probably increase and the grant percentage will shrink.

You should also ask about the average indebtedness of the college's graduates. Ending up with more than $20,000 in debt—not unusual at many private colleges—could limit your child's career choices.

▶ **Can I keep my outside scholarship?** For students who are academic or athletic stars, you will want to know how outside scholarship money is treated. Until recently, many schools simply used such awards to replace the grant portion of the financial aid package, leaving the student no better off. But today, more colleges are allowing students to enjoy greater benefits from the awards. Ask about your prospective school's policy.

▶ **Do you offer merit awards, and can my child qualify?** Apart from some highly selective schools, most colleges are dangling merit scholarship awards, and at times engaging in bidding wars, to get the best possible recruits. Even a B student may be highly sought after. Find out how your child's record compares with the SAT scores and grade-point average of the college's freshman class. If your child ranks in the top 20%, he or she is a good candidate for a scholarship.

▶ **How does early decision affect the financial aid package?** Well over 50,000 anxious students will probably apply for early decision this year—a jump of 30% from three years ago—in the belief they will have a better shot at their first-choice college. The downside: They have far lower chances of getting the best possible financial aid deal. "If you need aid, you should not apply early decision," declares Jayme Stewart, college counselor at York Preparatory School in New York City. "You can't be certain of the aid package you will get until April." Moreover, you won't have the ability to leverage competing offers, which can lead to a better aid package.

▶ **What is your appeal process?** Nowadays, colleges expect parents to negotiate aid packages. That doesn't mean you should automatically ask for more money. To persuade the financial aid officer to reconsider your package, you need to offer a specific reason, such as a higher award from an equally prestigious school or new information about your finances. Ask the aid officer what procedure you should follow to make an appeal and how quickly you need to deliver the information. "And be polite, not demanding," warns counselor Stewart. "The financial aid officer probably makes less money than you do."

▶ How to Respond to Aid Offers

If you're the parent of a college-bound high school senior, you've probably endured the tedium of filling out intrusive federal and college financial aid applications. By March, you should receive the Student Aid Report (SAR) from the Department of Education (DOE), followed in April by the moment of truth—the schools' financial aid offers.

The way you react to these letters can make the difference between a C awards package and an A+. To maximize your financial aid, follow these steps.

Phase One: The Student Aid Report. Two to six weeks after you've completed your Free Application for Federal Student Aid (FAFSA), which most colleges use to calculate your aid, the DOE sends you a copy of the SAR. That's the summary of the FAFSA information that's forwarded to up to six colleges you name. Here's what to do once the SAR arrives.

▶ **Look for your share.** The SAR contains your first clue as to how much of the tab Uncle Sam and colleges expect you to pay. To find that critical information, look in the upper right-hand corner of the first page for a number marked EFC, which is short for expected family contribution. A figure such as 08800, for example, means that your likely share of annual tuition and other expenses such as room and board will be $8,800. Federal aid, most state assistance and some private school awards are based on the EFC.

▶ **Update and correct the information.** This is your chance to fix any errors as well as to amend the information you supplied on the FAFSA, which you might want to do if you've completed your tax returns since you filled out the FAFSA. If your income tax bill turned out to be lower than you had estimated, you may be able to qualify for a more generous aid package. For example, if you claimed a Hope Scholarship or wrote off student-loan interest, you can adjust your SAR to reflect those changes.

Before you submit the corrections, call the schools your child has applied to. With deadlines fast approaching, some may prefer that you send a copy of the SAR, with the corrections marked on it, directly to the financial aid office. (In general, schools receive your SAR, including any corrections, electronically.)

▶ **Include additional schools.** If your child has applied to more colleges since you submitted the FAFSA, enter their names on the correction form—with one caveat. If you've already listed six, each add-on will bump an earlier choice. Instead, mail a copy of the SAR (with corrections) to the new schools. Don't drop one just because your child has lost interest. "You'll want to have plenty of financial aid packages to compare," says Kalman A. Chany, author of *Paying for College Without Going Broke.* "An offer from a rival school could serve as a bargaining chip down the road."

A New College Aid Formula Kicks In

Attention parents: There's a morsel of good news about financial aid: The formulas used by many private colleges have changed and the alterations will help more people than they hurt.

First, some background. When your child applies for financial aid, you must file one or both of two forms: the Free Application for Federal Student Aid (FAFSA), which covers government aid and is used by most public schools; and the College Board's CSS/Financial Aid Profile, which is used by private colleges.

Both formulas are designed to come up with an "expected family contribution"—the theoretical amount you and your child have available for college. If that amount is less than the full cost of college, the school—again, in theory—will make up the difference with grants, loans and work/study. To estimate your expected contribution using both formulas, go to www.finaid.org. Here are the most significant changes to the CSS (plus one to the FAFSA).

▶ **You can keep more of your savings.** Under the new CSS formula, parents are expected to contribute 3% to 5% of their assets toward college costs, down from 5.65%. The student's contribution has fallen from 35% to 25% of assets, which is what FAFSA still uses.

▶ **Emergency savings are protected.** You can now consider some of your savings an "emergency fund" that isn't available for college costs. The amount varies by family size. This year, for example, a family of four can shield $14,770.

▶ **Sibling rules change.** If you have younger children not yet in college, schools using the CSS formula will now assume that a portion of your assets and income can't be used for the older student's tuition bill. This year, 1.5% of your income, up to $1,670 per child, is expected to go toward younger kids future education. On the other hand, if you have two kids in college at the same time, you'll be expected to contribute more. Under the old CSS system, your expected contribution was halved if you had two kids in college and cut by two-thirds with three. Now parents with two in school will have to pay 60% of their expected contribution for each. With three, you'll pay 45%.

▶ **More of your retirement money is up for grabs.** Schools don't expect you to tap your 401(k), IRA or other qualified plans. But the new CSS model no longer allows you to earmark money outside of those accounts as retirement savings.

▶ **Adult ed doesn't pay.** In a change to FAFSA, taking college courses while your child is in school no longer increases the child's aid. Under the old formula, if you spent a few hundred dollars on degree courses, your kid's eligibility could go up by thousands. That's no longer the case.

Phase Two: Official word. Come April, if all goes well, your mailbox will be stuffed with acceptance letters and financial aid offers. The aid letter will indicate the amount of the award and spell out whether it will be in the form of coveted grants or scholarships, federal work/study (in which the student is paid by the college for usually minimal labor), loans or some combination. Here's how to get the school to sweeten the deal.

▶ **Tell the schools about any new hardships.** Keep in mind that schools base what you can pay this year on last year's income. If a recent event—say, the loss of a job or major medical bills—has left a hole in your budget, call the schools and explain.

▶ **Review your tax returns.** If you reported an IRA or pension rollover on your most recent tax return, make sure the college didn't mistakenly count that distribution (reported on line 15a or 16a of Form 1040) as income. According to Chany, you should also check to see if you were eligible to file a 1040EZ or 1040A (which you may have been able to do if you earned less than $50,000 and didn't itemize). If so, tell the financial aid office. Some schools will exclude assets such as your house from their financial aid formulas as long as you qualify to use a simple tax form, even if you filed a 1040 instead.

▶ **Play the merit card.** Colleges have been known to dig deeper into their coffers to lure topnotch students. Calmly discuss a better deal with an admissions or a financial aid officer. You could also fax copies of more competitive aid offers to bolster your case.

▶ **Cover your contribution.** You'll find a list of the college's preferred lenders in your aid package. If you accept an award that includes federal Stafford Loans, call those lenders first. They may be able to disburse your money faster by transferring it to the school or the student's account electronically. That said, if the lender doesn't offer good repayment options or ways for diligent borrowers to cut their rate in repayment—as banks backed by Sallie Mae (800-891-4599) or USA Group (800-562-6872) often do—keep looking.

Federal PLUS loans for parents and home-equity loans are also attractive ways to fill the gap. While low-rate federal student loans are probably the better deals, your freshman can borrow only $2,625 this year with a Stafford Loan (current rates: 7.59%

during school, 8.19% thereafter). PLUS loans (current rate: 8.99%) let you borrow up to the full amount of college costs (minus financial aid) and, like student loans, a portion of the interest you pay ($2,000 in 2000) is deductible. The interest on a home-equity loan (average rate: 9.61%) is also deductible.

▶ *Consider a 529 Savings Plan*

Every parent who is trying to save money for college should be aware of the opportunities offered by the new 529 college savings plans that are cropping up around the country. The plans—named for a section in the tax code—allow families to have tax-deferred savings for college. Although not appropriate for everyone, they can be very helpful for many families.

A 529 plan beats an Education IRA. Although they're called retirement accounts, Education IRAs are really special educational savings accounts. You do not get a deduction for the money you put away but, just as with the Roth IRA, money saved in an Education IRA can be withdrawn tax-free, as long as it is used for higher education expenses (tuition, books, room, board and the like). Problem is, you can save only a paltry $500 a year per child—barely enough to make a dent in college costs. Another consideration: If you contribute to an Education IRA, you cannot put money in a 529 plan in that same year for the same beneficiary.

For those reasons, you should probably favor 529 plans. State-sponsored 529 college savings plans allow families to save tax deferred for college until the money is withdrawn, at which point it's taxed at the child's rate. By the end of 2001, 43 states will have launched some type of 529 savings plan. Already, 529s hold some $7.5 billion spread among 1.3 million accounts.

First, some background. There are actually two varieties of 529 plans. The older version is the prepaid tuition plan, which allows you to lock in the future tuition of selected state colleges at today's rates. But with tuition inflation now averaging almost 5.2% (4.4% for public schools), that's a low rate of return. The newer variety of 529 is the college savings plan, which gives you more options.

These savings plans can be a boon for investors in top tax brackets who have young children and do not expect to qualify for financial aid—they're the ones who can benefit most from the tax-deferred growth. The money can be used to pay the costs of any college, regardless of where you live or where your child wants to attend school. Unlike Education IRAs, there are no income limits for participation in 529 savings plans, and you can put away anything from $2,000 (Iowa) to $100,000 or more per child (New York and others), either in lump sums or through automatic deductions.

Your money is placed in a mix of funds based on the age of your child—typically, the allocation is most aggressive for newborns and becomes more conservative as college draws closer. For all savers, the money will grow tax deferred until withdrawal, when it is taxed at the beneficiary's tax rate; for a child, that's usually 15%. (Many states also exempt the earnings on their own plans, and a few even allow a tax deduction on the money you invest if you do so in-state.) And unlike custodial accounts, 529 plans remain in the control of the parents.

If you don't like your in-state plan, many savings plans are available to out-of-state residents, and many are run by well-known investment firms. Among the better performers: Maine (Merrill Lynch), Massachusetts and New Hampshire (both Fidelity). Of course, you'll need to weigh your choice against any potential state tax breaks that you may receive for staying in-state, as well as the plan's fees and withdrawal rules. (For links to these plans, log on to www.collegesavings.org.)

The plans aren't perfect. In the meantime, keep in mind that 529s have plenty of flaws. For starters, if you prefer to manage your own investments, you may find 529s too limited. You must submit to the asset allocation of the state—and that's often a conservative ratio of bonds and stocks. If you should become dissatisfied with the plan's performance or if you move to a different state, it can be tough, if not impossible, to shift money into another plan without paying taxes and penalties, notes C.P.A. Joseph Hurley, a 529 plan expert in Pittsford, N.Y. Another potential liability: 529 savings are currently treated as a parental asset, "but these plans are so new that financial aid directors don't know what to make of them," says Kal Chany. "As families start accumulating more money in them, aid directors will want a bigger piece."

One final consideration: When you withdraw the money from your 529 plan, be sure to have additional funds set aside.

You can't use 529 assets to pay Uncle Sam without triggering taxes and penalties; that's because tax payments are not a qualified higher education expense. Bear in mind that you will also pay taxes—at your rate—if your child ends up not going to college.

▶ Test Yourself

1. **What's a good way for parents to decide on an allowance figure?**
   A. Calculate the equivalent today of the amount they received when they were their child's age
   B. Give them what the kid next door is getting
   C. Tie the amount to how much household work they routinely do

2. **What's the best way to teach good spending habits?**
   A. Learn them yourself, and then show your children by taking them on shopping trips
   B. Have your children read books on the subject
   C. Point out people who are spendthrifts

3. **How can you help minimize angst for your college freshman?**
   A. Teach them how to handle a checking account while they're still in high school
   B. Give them a high-limit credit card and have the bill sent to you
   C. Tell them to forget checking accounts and work on a cash basis

4. **What should you tell your kids about same-as-cash credit offers on consumer purchases?**
   A. To forget them
   B. That they're a good idea
   C. That they're sometimes a viable option

5. **Should you encourage your teenager to pick stocks?**
   A. Yes
   B. No
   C. Perhaps, depending on their maturity

Answers

1. **A.** Many parents feel comfortable with this, especially if they are of similar means as their parents.
2. **A.** Learning by doing is classic.
3. **A.** They'll need a checking account to survive, and you must teach them how to survive the account.
4. **A.** It's better for consumers—especially younger ones—to bear the costs at the same time they get the benefit.
5. **B.** Instead, you should be teaching investment fundamentals at this point. Once your child shows a good grasp of those, it's okay to let him pick stocks.

Step 8

Become a Smart Online Consumer

*Y*ou can't spend your way to riches, but, over time, you can increase your wealth if you save a great deal of money every time you shop or travel. In fact, there has never been a more rewarding time than today to be a savvy consumer. And the Internet may be the best friend a smart shopper ever had. (You can start by reading the box on page 164 to determine whether a free internet service plan makes sense to you.)

The key to maximizing your savings is information. You need to know where to go for the best deals and, in this chapter, we'll guide you to the fastest, most reliable places. And we'll also guide you to some of the non-monetary benefits of the Internet, such as how you can find and use the best websites to take care of a health problem. It's all part of being a smart consumer, 21st-century style.

▶ *The Shopping Revolution*

In other contexts the Internet seems perpetually overhyped, but when it comes to your money, its impact has already been momentous. Whether you're finding great deals on stereos, comparing the prices of insurance policies or balancing your stock portfolio, your life is affected by the Internet every day to a degree hardly imaginable even a few years ago. Online sales have grown from $20 billion in 1999 to about $39 billion in 2000, and are expected to exceed $100 billion by 2002.

Although the deep discounts now found online may not last, the Net is eroding the very idea of the fixed price tag. From online auctions to dynamic pricing, be prepared for more creative shopping models than ever.

How dynamic pricing shakes things up. Prices on the Internet are, of course, already a moving target. More so than brick-and-mortar stores, online retailers can change their prices quickly and easily. And as retailers become more sophisticated in capturing and analyzing individual customer information, more and more will attempt what is called *dynamic pricing*— charging different people different prices for the same product based on their past sensitivity to pricing premiums or discounts. Aha, but here's the twist: Consumers may not embrace this idea, as Amazon.com found out recently, when it was forced to offer refunds to irritated customers who divined that they were paying more than others for DVDs.

Likewise, it's unclear whether retailers' attempts to get customers to pay different prices can keep pace with technologies designed to thwart just such initiatives—notably shopping comparison sites, also known as *shopping bots*. As bots get more popular, retailers will probably begin bundling products (a camcorder *plus* batteries, a carrying case and videotapes) so comparison-shopping becomes more difficult.

The Best Way to Buy Things Online

Getting the best deal online doesn't have to be laborious. It can, in fact, be achieved by visiting only a few well-chosen sites. Begin with a shopping bot—and limit your detours to sites that fill specific gaps, such as delivering product advice, tracking down collectibles and keeping you on top of sales.

Profit from shopping bots. A shopping bot does exactly what any ardent bargain hunter would do: search hundreds of competing websites for the best price. But bots do so in seconds, making them the single easiest way to find a low price quickly. Bots are so popular that there's even a website devoted to helping you find one: **BotSpot.com** (www.botspot.com), which describes and links to nearly 50 shopping bots, including those that specialize in online bookstores and electronics merchants.

Although no single shopping bot covers every Internet merchant, you can limit yourself to one. Otherwise, what's the point? Ideally, you want a bot that reports shipping costs, as well as product availability, and lets you sift search results by

The new millennium has spawned a wave of free Internet service providers (ISPs) which can reduce your monthly Internet bill by $21.95. You can even go online free via The Simpsons fan-club site. Free ISPs, however, are best for Web surfers who seldom call customer service for tech support and don't mind looking at on-screen advertising or answering personal questions.

If you fit that profile, there are five sites you should consider. All have banner ads that can be moved but not closed. You must provide extensive personal information, which the sites say they won't sell (but checking the site's privacy policy for changes is always wise). All have free customer service, although it may be a toll call. (Some "free" ISPs charge as much as $14.95 per customer service request.) Each has more than a thousand access numbers throughout the country and a modem-to-member ratio (where available) of no more than 15 to 1—the ratio at No. 2 paid-ISP Earthlink. That's a rough gauge of your likelihood of making a connection.

ISP WEBSITE PHONE NUMBER	MEMBER-TO-MODEM RATIO	TOTAL ACCESS NUMBERS	CUSTOMER SERVICE HOURS/COST	WHAT WE LIKE
NetZero www.netzero.com 800-333-3633	8 to 1	1,400	24/free[1]	The biggest of the freebies; you can access a personalized home page from any computer.
Freei.net www.freei.net 253-796-6505	15 to 1	1,300	24/free	Freei.net lets you surf the Net anonymously.
FreeAccess www.altavista.com 877-584-5551	15 to 1	2,300	8 a.m. to 1 a.m. ET/ free	You can perform Web searches right from your home page.
Kmart's BlueLight.com www.bluelight.com 888-945-9255	10 to 1	3,000	24/toll call[2]	The site guarantees service calls will be answered within 30 seconds.
FreeLane www.freelane.excite.com 800-952-8772	N.A.	2,170	8 a.m. to 1 a.m. ET/ free	Excite provides e-mail, a personalized home page and a calendar.

Notes: N.A.: Not available. [1] In addition to regular free service, you can pay $14.95 per incident for platinum service, which guarantees immediate access to a rep for up to 72 hours. [2] 409-776-6515.

price. Most important, you should stick with a bot that tracks the largest possible number of websites. Based on those criteria, we've identified two top picks.

Our favorite is **MySimon** (www.mysimon.com), an independent site that searches about 2,600 online retailers. The streamlined design makes it simple for you to find competing prices on a specific item with a single keyword. If you have only a vague idea of what you want, you can browse within 15 shopping categories that are drilled down to hundreds of sublistings.

If you want to do all your comparison shopping and buying at one site, you may prefer our runner-up for best bot: **Yahoo Shopping** (shopping.yahoo.com), a giant bazaar of more than 10,000 stores, from big-name retailers like Dell, the Sports Authority and Clinique to small shops like Seeds of Change, a site that sells organic seeds and plants. Yahoo Shopping is actually a virtual shopping mall that links you to stores that advertise with the site or pay it a portion of sales revenues, but it also employs shopping-bot search technology. One advantage of the site is that you can store your billing information and avoid filling out order forms more than once. Another perk: Yahoo will e-mail you when the types of products you're interested in go on sale.

While general shopping bots are perfect when you're in the market for new and mainstream items, they have limitations. They generally don't search auction sites, they don't always tell you much about the products, and they don't help if you're interested in something other than a rock-bottom price—say, frequent-flier miles for your purchases.

Thinking outside the bot. Here are six worthwhile reasons to go beyond a broad shopping bot—or even to start your shopping elsewhere.

▶ **Auctions.** If you can't find what you want at eBay, you might want to throw a wider net. That's when an auction shopping bot may help. Our favorite is **Bidder's Edge** (www.biddersedge.com). The site tracks 170 auction sites and, like eBay, alerts you when the item you want comes up for sale. A lawsuit with eBay prevents Bidder's Edge from searching eBay, but Bidder's Edge does link you to eBay and automatically fills in that site's keyword search with the same words last used on Bidder's Edge, presumably to make it easier to compare searches on both sites.

To get the most out of an auction bot, keep your search as specific as possible.

▶ **Advice.** If you want advice before you shop, go to the shopping bot **DealTime** (www.dealtime.com), which features con-

▶ *The Best Ways to Pay Online*

You've found what you want to buy on the Internet. Now how will you pay? The obvious choice is a credit card, but seemingly every day a new online-payment option appears. In particular, so-called person-to-person services—which let you e-mail cash—are proliferating on the Net, especially at auction sites and the online storefronts of small businesses.

▶ **Credit Cards:** For all the new flavors of online payments, though, we think credit cards are still your best bet. Why? If your card number is stolen, you likely won't owe a cent. By law, you're not responsible for more than $50 in fraudulent charges, and last year Visa and MasterCard introduced zero liability on all of their credit and debit cards. Historically, American Express hasn't made you pay the $50. With a credit card, you also have the legal right to dispute a charge—and ask the card company to act as intermediary—if what you buy is defective or never arrives. (If you use a debit card, you'll miss out on some credit-card protections. For instance, your bank isn't obligated to help you with a merchant dispute.)

In addition, many credit-card issuers have added attractive incentives to get you to use their card on the Net. Pay with any American Express card online, for instance, and you're protected against loss or theft for 90 days (with a $50,000 annual limit per account). If the site doesn't accept returns, in many cases Amex will refund your money, up to $300 an item and $1,000 per account. The company also doubles the length of the manufacturer's warranty. Several Visa or MasterCard issuers, such as Capital One (www.capitalone.com), have similar promotions. The Webmiles MasterCard (www.webmiles.com) guarantees that if you buy something with the card and the merchant lowers the price within three months, they'll refund the difference.

▶ **Smart cards.** Visa and American Express have launched competing versions of souped-up credit cards known as smart cards, which are designed to add an extra layer of protection. In October, Amex introduced a new system called Private Payments, which enables consumers to pay for online goods using a randomly gen-erated number in place of their own account numbers. The number, which is created by software you install on your computer, is good for only one transaction, meaning that even if someone intercepted the number, that person couldn't use it.

sumer education links within the price comparison engine. (Hit "refine your search" after you run a price comparison.) The advice is divided into *The Basics* (useful facts about how a product works), *Terms to Know* (if you're too embarrassed to ask) and *Get Your $ Worth* (with picks in a variety of price ranges). With camcorders, for example, DealTime details the differences

Visa's new smart card, which began rolling out in September, comes with a small digital reader that connects to your computer. Not only do you need your account number to complete the transaction, you also need your PIN number and the card itself. The magnetic strip on the back of the card will be able to store more than 100 times the amount of information it can hold now, enabling you, perhaps, to purchase an airline ticket online, download it directly to your Visa card, automatically add the miles to your frequent-flier account and sweep the card through a reader at the airport gate to board the plane, says Al Banisch, a senior vice president with Visa.

▶ **Payment services:** If you shop at an auction or at a website run by a small business, you may not have the option to pay by credit card. To fill that void, person-to-person payment services such as **PayPal** (www.paypal.com), **PayMe.com** (www.payme.com), **Western Union MoneyZap** (www.moneyzap.com) and **eMoneyMail** (www.emoneymail.com) have popped up. With these services, which eliminate the need to mail a paper check, you in effect e-mail money using a credit card or bank account.

But what happens if you're unhappy with what you bought? Or, worse, the product never arrives? Unfortunately, payment services are so new that there are no hard-and-fast rules. Some e-mail services have begun to add fraud protections. PayPal (www.paypal.com) will refund your money (with a $5,000 annual limit) if something you paid for never arrives. Western Union (www.moneyzap.com) plans to roll out fraud protections this year but has yet to announce the details. Although you can fund your payment with a credit card at these sites, doing so probably won't help you if the product never arrives. In the eyes of the credit-card company, your transaction was with the payment website, not the merchant.

Sites that help fight fraud. Finally, no matter how you pay, the major auction sites can be an ally. Ebay automatically insures every sale against fraud, with a $200 limit and a $25 deductible; Amazon.com's auction site covers you for up to $250. If you are spending significantly more, consider using an escrow service like **www.iescrow .com** or **www.escrow.com**. For a fee of about 5%, both act as clearinghouses, holding your payment until it clears and guaranteeing the seller's product.

between analog and digital models, explains what you'll get in various price ranges and suggests picks in each category.

▶ **Sales alerts.** If you're particular about where you shop but still want to get the advantage of Web discounts, see if your favorite merchant will let you sign up for e-mail sales alerts. REI (www.rei-outlet.com) and Eddie Bauer (www.eddiebauer.com), for example, send customers sales notices by e-mail, notifying them when merchandise is being cleared out. Others, like Bloomingdale's (www.bloomingdales.com), will e-mail you when the items you like go on sale.

▶ **In-person shopping.** If you prefer shopping in person, the Web can still help you pay less. Before you hit the street, check out **SalesHound.com** (www.saleshound.com), a website that posts advertised sales at 520 stores in 165,000 locations nation-wide. Specify your zip code and the distance you're willing to travel (up to 50 miles), and you'll get a list of nearby stores that have sales in general or specials on the goods you want. Most SalesHound price reports are text only, which frustrated us when we spotted a La-Z-Boy chair that was advertised as "artfully shaped." Still, the site is useful if you know exactly what you want.

▶ **Earning rewards.** Low prices are nice, but earning frequent-flier miles, cash back or other rewards can sweeten any deal. You can find plenty of rewards sites on the Web, but be aware that many are stocked with caveats, such as minimum purchases or expiration dates. Plus, shopping through a portal takes longer than going directly to a retail site. Still, if you don't mind some rules, here are a few good options. At **ClickRewards** (www.clickrewards.com), you can earn miles good at 10 major airlines by shopping at over 75 affiliated sites, including BananaRepublic.com, CDNow and OfficeMax.com. The number of miles you earn depends on each merchant. All of the airlines let you transfer ClickMiles to your existing air-mile account, with a 250-mile minimum.

Another worthwhile rewards portal is **Beenz** (www.beenz.com), where you earn beenz currency (200 to a dollar) that you can spend at member sites like Borders.com, Beautyjungle.com and Art.com. You don't need to shop to earn rewards; you can earn 10 beenz for checking the daily edition of beenz news, 100 for lodging a customer service gripe at UGetHeard.com, 1,000 for referring 20 friends to Beenz.com or 2,000 for signing up for a movie-rental account at Blockbuster. Once you amass 1,100 beenz (a little over $5), your money (in dollars) is loaded onto your RewardzCard, a debit card good at any store, online or off, that accepts MasterCard (except gas stations).

Several Web portals, including **Ebates.com** and **CashBack-Club.com**, rebate the commission they earn for referring you to member sites. Our favorite in this group is **dash Inc.** (www.dash .com), a mall of 135 online stores such as L.L. Bean, Wine.com and clothing boutique Bisou Bisou. Depending on the merchant, dash rebates up to 25% of the purchase price in cash. What's the catch? You must download a tracking device—called the DashBar—so that dash can keep tabs on your whereabouts on the Internet. When you're shopping at a non-dash website, the DashBar flashes a savings alert if a dash merchant has a competitive deal. Dash does not resell information to third parties, and you can turn the bar off.

▶ **Using miles.** Frequent travelers who've earned more air miles than they'll ever need can spend them at **MilePoint.com** (www.milepoint.com). You can use points from America West, Continental, Delta, Hilton, Northwest, TWA and US Airways to defray up to 25% of the cost of products sold by 125 stores, including Orvis, Sharper Image and Amazon.com. Each mile is worth 2¢—a good rate by frequent-flier standards—and you can combine miles from various plans.

▶ *The Only Travel Sites You Need*

If it sometimes seems that there are more travel-related websites than places to travel to, well, it's indeed nearly the case: According to Web research group PhoCusWright, there are now more than 10,000 sites devoted to the subject. And while nobody tries to use all of them, the uncertainty involved in securing the best price on, say, an airline ticket, compels many of us to do exhaustive—and exhausting—searches. Most of this work is redundant, which is why you should focus on a handful of sites that are the best at what they do.

Travelocity.com *and* Expedia.com

What they're best for: Your initial search, especially for air fare

✈ 🚗 🖥 ❓ Travelocity and Expedia purport to be one-stop travel services, where you can do all the information gathering and booking

▶ **Symbols**

✈ **Air Fares**

🛏 **Hotels**

🚗 **Car Rentals**

❓ **Information**

🖥 **Online Booking**

💲 **Discounts**

🎁 **Package Deals**

you'll ever need. And to the extent that anyone offers that, they do. But we think the one thing these sites do better than any others is find the lowest published air fares—that is, the fares that airlines make available to everyone. Flight sections at both sites are extremely easy to use, and both offer some nifty tools for finding the lowest fares.

Is it actually necessary to check both of them? The answer, unfortunately, is yes. Travelocity and Expedia use different software to access different reservation systems and therefore yield different results. They've also negotiated deals with different carriers.

Besides airline info, both offer a ton of information on everything from packaged vacations to car rentals. Those sections are convenient for getting a general sense of the going rates, but won't necessarily produce the best deals.

CheapTickets.com and Lowestfare.com

What they're best for: Discount airline tickets

✈ ⊕ ▣ These sites are run by so-called consolidators, which buy large numbers of tickets from airlines at wholesale prices and resell them at substantial discounts. Again, experience shows that because the two websites have relationships with different carriers, you should always try both. For example, the best round-trip fare from New York City to London for an October weekend on Travelocity and Expedia was a Virgin Atlantic flight for $553.50. Cheap Tickets found a similar ticket for $510. Lowestfare came in considerably lower, at $307.

Keep in mind that bargain tickets are typically nonrefundable, nonchangeable and often ineligible for frequent-flier miles. Both sites also offer discounted cruises and vacation packages, but there's little to choose from, so we suggest that you stick to the airline sections.

SmarterLiving.com and BestFares.com

What they're best for: Last-minute, airline-sponsored deals

✈ ⊕ Most airlines offer heavily discounted last-minute fares at their own websites, but checking each site is time consuming. Instead, look to Smarter Living for a conveniently organized list of all airlines' last-minute offerings. It will also e-mail you all this information once a week. Best Fares also offers a compendium of last-minute deals—as well as every one of the thousands and

Other Ways to Fly for Less

Seasoned travelers know that the way to find a better fare is to be flexible, and what both Expedia and Travelocity have going for them—in addition to access to published fares—are tools that let you see how a few changes can lower your fare.

▶ **Finesse the system.** At Expedia, for example, you can search by "specific travel dates" or "flexible travel dates," and a link lets you experiment with date changes once your fares are displayed. Travelocity allows you to define your search based on your willingness to change days, change flight times or not change at all. At both sites, if you can be flexible about the days you travel, you can enter the cities you're traveling between to get a list of best fares, the airlines offering them and the dates they are available (displayed on color-coded calendars).

Travelocity, on the other hand, makes it easier to check out flights into and out of alternative airports—where fares may be lower. The "search for the closest airport" link gives you airport names, codes and miles from your first choice. By plugging in the airport codes on your original search page, you can see if your price changes.

▶ **See what you missed.** In an effort to get customers to book directly over the Internet, airlines have, in effect, created a new ticket category: special deals that are available only at the carrier's website. (Airlines are also rewarding travelers who book online with bonus frequent-flier miles. United, for example, was recently offering 3,500 miles for booking at their site.) So once you've got the best price from Expedia and Travelocity, visit the airline sites, especially if you're accumulating frequent-flier miles or know that the carrier dominates a particular route.

Airlines often mix news of these specials in with the last-minute fare sale notices they e-mail every week. To subscribe—which in some cases involves joining the frequent-flier program—go to the carriers' sites.

▶ **Try your luck at an auction.** You know what comes next: Name your price on the Net, and see if the site will meet it. We've always been dubious about beleaguered **Priceline** (www.priceline.com), the site that created and continues to popularize this auction system, because the site forces you to accept a nonrefundable flight before you find out what time it leaves and how many layovers it subjects you to.

If you can accept that lack of control, we will concede that Priceline can work, as long as you're savvy about how you bid. Here's our method: First, keep in mind that the maximum discount that you have a good chance of getting is 30% off the lowest published fare. So if you can't find a consolidator ticket that's 30% off, bid that amount. If you go for a deeper discount, you'll likely be denied. You might win the auction with a higher bid, but we think a small savings doesn't make up for Priceline's uncertainty.

Unfortunately, the site guarantees a flight only within a ridiculously large window, between 6 a.m. and 10 p.m.

The first rule of cruise booking: Never, but never, pay full price. The rates in those glossy brochures? They're like sticker prices on cars or hotel rack rates—all you have to do is ask and they come down.

How far down? That depends on how much strategy you're willing to apply. Here's how to get the best deal:

► **Check with several travel agents.** Unlike airlines, which are happy to sell you a ticket directly, cruise lines encourage passengers to use agents. Many who specialize in cruises can get you discounts of 10% to 50% off list prices. We suggest you contact at least three—check **www.cruising.org** for a list—because most have relationships with specific lines. Drill your agents on their specialties, and make sure that, together, they deal with many lines.

► **Plan early...** Snag the deepest discounts—up to 60%—by booking your cruise six months to a year ahead.

► **...or book at the last minute.** As with airlines, cruise ships are desperate to avoid setting sail with empty cabins, so last-minute deals—both through travel agents and online—can be huge. Two good sources are **www.i-cruise.com** and **www.uniglobe.com**. Just make sure you can get a reasonably priced and timely flight to the point of embarkation.

► **Sail off-season.** You'll find particularly great deals between Thanksgiving and the week before Christmas. Repositioning cruises, when ships move from Europe and Alaska to the Caribbean in the late fall, and back in the spring, are a cheap way to take extended trips.

► **Just ask.** Most people are part of some group or category that's eligible for discounts. Carnival, for example, takes up to $200 off early-booking discount prices for seniors with AARP cards. Holland America Line cuts rates by as much as 53% for kids up to 18 traveling with two full-fare adults. Repeat passengers get some of

thousands of travel deals available at any given time, making it, in our eyes, less appealing.

Site59.com

What it's best for: Last-minute package deals

🖥 💲 📱 Most travel sites serve—and offer the best discounts to—travelers who plan their trips at least several weeks in advance. But a handful of newer sites, including **LastMinuteTravel.com** and **11thHourVacations.com**, are a procrastinator's dream. Our

the biggest deals of all. Past guests on Seabourn and Cunard ships, for example, save up to 40%.

▶ **Find out what's included.** Price quotes sometimes don't cover gratuities, port charges and off-the-boat excursions, and they rarely cover air fare and alcoholic beverages.

▶ **Handpick your cabin.** Make sure your cruise agent selects your cabin after examining the ship's schematic. Rooms on mid-tier decks are not only cheaper than those higher up, they're often steadier too. Light sleeper? Avoid rooms with obstructed windows and those near elevators, staircases, bars and discos.

Illustration by Gentl & Hyers

▶ **Buy trip-cancellation insurance.** Cruise lines differ, but you can generally get a full refund if you cancel your cruise up to 60 days prior to sailing. But if you want to be covered against a last-minute or mid-cruise cancellation due to illness or other emergencies, you'll need trip-cancellation insurance, which runs about $7 for every $100 of coverage. Private insurers such as CSA Travel Protection (800-348-9505) usually offer more comprehensive coverage than policies sold by cruise lines.

▶ **Book your own flights, hotel…** Cruise lines book air fare and hotel rooms, but your agent may find a better deal. Just remember, you won't get transportation from airport to ship, so build extra time into your itinerary.

▶ **…and excursions.** Ship-sponsored port-of-call excursions can add a lot to the price of your cruise. Travel agents can often make similar arrangements, for a lot less money, before you set sail.

favorite is Site59. The site offers last-minute discounted package deals that often include hotel, air fare, car rental and, in some cases, dinner at a local restaurant. One recent packaged trip to New Orleans included round-trip air fare from New York City, two nights' accommodations and car rental for $328 per person. Some caveats: You usually have to travel within a week of booking. And for now, the deals are limited to 21 departure spots: Austin, Baltimore, Boston, Cincinnati, Cleveland, Dallas, Ft. Lauderdale, Houston, Los Angeles, Miami, New York, Orange County, Orlando,

Philadelphia, Phoenix, Portland, San Diego, San Francisco, Seattle, Tampa and Washington, D.C.

TravelWeb.com

What it's best for: Booking rooms in mainstream hotels

⊟ ⑦ 🖥 With 35,000 hotels in 170 countries, TravelWeb boasts the largest database of hotel rooms and resorts in the industry. Though a little sparse on graphics, the site offers prices, availability information, special deals and photographs of most hotels. The site has little in the way of descriptions or ratings of its huge roster of hotels. For that, we suggest cross-checking with a travel-guide site like **Fodors.com**.

PlacesToStay.com

What it's best for: Booking off-the-beaten-path B&Bs and inns

⊟ 🖥 A nice complement to TravelWeb, this site lists more than 10,000 places to stay, most of them independents (not chains, in other words). You can check availability and search by type of property, including B&Bs, cabins, even campgrounds. If you know roughly where you want to go but not the type of accommodation, the site will list your alternatives.

Weather.com

What it's best for: Weather predictions anywhere in the world

⑦ Getting an accurate weather forecast before you take off can save you from overpacking—or worse: being forced to buy clothes after you land. To make sure you bring the right stuff, check out **Weather.com**. The site provides current weather conditions, seven-day forecasts for domestic destinations and three-day forecasts for overseas locations, plus seasonal info so you can plan trips for the ideal time of year.

MapsOnUs.com

What it's best for: Maps and driving directions

⑦ Some people are born navigators; that is, they can take a map and quickly chart the fastest driving route. Then there are the rest of us, who need a Global Positioning System, a state trooper or even some more desperate form of help to get where we're going. MapsOnUs prints driving directions for the fastest, the geographically shortest and the most scenic routes. It will locate museums, malls and airports along your route. And it lets you map out as many intermediate destinations as you want.

Oanda.com

What it's best for: Currency-exchange questions

⑦ For the latest conversion rates for more than 160 different currencies, check out this site, which uses the so-called inter-bank rate, the best rate available. Oanda also generates handy, easy-to-print conversion charts that fit neatly in a wallet.

Zagat.com

What it's best for: Planning your meals in major U.S. cities

⑦ Some people feel they haven't visited a place until they've sampled the local cuisine—but hitting the most important eateries often means planning ahead. For the 32 U.S. and six international cities it surveys, there's no better way to get the lay of the culinary landscape than Zagat's website. Superior even to the well-known books, the site lets you parse restaurants by type of food, location, price and quality ratings.

▶ *The Internet Can Save Your Life*

Veronica Rippe was trying to do her own research on a debilitating kidney infection that didn't seem to be responding to the antibiotics her doctor had prescribed. Logging on to the Net, she typed in a few keywords: pain, fever, kidney, cyst. The search engine turned up a half-dozen websites—all, alarmingly, on polycystic kidney disease, described as potentially fatal. In tears, Veronica called her doctor, who told her, "You do have a serious problem, but it's not polycystic kidney disease and you're not going to die."

Tara DelGado, a lawyer and new mother in New City, N.Y., was suffering from a fever and sharp pains in her side one November evening. Her brother-in-law urged her to go to the emergency room right away, but she wanted to wait until morning—until he went online and found a checklist indicating that Tara might have appendicitis. Later that night, she underwent an emergency appendectomy.

Moral of the two stories: Medical information on the Net can scare you to death—or it can save your life.

Whether you're trying to quit smoking or research a catastrophic illness, the Internet is now the place to go. There are at least 15,000 health sites, and more are springing up all the time.

As rich a resource as the Web may be, it's also totally disorganized, which means a search can be rewarding or frustrating, depending on your skill (and luck). To make matters worse, info on the Web isn't checked for accuracy or timeliness. So how do you figure out where to go? Here's what MONEY learned after researching many of the Web's leading health sites.

For general health information, there's nothing like the Web. For the 68% of e-health consumers in the U.S. who classify themselves as healthy or "the worried well," the Web is fantastic: You can get more detailed advice on exercise, nutrition, health habits and bothersome conditions (think poison ivy or insomnia) than your physician would ever have time to give you. Start with a major omnibus site. Our favorite: **Mayo Clinic Health Oasis** (www.mayohealth.org), affiliated with the world-famous clinic. The site features medical news and Q&As on common treatments and conditions, and lets you e-mail questions to its staff doctors and dietitians.

The best of the major commercial sites is **CBSHealthWatch** (www.cbs.healthwatch.com), the consumer version of the Medscape site for medical pros. You can scan topics that interest you or join discussion groups on specific diseases. Another good first stop: the **Merck Manual** (www.merck.com/pubs/mmanual). Merck, which publishes this doctors' reference book on a not-for-profit basis, has also put parts of the plain-English *Merck Manual of Medical Information-Home Edition* online (www.merck.com/pubs/mmanual_home).

If you're feeling sick, the Web is no substitute for a flesh-and-blood doc. Use the Web to get background info and to help you frame questions for your doctor—but don't delay calling a live medical pro if you're not feeling well.

Online doctor visits may be the way of the future, but for now they're more of a curiosity. Take **AmericasDoctor.com** (www.americasdoctor.com), whose claim to fame is its free private chats with physicians. Logging on is easy; knowing whom you'll get is not. Our doctor's tag was AmDoc113. When asked about a cutting-edge treatment for chronic eczema, No. 113 had not heard of the treatment. When asked if we should seek a second opinion, the reply was, "That is always a possibility." Well, yes.

At **CyberDocs** (www.cyberdocs.com), M.D.s serve up diagnoses based on online-chat appointments and even issue some prescriptions (primarily refills and "lifestyle" drugs like allergy medicines). The price: $50 to $100. They also recommend follow-up visits with your own physician. A full complement of specialists is not available in all states, and scheduling an appointment is confusing.

Making your search specific enough to be useful may require a doctor's diagnosis. The Web is a wonderful tool to research a catastrophic illness or a complex condition. But type, say, "diabetes" or "cancer" into a search engine and you'll be swamped. "People get frustrated and give up," says Colleen K. Lindell, R.N., co-author of *Internet Medical and Health, Searching and Sources Guidebook.* To keep your search in control, follow these steps:

▶ **Learn about the exact area of anatomy you're interested in.**

▶ **Read a few layman's articles for general background and relevant terms.**

▶ **Refine your search.** A **google.com** search for "breast cancer," for example, yielded an unmanageable 85,000 results. However, using the "search within" function and adding "postmenopausal" and "stage" and "therapy" produced a more workable 295.

When you're ready for hard-core medical info, search the **Hardin Meta Directory** (www.lib.uiowa.edu/hardin/md), a massive but well-organized site for professionals run by the University of Iowa.

There are tons of alternative-medicine sites—and plenty of quackery. If you're interested in alternative medicine, you'll strike gold on the Web. But the conventional medical world's demand for precision and accuracy is not always shared by alternative practitioners, who often rely on testimonials and folk wisdom in lieu of costly clinical studies.

Be particularly skeptical of sites run by nutritional-supplement companies, especially those that say everyone must take vitamins, that losing weight is easy or that fluoridating drinking water is dangerous.

One comprehensive alternative site to check out is **HealthWorld Online** (www.healthy.net), a for-profit site that offers reports on topics like Chinese medicine and biofeedback.

Whether you need to find a doctor, a diet or the latest info on a dread disease, there's a site for you.

Places to start

▶ **www.intelihealth.com** Johns Hopkins University and Aetna U.S. Healthcare's site with questions on common ailments answered by the center's world-class doctors.

▶ **www.mayohealth.org** The Mayo Clinic Health Oasis offers general info and lets you e-mail questions to clinic doctors.

▶ **www.4women.gov** The National Women's Health Information Center has comprehensive information in English and Spanish.

▶ **www.nih.gov/health** The National Institutes of Health's gateway to the resources of federal agencies, including a list of diseases being studied by various institutions

▶ **www.cbs.healthwatch.com** Excellent consumer version of Medscape's professional site, run by former *Journal of the American Medical Association* editor Dr. George Lundberg.

▶ **www.drkoop.com** Run by former U.S. Surgeon General Dr. C. Everett Koop. Invaluable tool: drug interaction checker

▶ **www.webmd.com** Links the newly diagnosed to information and support groups

Hard-core research

▶ **www.lib.uiowa.edu/hardin/md** Hardin Meta Directory, a massive but extremely well-organized site aimed mainly at doctors; reviews and sorts medical links

▶ **www.nlm.nih.gov** The National Library of Medicine features MEDLINEplus, the layperson's search engine for medical research.

Special tools

▶ **www.centerwatch.com** Lists clinical trials by condition and geographic location
▶ **www.navigator.tufts.edu** Tufts University Nutrition Navigator steers you to the best diet and nutrition sites.
▶ **www.bestdoctors.com** Refers you to leading local doctors for $25

Cancer

▶ **www.oncolink.com** A site run by specialists at the University of Pennsylvania cancer center
▶ **www.cancernet.nci.nih.gov** The National Cancer Institute site
▶ **www.cancer.org** American Cancer Society site

Some reports, though, cost a few dollars. The ever-popular **Dr. Andrew Weil** (www.askdrweil.com) dispenses advice gratis on a range of holistic and alternative therapies while keeping one eye on conventional, science-based medicine. The nonprofit **World Research Foundation of Sedona, Ariz.** (www.wrf.org) collects information on alternative treatments, ranging from herbs to color therapy, from around the world.

Use Internet research to open a dialogue with your doctor. These days, doctors are seeing more and more patients who have done their own research. Most physicians have gotten used to it. Don't hesitate to ask what all your treatment options are, or to raise questions based on your searches—you may have turned up something your doctor missed. If you find a specialist who's doing important work, ask your doc for an opinion—and possibly a referral. But be sensitive; it's counterproductive to slap reams of printouts on your already overworked doctor's desk and demand that he or she read them then and there.

Double-check all information before you believe it. A recent issue of the medical journal *Cancer* ran this shocking report: Of 371 websites about Ewing's sarcoma (a rare bone cancer), 42% contained medical information that had not been subjected to stringent scientific review. Six percent contained outright inaccuracies, including one belonging to the *Encyclopaedia Britannica*, which stated that the disease had a mortality rate of 95% (the error has since been corrected); most medical experts project a survival rate of 70% to 75%.

Your best guarantee of accuracy? Finding corroborating information on two or more sites. And if a site has been proved wrong a few times, remove it from your list of bookmarks.

Also, follow an old journalist's rule and take the source of your information into consideration. Does a website steer you to a peer-reviewed medical journal, a litany of testimonials or a thinly disguised sales pitch? Bear in mind too that most medical information has a shelf life of only about five years. A good site usually notes the date of the research it publishes and when the site was last updated.

You can compromise your privacy without realizing it. Don't click on that banner ad asking how often you go to the bathroom unless you want to start getting mailers about prostate exams. Any personal data you enter on a website "could be captured by someone that you don't want to have it," warns Dr. Donald Palmisano, co-chairman of the American Medical Association's task force for privacy and medical confidence. Don't enter any personal information unless it's encrypted and the site's privacy statement promises not to sell data about you or contact you with unwanted offers.

Don't assume that buying drugs online will save you money. A University of Pennsylvania study published in the *Annals of Internal Medicine* found that Viagra and Propecia cost 10% more online, on average, than they did at five Philadelphia pharmacies. Avoid sites that sell drugs without a prescription, don't provide a way for you to ask questions of a registered pharmacist or don't provide a U.S. address and phone number.

Step 9

Make Great Real Estate Moves

*R*eal estate has been one of the greatest wealth generators in U.S. history, and it may well deserve a place in your portfolio. Unfortunately, many people don't get all the details right when they buy a home. They pick the wrong kind of mortgage, pay an interest rate that's too high, get a bad deal on the property or acquire a vacation home without completely understanding the financial implications.

The goal of this chapter is to delineate strategies that will allow readers to save money when they buy a home and to increase the odds that the purchase will turn into an excellent investment.

▶ *The Right Way to Buy a Home*

There is no one-size-fits-all strategy for home buyers. The wisest approach is determined by a wide range of variables. How much cash do you have available right now? How long do you plan to stay put? But if you ask yourself the right questions—and we'll show you which ones really matter—you can put together a strategy that suits your particular situation. Here's how to begin the home-buying process.

Look into the future. People move on average every seven years. Where will you be in seven years? Answering that question will help you determine what kind of home to buy and how to pay for it.

If you expect to move again in a short period of time, you'll want to look for low closing costs and a short-term mortgage that allows you to build up equity quickly. If one kid is on the way and the other is about to graduate from day care, you may want to strain your budget now for a larger house in a good school district. On the other hand, if your heart's desire is to settle into an older house and renovate it, you'd do well to think about a 20- or 30-year fixed mortgage with lower monthly payments. Whatever your plans, it's important that you have some time frame in mind.

See how you look to a lender's eyes. Chances are, the type of home you purchase depends on the loan you can get. So it's essential to know in advance how you look to lenders; you may be able to make some adjustments before knocking on their doors.

Your income and your level of debt will determine how much you will be able to borrow. Lenders believe that a household should spend no more than 28% of its gross income on housing costs (mortgage payments, property taxes and homeowners insurance). Multiply your monthly income by 0.28.

Now for a reality check. Go to the box on page 184 that helps you calculate the yearly costs of owning the house of your dreams. Divide your annual expenses number on line 4 by 12. If that figure is significantly more than 28% of your gross income, you'll probably have to settle for a smaller mortgage than you might like.

The second guideline concerns debt. Lenders look for your housing expenses plus long-term debt (which you have carried for 10 months or more) to total no more than 36% of your total income. The lower your debt-to-income ratio, the better your chances of getting a good rate. Add up revolving credit-card debt, student and car loans, current mortgage (if you won't be selling), insurance payments and alimony. For help with the math, try an online mortgage calculator such as the ones at the sites in the "Online Resources" box on page 185.

Another reality check: For every $50 or so of monthly debt above 36%, the amount that lenders are willing to lend you will go down by $6,000.

Count your cash. How much can you pony up for a down payment? To answer that question, you'll have to examine your whole financial picture. You don't want to be house-poor, so strapped for cash that you have to cut back on your 401(k) contributions or tap your emergency fund.

Your time frame is critical. If you plan to keep your new home for a long time, you'll want to put down as much as pos-

Once you have a particular home—or one of a particular size in a particular community—in mind, fill out this worksheet to get a rough idea of the annual out-of-pocket costs of owning that home vs. your present home. To estimate mortgage payments and tax-deductible interest, consult your lender or use an online calculator. (See "Online Resources" on the opposite page.) For taxes and approximate homeowner's insurance costs, consult your real estate agent. **Renters:** Enter annual rent on line 1 of the left-hand column, and any relevant upkeep expenses on line 3.

		CURRENT HOME	NEW HOME
1. Annual mortgage payments	**1.**		
2. Annual real estate taxes	**2.**		
3. Annual upkeep (cleaning, association fees, insurance, landscaping, repairs, utilities, etc.)	**3.**		
4. Total annual expenses (add lines 1, 2 and 3)	**4.**		
5. Amount of mortgage payments that is interest	**5.**		
6. Total tax-deductible expenses (add lines 2 and 5)	**6.**		
7. Tax savings (multiply line 6 by your top federal income tax rate)[1]	**7.**		
8. Annual after-tax outlay (subtract line 7 from line 4)	**8.**		

Note: [1] If your state allows a tax break for real estate taxes or mortgage interest, your overall tax savings will be somewhat higher.
Source: PricewaterhouseCoopers, LLP.

sible. Put down $20,000—instead of $10,000—on a 30-year mortgage for a $100,000 home and you'll save about $17,000 over the course of the loan. Plus, if you put down 20% or more, you won't have to pay private mortgage insurance, or PMI, which typically runs 0.25% to 1.25% of the total amount; the closer to 20% you come, the lower the charge.

If, on the other hand, you expect to move on in a few years, a smaller down payment may make sense, since you won't garner the long-term savings and may well earn more investing your money in stocks than you'll pay in effective interest and PMI. One danger of a small down payment: If the real estate market softens and you have to sell the house after only a couple of years, the price you get may not be enough to pay off the mortgage.

▶ **Gifts from friends or family.** Anyone may give up to $10,000 to any individual tax-free. If you're lucky enough to have indulgent parents or friends, you must present proof to the lender that the sum is a gift—and if you're putting down less than 20%, you must pay at least 5% of your down payment out of your own pocket.

▶ **Low-down-payment mortgages.** Both fixed and adjustable-rate mortgages with down payments of 3% and 5% are available through traditional lenders. Countrywide (800-556-9568) even offers a 0% down mortgage. The rates are the same whether you put down 5% or 20%, but borrowers who come up short will have the added cost of PMI.

▶ **Pledged-asset mortgages.** Whether these are wise or foolhardy will depend upon the performance of your investments. Borrowers who want to continue to profit from their investments—or to avoid the capital-gains tax they'd incur by selling—might consider a pledged-asset mortgage. Both Merrill Lynch (www.ml.com; 800-854-7154) and Fidelity (www.fidelity.com; 800-544-6600) offer such plans. Using your nonretirement accounts as collateral, the firm lends you up to an average of 39% (at Merrill) or 50% (at Fidelity) of the value of your accounts. In return, you must get your mortgage through a company selected by the brokerage—GMAC Mortgage at Fidelity and a subsidiary at Merrill. The advantage: You don't have to come up with any cash for your down payment. The drawbacks: You may not get the best rate on your mortgage. And if the assets fall below a number fixed by the lender, you get the equivalent of a margin call: Come up with cash or sell securities.

▶ **Help with closing costs.** Closing costs and fees can add as much as 5% to 7% of the purchase price. If liquidity is a problem, fold some of these costs into your mortgage.

Get the right rate. The two big issues are how long you think you will stay in your new home and how big a monthly mortgage payment you can handle.

▶ **If your time horizon is short.** If you think you'll remain under one roof 10 years or less, consider a hybrid adjustable-rate mortgage. ARMs are fixed for the first three to 10 years, then adjust every year after that. Recently, a seven-year hybrid ARM was 7.61%.

▶ **If you plan to stay put.** Don't go for an ARM if you think you won't move for 15 or 20 years; once the adjustable portion kicks in, your rates could climb sharply, wiping out any earlier savings. Comparison shop for a 20- or 30-year mortgage with the lowest possible rate. You may also want to consider paying points. Each point—1% of the principal—typically trims your interest rate by .25%. And points are tax deductible.

Q. I know that I can add the cost of home improvements to the cost basis of my home when I sell it. But what if my wife and I get estimates from professionals, then do the work ourselves? Can we add the professional value of our labor to the cost basis?

A. No. Even if you were professional contractors, the IRS would not permit you to count the value of your labor in calculating the cost of improvements to your own home. You can, of course, count the value of the materials you use.

Q. I just received notice that the lender holding the second mortgage on my house has filed for bankruptcy. I'm worried about how this will affect me. Will my credit rating suffer? Will I have to pay off the loan or negotiate a new rate?

A. Do nothing except keep up your payments and make sure you have copies of your original loan agreement. Your mortgage is an asset belonging to the troubled lender. A creditor will either take possession of the loan or sell it. Either way, you will be notified to send your payments to the new owner. The loan terms, however, should not change, and your credit rating is unaffected by the original lender's insolvency. If there are any hassles, though, a copy of the original contract will settle the matter.

► **New twists.** To get the best rate, look for a locked-in rate when you get pre-approved, sometimes available for no extra charge, or a float-down option, for a $250 fee, which lets you take advantage of a lower rate should one materialize before you close.

Build fix-up costs into your mortgage. Not long ago, if you bought a home and needed extra funds to turn it into the house of your dreams, you had to tap into your savings, cash out some investments or—worst of all—max out your high-interest credit cards. But Fannie Mae's HomeStyle program has enabled banks to offer loans for the cost of a house plus its planned renovations.

Here's how HomeStyle loans work. Imagine you see great potential in a run-down Victorian selling for $100,000. If an appraiser then determines that, when properly restored, the house's value will jump to, say, $150,000, you'd receive a mortgage for $150,000, less your down payment. (Under the HomeStyle program, you can borrow as much as twice the pre-renovation value of the property.)

These loans are backed by Fannie Mae, which you can contact at 800-732-6643 for a list of participating lenders in your area. But the maximum loan amount is $252,700, so would-be country squires need not apply.

If your sights are set on more expensive digs, some local lenders now offer similar mortgages with considerably more ample credit limits. For instance, Connecticut's Webster Bank (888-681-7788) will finance fixer-uppers appraised at up to $2 million after improvements.

▶ *Hiring the Home Team*

If you use the wrong people to help you buy a home—or simply manage them poorly—you might overpay, have trouble getting a mortgage or face costly, unexpected repairs.

Consider the story of David Holcombe, a senior financial analyst at Eagle USA Air Freight in Houston, who knew the 70-year-old house he bid on would need work. The home inspector who had been referred by his realtor turned up minor problems but no big-ticket repairs.

Two months later, Holcombe discovered what the inspector had missed: a major flaw in the central air and heating unit. "When I bought the house, it was still warm out," explains Holcombe. "By November it was getting cold, so I called in a specialist. Right away, he found a crack in the heat exchanger. I had carbon monoxide coming through the vents." Replacing the cooling and heating system cost $4,500, far more than the $2,500 repair allowance he'd gotten from the seller for electrical and carpentry work. To make matters worse, that repair work totaled a higher than expected $3,500.

How can you avoid such problems? Real estate agents, inspectors, lawyers and mortgage brokers work with one another all the time. You're the outsider. Letting your agent be your guide, as Holcombe did, may seem natural, but it may not be in your best interest. The middlemen you are referred to make more money from the agent than they will make from you. (Federal law prohibits certain referral fees; nevertheless, real estate pros do have mutual interests.)

How Sellers Can Prep

If you're buying a home, you're also probably selling one. Here are some low-cost ways to spruce up your home before the potential buyers arrive.

▶ Nothing beats a fresh coat of paint; if that's too pricey, paint the shutters and the front door, and spend $200 to $500 to have the house pressure-washed.

▶ David Schoner, a Coldwell Banker manager in Short Hills, N.J., explains that "the front door says a lot." Install a new $20 to $35 brass kickplate and exterior lighting fixtures ($25 to $200).

▶ Trim the hedges to make your house look bigger and brighter. A landscaper's day: $300 to $500.

▶ Replace the wall-to-wall carpeting, at $4.99 to $25 a square yard.

▶ Reface the kitchen cabinets, which runs about $2,500 to $3,000.

Rule No. 1: Don't dismiss agent recommendations, but treat them just as starting points.

The real estate agent. With this middleman, your goal should be to ensure that the agent is working on your behalf, not the seller's. A traditional listing agent represents the seller and therefore looks for the highest possible price.

What to do: To avoid this conflict of interest, consider using a buyer's broker. Even though this agent, like the seller's agent, earns more if you buy a more expensive house, he or she typically doesn't make any money if you can't find one you can afford. By some estimates, you can save 5% or more by using a buyer's broker.

In most cases, buyer's brokers earn their keep by splitting the 5% to 7% sales commission with the seller's agent. Some ask for 1% to 3% of your target price up front, but that retainer is generally paid back at closing. Since many work as seller's agents at other times, sign a contract up front establishing your relationship and fees.

Resources: Check with the **Real Estate Buyer's Agent Council** (800-648-6224; www.rebac.net) for buyer's brokers in your area.

The mortgage broker. If you want help finding a loan, you can do what roughly half of mortgage applicants do: Hire

Fight High Home Heating Costs

One way to save money every year is to spend less to heat your home. Below is a list of energy-saving home improvements, plus estimates of how much they could cut your heating bill (according to the Department of Energy or the manufacturers) and how long you'll need to recoup the cost. The figures assume a $728 heating bill for a 2,000-square-foot home.

1. **Get a programmable thermostat:**
   Lowers the heat while you sleep and raises it in the morning.
   Cost: $40 to $250
   Annual savings: 10%, or $73
   Time to recoup: six months to three years

2. **Add weatherstripping to your windows and doors:**
   Prevents heated air from escaping
   Cost: $5 for stripping that you replace annually
   Annual savings: 15%, or $109
   Time to recoup: two weeks

3. **Buy low-emissivity coated windows:**
   Reduces amount of radiant heat lost through windows.
   Cost: $1,800 (assuming 10 windows at $180 each)
   Annual savings: $300 to $350
   Time to recoup: five years

4. **Insulate walls and attic:**
   Fiberglass or cellulose insulation maintains even temperatures.
   Cost: $740 to $1,340, depending on thickness
   Annual savings: 10% to 20%, or $73 to $146
   Time to recoup: nine to 10 years

5. **Insulate your hot-water heater:**
   Precut blankets wrap around the heater to prevent heat from escaping.
   Cost: $12 to $20
   Annual savings: $5 to $28
   Time to recoup: eight to 18 months

6. **Insulate your furnace pipes:**
   Fiberglass tubing prevents loss of heat into surrounding pipes.
   Cost: $10 to $20 per 10 feet
   Annual savings: $15 (assuming an average of 10 feet)
   Time to recoup: eight to 18 months

7. **Use heat-reflective paint indoors:**
   Prevents the loss of heat into your home's interior walls.
   Cost: $245
   Annual savings: 6% to 10%, or $44 to $73
   Time to recoup: three to six years

a broker to match you up with a lender. The broker's 1% to 3% fee is usually paid by the lender. But because the lender can pass that payment on in the form of a higher interest rate, paying too high a rate should be your primary concern.

What to do: To make sure you're getting the best rate, don't leave all the work to the broker. When Libby Schnee's mortgage broker wasn't returning her calls, the New York public relations manager made a couple of her own. "Where I work, we had a relationship with Citibank," says Schnee, "and I got a lower rate than the broker did." When Schnee asked her broker to match Citibank's rate on a 30-year fixed-rate mortgage, she did.

Check rates in the newspaper or on the Web to make sure your broker's is competitive. And look for a broker who works with at least 10 lenders in a large market or five in a small area.

Resources: Check mortgage rates at **www.hsh.com** or **www.quicken.mortgage.com**. For names of brokers, contact the **National Association of Mortgage Brokers** (703-610-9009; www.namb.org).

The appraiser. This middleman is basically behind the scenes and out of your control—unless there's a problem. Your lender hires the appraiser (and passes the $300 or so fee on to you) to make sure the home's value is in line with the price. As long as the appraisal is equal to or higher than the selling price, you'll get your loan. Lower, and you may have to increase your down payment to qualify for a mortgage—or not get one at all.

What to do: Make sure your purchase contract includes a clause that lets you void the sale if the appraisal comes in below the selling price. If that happens and you still want the house, here's what to do next.

Get a copy of the appraisal (which you are entitled to by law) and look for obvious reasons for the gap. "Square footage is a common discrepancy," says Marge Fraser, president of the Real Estate Education Center in Sterling Heights, Mich. "People think they're buying 2,000 square feet when what they've got is 1,600 square feet plus a garage." Your broker may be able to convince the appraiser to raise the value by pointing out comparable recent home sales. If not, you may want to spend another $300 to $600 for your own appraiser, but there's no guarantee the bank will accept that second opinion.

Resources: For a referral, get in touch with the **Appraisal Institute** (312-335-4100; www.appraisalinstitute.org).

The lawyer. In many parts of the country, you'll need a lawyer to review the purchase and sales agreements and accompany you to the closing. Hiring one will cost $500 to $1,500, depending on where you live.

Your chief objective should be finding an attorney who can anticipate problems you might not think of. For example, P.J. Garrity, a real estate lawyer in Arlington, Mass., represented a buyer who had to vacate his house by a certain date. On the walk-through the day before the closing, they discovered serious water damage. Because Garrity had made sure the contract contained a clause specifying that the seller had to pay any costs incurred if the closing didn't take place on time, her client's additional expenses due to the delay were covered.

What to look for: Real estate experience is essential. Find a pro who closes approximately 10 sales a month and specializes in the kind of property you're buying.

Resources: You can link to your state bar association's legal referral program at **www.abanet.org**.

The inspector. On your behalf, the inspector will examine the foundation, roof, heating, electrical and plumbing systems and walls, windows and doors for $250 to $500. But—as David Holcombe's expensive story illustrates—it's in your interest to find a tough inspector who'll flag deal breakers.

What to look for: Make sure that your inspector belongs to the American Society of Home Inspectors (ASHI), whose members must pass proficiency tests and agree to a conflict-of-interest policy that prohibits, among other things, payments from a real estate agent.

Most inspectors are generalists who look for readily visible defects. Holcombe, for example, could have avoided extra repair costs if he'd hired an inspector who specialized in heating, ventilation and air conditioning (HVAC). If you have any reason to suspect termites or other hidden problems, hire an additional inspector. Any home more than 20 years old is likely to have asbestos (in the insulation or floor tiles) or lead paint.

Resources: To reach **ASHI**, call 800-743-2744 or go to www.ashi.com. For the name of a state-certified lead inspector, call 888-532-3547 or go to **www.leadlisting.org**.

▶ *Are Two Homes Better Than One?*

Walter Braswell knows what the good life feels like. He and his family live in a comfortable suburban New Jersey home and he holds down a high-paying job as general counsel for a large utility company, but what completes the picture is his vacation house—his "reward," as he puts it—on Martha's Vineyard. Ten years ago Braswell paid about $155,000 for the house and the land; what he got in return was a three-bedroom cottage for family vacations that he also rents out for extra income. Today, Braswell estimates that the Vineyard retreat is worth $265,000. The investment has a water view, but it also comes with a never-ending set of financial duties and homeowner concerns.

When Americans think of the ultimate sign that they've made it, they don't envision driving an expensive car or holding an executive position. Rather, as a recent survey by Roper Starch Worldwide reveals, they picture a vacation house much like the Braswells'.

Unfortunately, whether you're buying for rental purposes or pure pleasure, a vacation house can harbor a number of unforeseen costs and hidden burdens.

A second home can be a fickle investment. Let's say that back in 1982 you had bought a vacation home in Jackson Hole, Wyo. If you had sold in 1987, you would have lost 40% to 60%. But if you'd been able to hold on for just three more years, you'd have doubled your original investment.

That's how it goes in the vacation-home market, economists caution. Whereas primary residences generally appreciate in value at about the rate of inflation, second-home prices can be like shooting stars, burning brightly for a short while before flickering out. And even if you're lucky enough to buy into a vacation area just before it takes off, it's still possible that you'd earn a better rate of return investing in securities. In the Jackson Hole scenario, that 100% gain over eight years works out to be growth of about 7% a year; during the same 1982-90 time period, the S&P 500's average annualized rate of return was 18.5%.

Smart strategies: To up the appeal of your property, buy a property that has the characteristics other vacationers favor. Most potential second-home owners want a single-family house as opposed to, say, a condo, and they prefer a choice location on the beach, followed by mountain and lake settings.

Of course, it's impossible to predict which locales will be hot a few years from now. But real estate experts say you'll increase your chances of landing in a desirable market by devoting a few weeks to research. Once you've narrowed down your search, start reading local newspapers. Scout for information about new housing developments (which could decrease future demand for your property) and local property taxes—namely, whether they're going up, another potential detriment when you're trying to sell. Talk to residents, store owners and civic leaders for insights about where the town is heading.

"It's hard to get away." According to U.S. Census figures, owners spend a median of just 28 nights in their vacation homes. Ten percent don't stay overnight at all, while another 20% use their places for seven nights or less. How to explain this seeming contradiction between the strong desire to own a second home and the tendency not to use it all that much? "People forget [when they buy] that they have busy lives, that it's hard to get away, that they don't have much flexibility in their schedules," says Bob Moles, president and CEO of Century 21 Real Estate.

Just ask Walter Braswell. When he and his wife Adele were searching for their Martha's Vineyard property back in 1989, they waited until they found one they could imagine "rushing to on the weekends," he recalls. They spent much of the past decade doing exactly that—and then their young children grew up. "Our kids are at an age where they're so busy during the summer that we can't use the house as much as we'd like to," Braswell admits.

Smart strategies: Restrict yourself to a property that's within 300 miles of your primary residence. "You should buy your house thinking you'll be able to use it once or twice a month," says Penny McLaughlin, a RE/MAX Unlimited real estate consultant on Bainbridge Island, about seven miles off the coast of Seattle. In addition, make sure you have viable, affordable transportation options. If getting to your vacation home is a problem, it doesn't matter how close it is to your primary residence.

Costs you can count on. These days, interest rates on secondary home mortgages are typically no more than one percentage point higher than primary mortgage rates, and lenders usually will accept a down payment of just 10%. Coming up with the money to buy a property is one thing, however; having the wherewithal to maintain it is quite another. (To determine if you have the cash to keep up a second home, see the box on page 196.) Not only will you shell out monthly mortgage payments, you'll also incur the same costs you do at your primary residence, including furnishings, property taxes, repairs and utilities. If you purchase a condo or buy into a vacation community, you'll face association or maintenance fees as well. And don't forget the cost of traveling to and from your second home.

Insurance is another potentially hefty expense. In fact, you may pay more for a homeowners policy on your second home than you do for your primary residence. That's because vacation properties often stand empty and are considered vulnerable to damage and theft, not to mention beachfront weather.

To cut your insurance premiums, protect your property as much as possible. Install smoke detectors, as well as an alarm system. Seek out insurance companies that offer coverage tailored to the second-home market. The Chubb Group, for example, has a vacation-home product available in more than a dozen states.

Smart strategies: Compare the additional monthly expenses with the amount you usually save each month. If you'll still be able to salt away part of your income, buying a second home is a judgment call. But if what you'll spend is about equal to what you currently save, you should ask yourself what that means for the future. "A retirement property without retirement funds ain't no fun," warns Daryl Jesperson, president of RE/MAX International. "There's a difference between what you can afford and what you can comfortably afford."

Knowing your way around rentals. Many second-home owners believe that their property will pay for itself if they rent it out occasionally. That's often wishful thinking. Even if there's strong rental demand for your house, turning your home over to tenants is likely to boost your expenses. How? For starters, you'll need to hire a cleaning service every time a renter leaves; you'll also pay a heftier insurance premium, since having other people in your home opens you up to liability coverage and the increased risk of property damage.

You may think such hassles are worth it because you can use your rental home as a juicy tax deduction. Well, think again—the IRS rules governing rental real estate are complicated and not altogether favorable. (No wonder experts recommend hiring a good accountant when you purchase your second home.)

Can You Afford a Second Home?

Worksheet A estimates the cost of owning a second home for personal use. Worksheet B estimates the cost of owning a home to rent out. If your adjusted gross income exceeds $100,000 or your rental losses top $25,000, ask a tax pro to fine-tune your numbers to account for tax phaseouts. Or use the additional worksheets on our website at www.money.com/contents.

A. Personal use

ANNUAL EXPENSES:

1. Mortgage payments	1.
2. Real estate taxes	2.
3. Upkeep (cleaning, association fees, insurance, landscaping, repairs, utilities, etc.)	3.
4. **Total annual expenses** (Add lines 1, 2 and 3.)	4.

ANNUAL FEDERAL INCOME TAX SAVINGS:

5. Mortgage interest	5.
6. Real estate taxes	6.
7. Total tax deductible expenses (Add lines 5 and 6.)	7.
8. **Tax savings** (Multiply line 7 by your top federal income tax rate.)[1,2]	8.
9. **Annual after-tax outlay** (line 4 minus line 8)	9.

B. Rental

ANNUAL INCOME:

1. Rental income	1.

ANNUAL EXPENSES:

2. Mortgage principal	2.
3. Mortgage interest	3.
4. Real estate taxes	4.
5. Upkeep (advertising, cleaning, maintenance, insurance, landscaping, repairs, utilities, etc.)	5.
6. **Total annual expenses** (Add lines 2, 3, 4 and 5.)	6.

7. Net cash from the rental (line 1 minus line 6)   7. _____

8. Depreciation (To estimate, add purchase price, closing   8. _____
   costs and improvements and divide the sum by 27.5.)[3]

9. **Taxable profit or loss** (Line 7 minus line 8, then   9. _____
   add line 2. Caveat: If this calculation results in a
   loss of more than $25,000, enter only –$25,000.)[4]

10. **Taxes** (Multiply line 9 by your top federal tax rate.)[1]   10. _____
    ▶ If the numbers on both lines 7 and 9 are positive,
      your rental is a moneymaker. CONTINUE TO LINE 11.
    ▶ If the number on line 7 is positive and the number
      on line 9 is negative, **you have sheltered your net
      cash and cut your taxes** by the amount
      on line 10. **STOP HERE.**
    ▶ If the numbers on both lines 7 and 9 are negative,
      you are losing money, but you will cut your taxes
      by the amount on line 10. **STOP HERE.**

11. **Annual after-tax income** (line 9 minus line 10)   11. _____

Notes: [1]2000 rates on taxable income for single filers: **15%**—up to $26,250; **28%**—$26,251 to $63,550; **31%**—$63,551 to $132,600; **36%**—$132,601 to $288,350; **39.6%**—$288,351 and above. For married joint filers: **15%**—up to $43,850; **28%**—$43,851 to $105,950; **31%**—$105,951 to $161,450; **36%**—$161,451 to $288,350; **39.6%**—$288,351 and above. [2]If your state allows a tax break for mortgage interest or real estate taxes, your overall tax savings will be somewhat higher. [3]You are required to claim depreciation, but doing so will decrease your basis thereby increasing your gain upon sale. [4]The maximum allowable loss is $25,000 a year for taxpayers with AGI of $100,000 or less. The $25,000 maximum phases down by 50¢ for every $1 of AGI above $100,000 and phases out at AGI of $150,000. Source: Price Waterhouse Coopers, LLP.

If you use your vacation home for no more than 14 days a year or 10% of the days it's rented (whichever is greater), the property is no longer considered your personal residence for tax purposes; it's considered a rental property. As a result, you can deduct rental expenses against your rental income. If your expenses exceed your rental income, you can deduct up to $25,000 a year in losses against your other income—as long as your adjusted gross income is $100,000 or less and you make key management decisions such as choosing tenants.

If, however, you use your second home more often, you can deduct your rental expenses only to the extent that they offset your rental income. Any net losses must be carried ahead and used to offset rental income in future years.

Smart strategies: If you figure you won't be using your house for most of the year, you'll want to purchase one that's attractive to renters. That means finding a home within commuting distance of a major metropolitan area. Not only will such a location offer a broader range of attractions and services, it's also more likely to draw off-season tenants.

Keep in mind that it's sometimes better to sign long-term leases than short-term ones. This will reduce the wear and tear on your property, save you money on cleaning fees and generate a more reliable rental income. You may want to consider employing a management company to help you find tenants. Although such outfits typically pocket 10% to 30% of the rent, that may turn out to be a small price to pay for having your house regularly booked.

A place for retiring types. Should you purchase a second home with an eye on retirement? Keep in mind that falling in love with an area during its ideal season is different from living there year round. And while a condo may seem roomy enough when you're just crashing there for the weekend, as a full-time resident you may come to miss walk-in closets and a well-equipped kitchen.

Smart strategies: If you want a second home you can retire to, spend time in the community during the off-season before you buy. Check out whether there are enough other things for you to do—and enough people to talk to. And make sure you can add on to the property if you're so inclined.

Retirement was also a consideration when the Braswells bought their Martha's Vineyard vacation home. As Braswell sees it, the costs of owning a second home are outweighed by something you can't put a price tag on: relaxation. "When I get on the ferry to come out here," he says, "and I know I'm heading for great beaches and great golf, it's like I'm leaving my troubles behind me."

▶ *Test Yourself*

1. **When considering you for a loan, banks usually want to be sure that your monthly housing costs do not exceed ___ percent of your gross income, and that the sum of**

housing costs plus long-term debt payments are not more than ___ percent of income?

A. 36 and 28 percent

B. 26 and 38 percent

C. 28 and 36 percent

D. 38 and 26 percent

2. **When choosing a mortgage, you should usually select a fixed-rate loan over an adjustable-rate loan when...**

A. You plan to remain in the house for five or more years

B. Your income may change sharply within the next three years

C. You believe that interest rates are headed down during the next four years

D. You are unable to decide what fixed rate is best

3. **What does it mean to pay "points" on a mortgage loan?**

A. You are pre-paying a percentage of the loan principal in order to obtain a lower monthly payment

B. You are pre-paying a percentage of the interest in exchange for getting a lower interest rate

C. You are pre-paying a mortgage broker to get him or her to work harder on finding you a loan

4. **Most real estate agents represent the ...**

A. Seller

B. Buyer

5. **Mortgages whose interest payments rise or fall in step with prevailing interest rates are called ...**

A. Step up mortgages

B. Adjustable rate mortgages

C. Balloon mortgages

D. Fixed rate mortgages

6. **What is the difference between an appraisal and a home inspection?**

A. The buyer pays for the inspection in order check the home's defects while the seller pays for the appraisal in order to prove the value of the house

B. The bank requires the inspection to make sure the house is free from defects while the seller demands the appraisal to support his list price

C. The lender requires the buyer to pay for the appraisal to establish the home's worth, while the buyer pays for the inspection on his own to check for defects

D. There's no real difference, they are the same thing

7. **Assuming that you and your spouse's (or partner's) parents are both well-off, and they want to help you raise a down payment for a home, what is the most they can give to you and your spouse in a single year without triggering the gift tax laws?**

A. $10,000

B. $20,000

C. $40,000

D. $80,000

Answers

1. **C.** In general, your housing costs must be at or below 28%, and that sum plus your long-term debt must be under 36% of gross income.

2. **A.** A fixed-rate loan is appropriate for owners who prefer to keep their monthly payments constant, whether interest rates rise or fall. But if you are planning to keep the house for only five years, an adjustable rate mortgage is almost always cheaper.

3. **B.** Otherwise known as the "loan discount cost," points are a portion of the interest that the buyer pays at closing in order to get a lower mortgage interest rate.

4. **A.** Most agents, unless they are exclusive buyer agents, work for and are paid by the seller. So their duty is to get the seller the best possible price during a negotiation.

5. **B.** The interest rate on an adjustable rate mortgage rises and falls—often yearly—according to some index, such as the rate paid by a one-year Treasury bill.

6. **C.** Even though the mortgage lender will order a home appraisal, a buyer pays for it—and should also hire an inspector to look for potential problems in the home.

7. **D.** While the limit on a gift from one person to another is just $10,000, the parents in this example can actually give a total of $80,000 without running afoul of gift tax limits. Here's how it works: Your father gives $10,000 to you—and $10,000 to your spouse—for a total of $20,000. Your mother gives $10,000 to each of you for a total of $20,000. Your spouse's father gives $10,000 to each of you for a total of $20,000. And your spouse's mother gives $10,000 to each of you for a total of $20,000. Grand total: $80,000. We should all be so lucky!

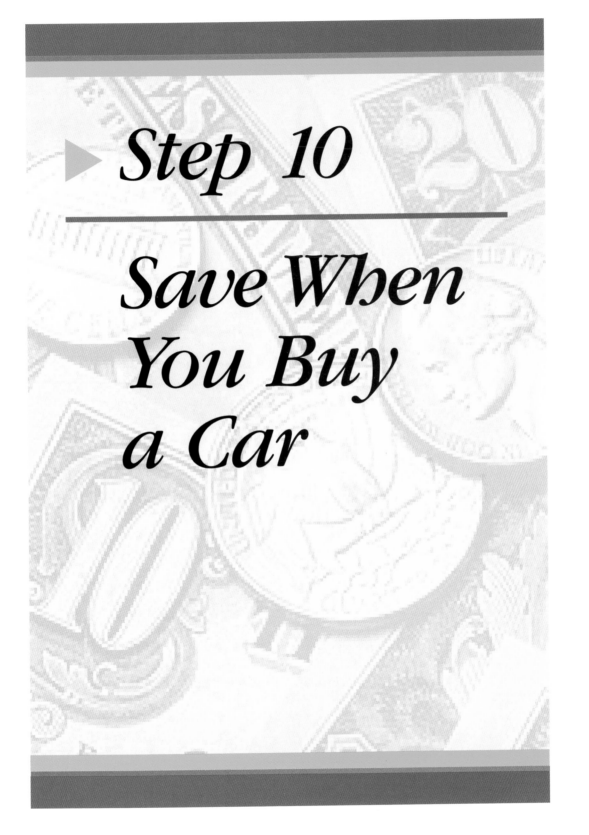

Step 10

Save When You Buy a Car

*S*hopping for a car has long been one of the most daunting—and needlessly expensive—exercises that a consumer endures. For good reason, the car dealer has become the butt of innumerable jokes. If anyone has some glowing things to say about dealers outside their immediate family, well, we haven't heard them.

In recent years, however, the car buying process has changed radically. It's much easier to get a great price today, and you can now avoid dealers completely if you wish. (From a quality of life viewpoint, this is clearly desirable, although it probably won't get you the lowest price.)

If you employ the right strategies, you can now save a small fortune every time you buy a car—and get better value for the vehicle you decide to trade in or sell. This chapter will examine the ins and outs of getting the best deals. We also will provide some crucial information on car safety that will help you avoid potentially serious accidents. After all, if you're badly hurt while driving, who cares what kind of deal you got on the car?

▶ Car Shopping Strategies

Shopping for money. When you go to a car dealership to negotiate for a new car, you're in a stronger position if you have a loan pre-approved. Unless your model has a special low-rate financing offer backed by the manufacturer, a local bank or credit union is likely to give you a better deal on a loan. And in most cases, you can take a rebate in place of any low-rate financing and use that to lower your purchase price.

Credit unions typically charge one-half to one percentage point less in interest than banks do. You may be eligible to join a credit union where you work or through a professional association or organization.

If you don't have ready access to a credit union, check out your local bank offerings. Find the best rate in your area by visiting **Bankrate.com**. It gives five or more quotations for each major city, including the lowest rate available.

When you get a pre-approved loan, that commitment usually is good for a month or more. So you can shop for the car you want knowing your financing is ready to go.

Show the right attitude in the showroom. Before you head for the dealership, you'll need to do some homework. To negotiate the best deal on the car you desire, find out the *dealer's invoice price* (see the "How to Get Real-World Selling Prices" box on the following page), whether *rebates* or *dealer incentives* are available, your target price and determine where you should start bidding. You want to start as low as you reasonably can, but not so low that you will seem like an uninformed buyer just making a low-ball offer.

Pull together a folder containing printouts or copies of your research and bring them with you to the dealership when you go shopping. When you step into the showroom, establish quickly that you are a serious buyer, not a browser. If you come across as "just shopping," the salesperson will be eager to move on to a likelier sale. Don't say: "I'm looking at the Ford Taurus." Instead, say: "I plan to buy a Ford Taurus LX within the next two weeks and I know pretty much how I want it equipped. I will buy where I get the best price. Let's talk about it."

That keeps you in control. The salesman wants to know as much about you as possible to start spotting potential profit points. Stay pleasant, but just turn away questions and say: "We can talk about me later. Let's talk about price."

Focus on the invoice price. As soon as you can, try to switch the discussion away from the MSRP (*manufacturer's suggested retail price*) or *list price* to how much you intend to bid over the dealer's invoice price. However, even as you start quoting figures, a salesperson may claim that you don't have the right invoice price for the car. Although he or she may be convincing, don't get nervous. The truth is that the salesperson may know less than you do since traditional dealer training focuses on the MSRP and many dealers do not give their sales team the invoice prices.

▶ How to Get Real-World Selling Prices

Once you have settled on a model, it can be tempting to go to a selling site and quickly make a deal. Before you do, check out several independent price sites. We recommend **Edmunds.com**, Kelley Blue Book's **Kbb.com** and Microsoft's **CarPoint.msn.com**, all of which provide full invoice prices and the cost for options.

Good bargainers always start negotiating with the invoice price, but the tricky step is to determine how much over (or occasionally under) invoice to set your target price for a certain model. In general, a good deal for a new car is 2% or less above the dealer's invoice price. The price you can get varies greatly with how strong demand is for a given model, but recently introduced Web data can really help you figure out whether a price is fair.

For instance, Edmunds.com has just begun posting so-called *true market value* prices. Edmunds determines a car's market value by factoring in the supply and demand for a given model and spot-checking more than 400 major dealers around the country. The service is still new, but it's promising. In 2001, Edmunds plans to improve on the numbers by offering prices that reflect regional differences. The popular Lexus RX 300 sport utility, for example, was recently selling for higher prices in the Northeast than in California. To double-check Edmunds' market price, go to **Autoadvisor.com**, a service that shops for the best price for clients. It posts target prices in dollars above (or occasionally below) invoice.

Another website, **Carclub.com**, affiliated with the J.D. Power research firm, expects to begin posting regionalized average selling prices for all models in the biggest metropolitan areas later this year.

The detailed information offered by these sites is useful as a starting point in your negotiations. "When I went to a dealer and showed them the Edmunds printout, it saved a lot of time," says Byron Glueck, 31, a software developer from Charleston, S.C. "They stopped trying to give me the usual spiel and negotiated seriously." Glueck got his fully loaded 2001 Audi A4 Quattro for $28,100—$800 below the Edmunds market price.

This is when you pull out your research and say: "This is the invoice price for the car I want with the equipment I want."

Though your target should be no more than 2% above the invoice price ($400 over a $20,000 invoice price, for example), you need to leave room for the dealership to budge you a little. (If you're also entitled to the consumer rebate that was offered recently make it clear now—or at the very end of your discussion—that all negotiations *exclude* this figure. That rebate belongs to you.)

At this point, the salesman is likely to say something like: "I think this is way too low, but I will take your offer to my sales manager and see what I can do for you." He or she may not even intend to talk to the sales manager, but plans to keep you waiting in the glassed-in office to pressure you into a higher offer before even seeking approval. Tell him or her you do not intend to wait long. Then don't just sit there. Wander around the showroom or go outside to look at other cars. That usually brings the salesman back quickly. It's likely he will bring the news that your initial offer was not good enough. At this point, if you started the bidding at the invoice price, agree to go 1% over invoice.

If the dealership has a car with the color and equipment you want, and the salesman offers you 2% over invoice, accept the offer. If not, get the best offer and take it to another dealer. If the second dealer beats the original offer, keep the competition going—play it back to the first dealer. When you hit your target or come as close as you think you can, agree on the price. Now—and not before—is the time to talk about a trade-in. (See "Making the Trade" on page 210 for trade-in strategies.)

If your research reveals that the car you want is offering a dealer rebate or dealer incentive (an incentive fee that manufacturers offer dealers to push slow-selling cars), that's a signal that you should negotiate hard, and here are some strategies you can follow. Say you find out that Ford is offering a $500 dealer rebate on the Taurus you're eyeing. Try to capture at least half that money by bidding $300 below invoice and make it clear to the salesperson how you got that figure by saying something like: "Since the dealership stands to get a $500 payment from Ford as a sales incentive, $300 below invoice seems fair." Then follow the negotiation strategies outlined above.

Closing the deal. Don't let your guard down at this crucial moment or you might close out your savings. The salesman may call it "doing the paperwork" or some similarly innocuous description. But the finance manager you are about to meet hopes to boost dealer profits at your expense with attractive-sounding offers of mechanical and financial add-ons. In most cases, just say no. But there are some exceptions.

If you already have financing approved, just say so and you can avoid the financing pitch. The one exception: if you already know that the manufacturer is sponsoring a promotional deal with really low rates.

▶ *Shopping for a Used Car on the Net*

Car lots and classified ads used to be the only way to buy a used car. But now consumers are turning to their computers to help them get a good deal.

Used-car buyers have been slower to embrace the Web, with about 30% of buyers now doing research on the Internet, compared with half of new-car buyers. And many shoppers remain reluctant—and rightly so—to buy a used car online because you need to see the vehicle to check its condition. But online used-car listings are extremely useful for searching out the used car you need.

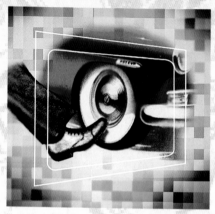

If you are not sure of the model you want, start with **Netscape**'s used-car selector, which shows you choices that meet your price and model specifications. Once you decide what you want, check listings from both dealers and individuals selling used cars at **autotrader.com**, the biggest used-car site. You put in your zip code and the model you want and get a list of available vehicles near you.

Illustration by Brian Stauffer

Cars.com also has extensive used-car listings. It picks up local newspaper classified ads from many major newspaper chains, including the Tribune Co., Gannett and Knight-Ridder. To check how the price quotes you see compare with the average selling price for that vehicle at dealership lots, visit **www.nadaguides.com**, the pricing site of the National Auto Dealers Association.

Of course, beyond the price, it's vital to check out the condition of any used car you want to buy. Take the car to a mechanic for a full diagnostic workup before you put any money down. That should cost about $100.

The next pitch you are likely to hear is for an extended warranty. Whether you want to consider this depends on how long you expect to keep the car. If it is the three years or less that matches the typical warranty, reject it immediately. If, however, you are almost sure you will keep your car for five years or more, you might consider an extended warranty contract. Ask about when the extended-warranty coverage kicks in and what it covers. (So-called "power train only" warranties, for instance, may exclude expensive electronic repairs common in today's cars.) An extended warranty can cost $400 to $1,200, so be sure you know how long the manufacturer's warranty runs. Volkswagen and

Hyundai extend power train coverage for 10 years and luxury models Lexus and Infiniti for six years.

The latest vogue in add-ons (replacing rustproofing now that almost all new cars are rustproof to start with) is security etching. Having your vehicle identification number etched into the glass on your windows may, as claimed, make your car somewhat less likely to be stolen. But it is certainly not worth the $1,100 some dealers are charging.

▶ *Strategies for Buying a Car Online*

Eileen Horwath is among the new breed of Web-savvy car shoppers. Looking for a Honda Civic that fit her budget, the 24-year-old San Franciscan never even considered stepping into a dealer showroom. Instead, she went to several auto sites on the Internet and swiftly got a $15,000 offer for a new 2000 Civic EX coupe from **Carsdirect.com**. Six days later, she had the black compact delivered to her—at the office.

The experience was a breeze and a real deal too. The Honda was $1,350 below sticker price, even less than the cost of some year-old Civics. "I didn't worry at all about buying on the Internet," says Horwath, an analyst with a corporate strategy consulting firm. "I had much more trepidation about going into a car dealership."

Gone are the days when car shopping was as intimidating as a trip to the dentist. Now it's become positively painless. Thanks to the emergence of several major online car buying and pricing services, the Net is changing the way many people buy cars. In fact, it's becoming the go-to source for detailed information about vehicles. And consumers are taking notice. Nearly 50% of all new-car buyers have used the Internet to do research, according to CNW Marketing/Research, and about 3.5% actually bought through an Internet service in 2000.

You need an online road map. Even if you're not as daring as Horwath, the Web can be a powerful tool for car shopping. It provides access to loads of valuable information once available only from the auto manufacturers and their vast network of dealers. Better yet, it makes it easy to obtain the most important number for buying a new car: the dealer cost, or invoice price. As smart shoppers know, this number—not the manufacturer's suggested retail price, or sticker price—is the starting point for a good deal.

While the Internet is definitely empowering, it can also be confusing and downright maddening. More than 50 sites give invoice prices alone, and at least 15 sites sell cars—all with a wide divergence in prices, speed and quality of service. Worse, a thicket of state regulations stands in the way of certain online transactions.

Illustration by Brian Stauffer

What's a harried consumer to do? To help speed your search, we reviewed dozens of auto sites and picked the best, fastest and easiest for all stages of the shopping and buying process. Keep in mind that this step-by-step approach will make you a better consumer, even if you buy from a dealer rather than making the purchase online.

Pick your model and options. Not sure what car you want? A great place to start your search is **Netscape.com**'s auto site. Go to the Decision Guides section, and you'll be directed to Netscape's CarMatch service. It allows you to shop for new cars based on your desires, from make, model and size to price.

In our site test we decided to search for a new station wagon. After you put in what you're looking to spend, you answer questions about how much certain features matter to you—more head- or legroom or greater cargo space, for example. When we selected wagons under $30,000, it gave us five models. We knew from past test drives that we liked both the Volkswagen Passat and the Subaru Outback. To check them out in greater detail, we set up a side-by-side comparison of the two models, a fantastic feature that really shows the power of the Web. (You can do similar searches in the Car Guide section of money.com.)

We soon learned that the VW had the advantage in two key areas: power (190 hp vs. 165 hp) and cargo space (39 cubic feet vs. 34 cubic feet). Satisfied that the 2000 VW Passat GLS V6 wagon was the best car for us, we clicked ahead to get a price. With automatic transmission and a CD player, the sticker price was $26,200, and the dealer invoice cost was $23,963. The printable page showed the base cost plus the breakout for various options, very valuable information indeed.

Beyond comprehensive sites like Netscape (and money.com), it's also worth browsing the auto company corporate websites. **GM.com**, **Toyota.com** and others offer online brochures and provide detailed information on colors and standard and optional equipment. But remember that these are basically ads for cars; the sites are far less interactive than those of other car services.

At some point during the search for the right model, it's worth test-driving several cars. Nothing beats getting behind the wheel to get a feel for a new car.

Snare an online offer. Once you're armed with cost information, it's time to start making a deal. Of the approximately 15 sites that provide online selling, three offer the best prices: **Carsdirect.com**, **Autonation.com** and **Driveoff.com**. Web research firm Gomez Advisors recently ranked Carsdirect and Driveoff Nos. 1 and 2 among the 13 sites it surveyed. (Autonation wasn't in the survey.) Each of these services provides a firm price for the car you want and then locates it through a cooperating dealership or sells it to you directly. Check all three to find the one that offers the best coverage in your area.

▶ **Carsdirect.com** typically quotes among the lowest prices on the Web, but it often cannot get the hottest-selling cars, which dealers want to keep to sell themselves. And because of state laws and regulations, you can't use Carsdirect

Illustration by Brian Stauffer

in 11 states (Alaska, Arkansas, Hawaii, Kansas, Montana, Nebraska, Oklahoma, Tennessee, Texas, Utah and Wisconsin).

▶ **Autonation.com** is also very competitive on price. The company has 400 car dealers in 25 of the biggest cities and is beginning to expand its reach in the Northeast and upper Midwest.

▶ *Making the Trade*

More than half of new-car buyers with old cars trade them in to the dealer. By doing so, however, you could lose at least $2,000 on the deal, or considerably more if your car is in good condition. Here's how to avoid this costly car-buying mistake by selling your car directly—plus advice on getting the most for your trade-in if you prefer sticking with the dealer.

First, some background on why trade-ins can be a lousy deal. Dealers make more money selling used cars than they do selling new ones—no surprise when you consider that their typical used-car markup is 15% to 20% vs. 3% to 8% on a new car. Not only do they pay you well below what your car will sell for, but you're at a disadvantage if you try to negotiate for more. When it comes to calculating your car's value, good information is hard to find.

Used-car values, unlike new-car prices, are far from uniform. You can find out the exact invoice price on a new Honda Accord LX, but if you're trading in a similar 1997 Accord, you might get anywhere from $8,000 to $12,000 from a dealer, depending on the mileage, the condition, where you live and whom you ask.

You can get estimates of your car's trade-in value from the **Kelley Blue Book** website (www.Kbb.com) and *Edmund's Used Car Prices* ($9.95 for the book; free estimates at **www.edmunds.com**). But your dealer will likely refer to a price guide that's not sold to the public, such as his regional *National Auto Dealers Association Used Car Guide*. NADA has just made those trade-in values available to the public online at **www.nadaguides.com**. If you don't have Web access, your best shot at seeing the printed guide is to ask your lender or insurance agent. (The consumer edition reveals only the average used-car selling prices.)

NADA calculates trade-in values quite differently than Kelley and Edmund do. Consider this comparison: If that 1997 Accord LX is in good condition and has 45,000 miles on it, NADA awards a trade-in value of $12,450, Kelley $10,725 and Edmund $10,650. NADA's trade-in value assumes the car is ready to sell, which is why a dealer will pay you much less if your car has dents, scratches, stained seats or old tires. Edmund's data is based solely on sale prices at wholesale auctions, where many cars haven't been reconditioned. The Kelley Blue Book mixes auction data with surveys of what dealers pay.

Using the Kelley Blue Book website is the closest you'll come to predicting what a dealer would pay. The site lets you input your car's mileage and condition and your location—factors that can account for huge variations. If that Accord is in excellent condition, the Kelley Blue Book value rises $750 to $11,475. If that same car is sold in Southern California rather in New York City, its trade-in value goes up another $750 to $12,225—a reflection of the popularity of Hondas in California and the likelihood that the car has been subjected to more bad weather in New York.

Now that you have at least an approximate idea of what a dealer might pay, here's more on your alternatives.

▶ **Sell it yourself**. Only 20% of new-car buyers sell their old cars, but more should. On a car with a $10,000 trade-in value, you could net another $3,000. The challenge is coming up with an asking price. For starters, don't set your sights on getting a dealer's selling price (a number you can find at the NADA and Kelley Blue Book websites and in their consumer guides). Dealers generally recondition cars and supply a 30-day warranty; that adds as much as 10% to the value. What you want to look at is what private sellers are asking for cars like yours. You'll find that information in the classifieds or online at **AutoTrader** (www.autotrader.com).

Set your asking price close to the asking price for cars with similar mileage—and then expect to get about 10% less. Remember that 1997 Honda Accord? When we searched a Los Angeles zip code at AutoTrader, we found private sellers asking about $15,500 for similar cars. A price 10% below that would be $13,950, or $2,475 more than the Kelley Blue Book trade-in value for a car in good condition in Southern California.

What if you're uncomfortable selling a car directly? Here are four tips to make it less intimidating: 1) Get a diagnostic report on the car from a shop certified by the **American Automobile Association (AAA)**, which you can show would-be buyers. (For a link to your local AAA site, go to www.aaa.com.) 2) Advertise for free on the Web at Autotrader.com and **Yahoo.com**; both let you request e-mail responses instead of phone calls. 3) Ask the caller or e-mailer how he will pay for the car; this can eliminate all but serious buyers. 4) Once you get your price, insist on cash or a cashier's check.

▶ **Trade it in**. To get the best possible price—the Kelley Blue Book trade-in value for your region and your car's condition—you'll need to do two things. Start by getting competing offers. Call dealerships for the brand you're selling and ask the used-car manager for an approximate offer. If you live near one of the 40 **CarMax** used-car superstores in California, Florida, Georgia, Illinois, Maryland, North Carolina, South Carolina, Texas, Virginia or Wisconsin, you have yet another option. (Go to carmax.com for store locations.) CarMax appraisers will give you a free on-site estimate, which will likely be below the best price you could get from a dealer, along with a seven-day commitment to buy your car.

If you decide to hire a buying service to shop for your new car, the firm will sell your old car as well for an additional fee. **AutoAdvisor** (800-326-1976; www.autoadvisor.com), which charges $395 for new-car buying, will shop your old car for an extra $63. **CarSource** (800-517-2277; www.carq.com) adds $100 to its $375 average fee to shop your old car.

Since they're selling the car to dealers or wholesalers, you'll get the best available trade-in value—probably even better than what you'd get yourself from a dealer—but likely not as much as if you sold it yourself.

It's worth shopping Autonation if it's available in your area. In Tampa, an Autonation stronghold, we found a well-equipped 2000 Ford Taurus LX for $17,368, including a $1,000 consumer rebate—$200 to $350 below online competitors and about $400 below Edmunds' true-market-value benchmark. Autonation.com recently formed an alliance with America Online (which was slated to merge with Time Warner, MONEY's parent company).

▶ **Driveoff.com** is allied with dealers in such a way that it can operate even in Texas, the most difficult state for online services to crack. Driveoff usually will give you price quotes from two or three dealers at varying distances from your zip code, a convenience that sure makes it easier to locate a car. The other good news is that the site, which is now owned by Microsoft's CarPoint website, is also extremely competitive on price, especially in areas where Autonation is less dominant. In the Los Angeles area, the Driveoff price for a well-equipped Jeep Grand Cherokee Laredo sport utility was $26,045 after a $1,500 consumer rebate—$400 below Autonation and $700 under Carsdirect.

Look for financing. Nearly all auto sites have a link with an auto financing site. But before you click your way to a new loan, it's best to head to the financial services website

Illustration by Tavis Coburn

Bankrate.com. It will show you the benchmark information you need: the current national average interest rate for car loans and the best rates being offered by banks and other lenders in your area.

Another solid online resource for competitive bank loans is **LendingTree.com**. The best rate we got in a recent test was 1.5 percentage points below the national average car loan of 9.13%. Assuming you have good credit, you can probably get approval in an hour or less.

Even with those choices, though, don't overlook the car-selling sites completely. Some, like Driveoff.com, offer competitive financing along with the lightning-fast service you'd expect from an electronic retailer.

▶ *How Safe is Your Car?*

The image of Ford Explorers mangled after their Firestone tires failed is a stark reminder that danger still lurks behind the wheel. But as the confusion over the Firestone recall shows, it has become more difficult than ever to know if the car you're driving is safe.

Decades of innovations like air bags and improvements in auto design, combined with tough nationwide drunken-driving and seat-belt laws, have made it much safer to be on the road. Since 1979, the rate of highway traffic deaths has dropped by 50%, from 3.2 to 1.6 per 100 million miles traveled. Despite this progress, more than 40,000 people die in auto accidents each year.

Yet cars are so reliable today that few people pay attention to what matters most on the road—the tires, brakes, air bags and seat belts. "Modern cars are so trouble-free that people have forgotten that vehicles need maintenance," says David Van Sickle, consumer and auto information director for the American Automobile Association. "Failure to check tire pressure and do other maintenance can have serious safety consequences."

Taking care of your tires. Tires that don't have enough air can kill you. Underinflated tires flex too much and build up heat, which can lead to blowouts and tread separation, where the tread peels away from the body of the tire.

How low is too low? The answer: Just four or five pounds per square inch (PSI) too low can be dangerous, tire safety experts say. With such a narrow margin for safety, it's important to check your air pressure at least monthly. But don't rely on the recommended pressure noted on the tires themselves. Instead, you should follow your car maker's pressure recommendation. Car makers usually post it on a metal plaque on the driver's side door pillar or inside the glove compartment. It may also be in the owner's manual. On European brands, it may be inside the gas-cap cover.

▶ **Checking pressure.** As for how you check your pressure, be wary of gauges at service stations, since their readings are often inaccurate and inconsistent. Instead, buy your own tire gauge at an auto-parts store (it should cost no more than $5 or so). Test the pressure of each of the tires when they are "cold," before the car has been driven. If you must add or subtract air, always retest the tires with the gauge afterward to get an accurate reading.

▶ **Heavy-load alert.** Tires are often weakened by the stress of hauling gear or by towing a boat or trailer, especially if you are driving for long periods at speeds over 65 mph. This can heat up the tires and cause them to blow out.

You may think that it helps to let air out of your tires as a precaution during these situations. But, in fact, the opposite is true. To make sure your tires hold up under heavy loads, you may actually need to add an additional five pounds per square inch to each tire. Consult the owner's manual for the heavy-load pressure recommendation.

▶ **Danger signs.** If when driving at highway speeds you hear a muffled thumping noise or feel a shimmy in your steering wheel, it may be a sign of trouble. The noise may indicate tire tread problems that require immediate attention. The shimmy may mean your wheels are out of alignment, which can cause tires to wear prematurely.

Get a jump on tire problems by checking their condition every six months. Stick a penny in the tread. If the tread does not reach the top of Lincoln's head, you need new tires. Keep in mind that most tires usually last 40,000 miles, and it's prudent to have a mechanic check your alignment every 5,000 to 7,000 miles.

▶ **Ratings count.** It's not just cars that are rated for safety. The government also rates all tires that are on the market. The ratings are generally noted on the side of a tire—A is the best, C is the lowest—and you can also check the website of the **National Highway Traffic Safety Administration** (www.nhtsa.gov/cars/testing/tirerate). If you drive long periods at high speeds or with heavy loads, you should have tires rated B or better for resistance to heat.

What you need to know about brakes. It used to be that brakes needed to be replaced when they squealed. Today, however, many cars have anti-lock braking systems (ABS) equipped with sophisticated sensors that monitor the rotational speed of the wheels to help you gain better control over brak-

For every recall that garners national attention, there are countless others that get little if any notice. Automakers say they routinely notify all owners affected by recalls for whom they have an address, but it isn't always so.

The good news: Many automotive websites now offer free services that will notify you of recalls by e-mail. All you have to do is register with the site and provide them with your e-mail address. The best of them are **carpoint.com** and **autobytel.com**. They cull recall information from the National Highway Traffic Safety Administration. You can also keep track of recalls by checking NHTSA's website (**www.nhtsa.gov**). Select "recalls" and type in the year, make and model of your vehicle. You should get a list of all recalls that have been issued for your car.

ing. Better yet, many cars with ABS brakes automatically check them out for you with computerized diagnostics as soon as you start the car. That's why it's so important to watch the brakes' dashboard warning light. If the light goes out after about two seconds, the system is working properly. If the light stays on, it's a sign of potential trouble that requires a trip to the mechanic.

▶ **Test your stopping power.** Every six months or so, you should apply this simple brake test. Find an empty parking lot or quiet road and accelerate to 50 mph; then hit the brakes hard. If the brakes are in good shape, you should stop within 100 feet.

Remember that if you have traditional brakes without an automatic anti-lock assist, you'll need to pump the pedal to keep the wheels from locking. With anti-lock brakes, hit and hold the brakes even if you feel a pulsating in the pedal.

If your car has trouble passing the test, it means you won't be able to stop on a dime in an accident, and you may have trouble stopping your car fast enough in rough weather. Time to bring it in for service.

▶ **Listen up.** Even if you can stop on a dime, unseemly noises warrant a service visit. If you hear a squeal when you hit disk brakes or a grinding noise with drum brakes as you're doing this test, it means that, at a minimum, the shoes in drum brakes or the pads in disk brakes need replacement. If the car pulls to the right or left when you brake, that is also a trouble sign. A thorough brake overhaul—which you probably need every 30,000 miles in any event—should cost from $150 to $300, depending on your vehicle.

Air bags should help, not harm, you. They're one of the biggest lifesavers to come along in decades. Air bags have saved nearly 5,000 lives since 1990, according to the National Highway Traffic Safety Administration (NHTSA). But airbags have also been linked to more than 160 deaths, which means it's prudent to maintain this safety device and to learn how to use it properly.

▶ **Maintenance.** Every time you start the car it runs an automatic diagnostic test of your air bags. The results of the test will show on your dashboard's air-bag light, which usually looks like an expanded air bag or reads SRS for Supplemental Restraint System. If the light stays on, it's signaling a problem and the air bag should, of course, be checked immediately. Go to a dealership, not an independent mechanic. Dealers will have the electronic diagnostic equipment that should be able to identify the problem in the air-bag system.

If you need to replace the air bag—as you would after an accident or any time it deploys—make sure you ask for a new bag and get proof that it's authentic. There's a vigorous trade in used and black-market air bags. Tell your car dealer you expect to see the invoice from the manufacturer. Check that the serial number on the invoice matches the one on your new air bag.

▶ **Sit right.** We all know air bags are dangerous if you sit too close to them. That's been especially true for children and smaller adults, who account for many of the air-bag-related deaths. But the safety devices can be dangerous for everyone.

How close is too close? According to NHTSA, drivers should be at least 10 inches from the front of the air bag. Anything closer puts you in danger of being hurt by the force of the air bag should it inflate. If your car has an adjustable steering wheel, tilt it as far down as is comfortable, so it's pointing the bag at your chest instead of your head. NHTSA's website (www.nhtsa.gov) actually has a detailed diagram of the proper way to sit.

Handle seat belts and child seats with care. Three out of five people killed in traffic accidents would have lived

▶ *Protecting Your Most Precious Cargo*

Children are particularly vulnerable to severe injury in car accidents so it's crucial that infants, toddlers and young children are placed in the best child seat (or booster seat for older children) you can afford. Magazines such as *Parenting* (www.parenting .com) or *Consumer Reports* (www.consumerreports.org) often rate child seats, so check out their websites.

When it comes to child safety seats, the best news to come along is the addition of child-seat anchors in cars. The anchors bolt in the seat and make it far more secure than using seat belts. This feature is standard in the Chrysler 2001 minivan and will be required in all cars starting with the 2003 models.

In the meantime, there's a lot you can do to make sure that the seats are functioning properly and safely secure your child.

▶ When placing your child in the seat, cinch the belt as tightly as possible so that the seat cannot move more than one inch to the front or side. Position the clips on the belt harness at the level of the child's armpits.

▶ Check at least once a year for cracks or spiderwebbing in the fiberglass that could mean you need a replacement.

▶ Get the right seat. If you buy a convertible seat in the $50 to $70 range, you can first install it in a rear-facing position for babies weighing under 20 pounds in order to keep your child out of danger. But when the child grows, you can switch to a front-facing position. And remember, once your child is over 41 pounds, she'll need a separate booster seat that works with regular adult seat belts.

---

had they been wearing their seat belts, according to estimates by federal safety regulators. But few of us pay much attention to belts. We assume that they are in good condition and functioning properly. Yet that isn't always the case. So how can you tell if your seat belts are up to the job?

▶ **The fit test.** The belts should unreel smoothly when you pull them, then retract snugly around you. The best belts, in recent-model cars, have so-called pre-tensioners that make the belt retract slightly to hold you in place during an accident.

▶ **The visual test.** On older cars, look to see if belts are frayed or torn. If your belts don't fit well, check the "retractor" —the spool-like device that tightens the belt—near the floor. "In a family car, you may find crayons, McDonald's wrappers or anything else caught in the retractor," says the AAA's Van Sickle.

▶ **Post-accident vigilance.** An accident can seriously weaken belts. Look at any belt that was in use during the accident for signs of "tear strips," a patch of torn threads down near the retractor.

If your seat belts fail these simple tests, go to a dealership or a mechanic who is certified for such work. A replacement should cost $150 or less.

Index

Insurance, 91-108
    auto, 97-98
    homeowner's, 99-102
    life, 92-98
    long-term care, 105-06
    savings, 102-04
Internet
    banks, 55-56
    best financial websites, 48-56
    free service, 164
    health information, 175-80
Internet brokers, 53-54

K
Keogh plans, 74

L
Living trusts, 112

M
Money-market funds
    selecting, 45-47
Municipal bonds, 42-43
Mutual funds
    bond, 25, 43-45
    the MONEY 100, 28-30
    picks for 2001, 25-27

N
Net worth
    calculating, 5

O
Online shopping
    shopping bots, 163-68
    travel sites, 169-75

R
Retirement
    and company stock, 82-87
    portfolios for, 81
    postponing, 87-90
    early retirement, 66-69
    tax-deferred plans, 74

S
Salaries
    negotiating, 127, 130-32
    websites, 133-38
Simplified Employee Pension (SEP),
    74
Social Security
    benefit estimate, 66
    early retirement, 65
Stock market forecast, 8-19
Stocks
    case for midcap stocks, 19-26
    "folios," 40-42
    100 stocks for long-term investors,
        14-16
    picks for 2001, 19-27
    technology, 31-38

T
Tax-deferred retirement plans, 74
Taxes
    estate, 111, 113-15
    gift, 116-18
    websites, 56
Technology funds, 35-36
Technology stocks
    smart ways to buy tech, 31-38
Trusts, 111
    credit shelter (or bypass), 111, 113
    family limited partnership, 115-16
    generation-skipping, 115-16
    minor's, 115
    Qualified Personal Residence Trust
        (QPRT), 114
    QTIP, 113

V
Vacation homes
    affordability, 196-97
    buying, 193-94
    renting, 195, 197-98

W
Wills, 112